# Praise for Satire In The Trump Era

"*The Halfway Post* boldly says the quiet part of contemporary Republican politics out loud, cleverly using conservatives' own disdain for political correctness as a cudgel against the GOP's various bureaucratic excesses, mental redundancies, and ideological incongruities."

"It's unbelievable how many sources *The Halfway Post* has collected who will talk so candidly and intimately about the deepest workings of our government. Literally unbelievable."

"A masterfully accurate portrait of the Trump years, as well as the gamut of Donald Trump's deranged vulgarities, ranging from his passion for alluding to incest to his fingers' uncanny resemblance to chubby, little sausages."

"Every print of this book should be burned for obscenity. I only wish there was a way to acquire all the copies without giving Dash MacIntyre any royalty money. I'd say ban the book nationally, except that banning books inevitably makes them more notable and widely read."

"Dash MacIntyre is certainly going to Hell, and I look forward to meeting him there and having cocktails over polite, affable palaver."
—Jesus

"If anyone should be able to take a joke, it's Me! Whereas many devout worshippers of Mine will be horrified at the collected heretical blasphemies throughout this book, I'm quite tickled!"
—God

"*The Halfway Post* has more perspicacious, anonymous sources than any other news company in America, and gets right to the heart of the Trump Administration's negligent soullessness. There is no better insight into the grotesque personal idiosyncrasies of the public figures orbiting the Trump White House."

"Just garbage."

"Dash MacIntyre is almost certainly America's premier satirist of white supremacist semen jokes."

"This is the book President Trump does not want you to read! I would not be surprised if he sues the author for $5 billion in frivolously alleged damages to the Trump brand, only to drop the lawsuit when it eventually comes time for a depositional inquiry into the President's personal records and finances for fact-gathering in service of dethroning the claims made in this assemblage."


"The most true book you'll ever read. Also, the most filled with lies."


"I can't wait until a bunch of radical SJWs addicted to the cheap high of mindless persecution outlaw a bunch of the words and phrases used in this anthology so the radical Left turns on Dash MacIntyre, as credentially liberal-minded as he is, and call him worse than Hitler as they roll out the guillotine and chop off his head!"


"These puckish headline fibs and farces of US politics in the MAGA Era capture the spirit of a once peerless democracy buckling and threatening to collapse under the weight of a demagogic, ethno-nationalist movement on the right celebrating cultural narcissism with unpatriotic conceptions of discriminatory citizenship and scientific ignorance exhilarated by professing undeservedly that all opinions are equal, and that therefore all inconvenient expertise, statistics, fact-checking, and serious journalism from even the most esteemed authorities and legacy institutions must be a hoax. ... Amusing throughout, though occasionally unnecessarily distasteful and frankly crude."


"Your book is a total piece of s***, you communist a**hole. Don't walk across the street in front of my car. You will not like the results of the sudden brake failure and throttle-sticking issues my car will have."


"Magnificent commentaries... Superb pieces that reconfigure our society's distinctive cultural power dynamics, and offer a tour de force burlesque of the degradations in our modern populist aesthetics haunted electorally by competing generational angsts dominated by intersectional, Millennial cosmopolitanism on the Left and brutalist Baby Boomer nativism on the Right... Astute observations on the absurd politics of America in the late 2010s sprinkled with inescapably prudent judgments on late-stage capitalism's egregious corporatism exploiting the last halcyon vestiges of the mid-20th Century New Deal's idealistic federalism alongside the obvious orchestrations of white supremacist rage posing as economic fragility juxtaposed against liberals' cultural revolution of post-modern marxist humanism rooted in a burgeoning digital dystopia of deconstructive, neo-Jacobin identity politics... wait, which book am I reviewing again?"


"*The Halfway Post* employs such an erudite, sophisticated vocabulary for its saucy descriptions of objects that have allegedly been up Rudy Giuliani's butthole."

# SATIRE
# IN THE TRUMP YEARS

*The Best Of The Halfway Post*

**DASH MACINTYRE**

**Published by The Halfway Post**

Printed in the United States of America
Second edition

Book design, cover, illustration, and jokes by Dash MacIntyre

Library of Congress Control Number: 2021902586


**Publisher's Cataloging-In-Publication Data**

Names: MacIntyre, Dash, author.
Title: Satire in the Trump years : the best of the Halfway Post / Dash MacIntyre.
Description: St. Louis, MO, USA : The Halfway Post, [2021] | Summary: A best-of collection of comedic,
    satirical news articles written for the author's website, HalfwayPost.com.
Identifiers: ISBN 9781736581902 (paperback) | ISBN 9781736581926 (ebook)
Subjects: LCSH: Trump, Donald, 1946---Humor. | Presidents--United States--History--21st century--
    Humor. | United States--Politics and government--2017---Humor. | Right and left (Political
    science)--United States--History--21st century--Humor. | Political satire, American. | LCGFT:
    Humor.
Classification: LCC PS3613.A272542 S28 2021 (print) | LCC PS3613.A272542 (ebook) | DDC 817/.6--dc23


ISBN: 978-1-7365819-0-2  (Paperback)
ISBN: 978-1-7365819-2-6  (Ebook)



For more information, please address:

DashMacIntyre@gmail.com
TheHalfwayPost@gmail.com

This is a work of satirical fiction and Dadaist caricatures of American politics from 2017 to 2021. All
characterizations, quotes, and the situations in which public figures, companies, and organizations are
described as participating in this book are entirely made up.

# About

# *The Halfway Post*

*The Halfway Post* has been the newspaper of record for Dada journalism since the summer of 2017. Its satire has earned the most coveted rating in the satire industry of "Pants On Fire!" by *PolitiFact*.

Follow *THP* on your favorite social media platform:

DashMacIntyre.Medium.com
Twitter.com/HalfwayPost
Threads.net/@TheHalfwayPost
Facebook.com/TheHalfwayPost
TheHalfwayCafe.Substack.com
Spoutible.com/TheHalfwayPost
Post.News/DashMacintyre

# Notice

This satirical collection is protected by numerous judicial interpretations and legal precedents established by the Supreme Court in validation of broad, inalienable rights to free speech via the First Amendment, no matter how triggered unfunny MAGA fans might be by its untiring criticism of their cultural, ideological, and personal flaws. Any attempt to sue the author or publisher of this book's obvious comedic fictions would prove further how deserving they are of its mockery.

In the iconic words of Donald Trump, "I don't take responsibility at all" that the real-life deranged behavior of the public persons lampooned here may make my parodying exaggerations seem indistinguishable from reality.

The book's only non-exaggeration is this picture of what Donald Trump looks like in the morning before beginning his daily, two-hour regimen of cosmetic styling:

# Trump Says His Favorite Bible Story Was When Jesus Built The Ark

June 13, 2017
Washington D.C.—

President Donald Trump has always had a shaky grasp of Christian theology, and today he committed perhaps his greatest Bible gaffe yet.

During a prayer breakfast event Mr. Trump was asked what his favorite story from the Bible was, and he gave one of his trademark rambling answers.

The following is a transcript of Trump's response:

"My favorite Bible story? Gosh, there's so many to choose from I don't even know where to begin. How could you pick just one? They're all my favorites. I love them all. Great stories. Some of the best stories of all time. Maybe I'll be in one some day. People always tell me they'd love it if I was in one. They say the Bible is great, and has great morals, but they'd like to see an *Art of the Deal* chapter. But Jesus knew a little about deals. He made some great deals. He made the deal for us all to get into Heaven. One of the best deals of all time. Too bad Jesus didn't get into business. I'd love to do deals with Jesus. Me and Jesus would make a great team, wouldn't we? Wouldn't that be something? We could write a book together. *The Bible Part 2*, by Donald J. Trump and Jesus. Trust me, no one wants that more than me. I'm one of the great Bible lovers of all time. I read it every day. I can barely put the Bible down I read it so much! You know, a lot of people don't know this, but the Bible is actually very long. Very long. I thought *Art of the Deal* was long, but it's not long like the *Bible*! It's filled with so many tremendous stories. But my favorite story? I think I'd have to go with the one where Jesus builds the ark. Who doesn't love that one? It's a classic! The way Jesus built that ark, and led all the Jews out of Egypt on it, and out of slavery. It taught me so much. And He showed such incredible strength when He sent all the plagues down on the Egyptians for not believing in His stone tablets of the Ten Commandments. I think about that story all the time when I'm making deals for America. I imagine Jesus looking out over the side of the ark waving goodbye to the Pharaoh as He sails for the Promised Land. And Jesus sitting down in the captain's cabin writing all the pages of the Bible by candlelight until the animals could be delivered to Bethlehem. And who could forget all the phenomenal adventures Jesus had along the way? Like His battles with the Cyclops, and then the Minotaur. And the Trojan War that lasted for years and years. It's just amazing how clever Jesus was to build the wooden horse and hide inside. Whenever I have a problem I ask myself what Jesus would do. That question always helps me decide exactly what to do as president!"

# Shocking Birth Certificate Discovery Sheds New Light On Donald Trump's Orangutan Ancestry

June 15, 2017
St. Louis, MO—

*The Halfway Post* recently sent an amazing, great guy (you'd love him) down to Borneo in the South East Pacific to sift through all the biological records of President Donald Trump's birth and early childhood, and the stuff our guy is uncovering is astounding.

It'll really blow your mind. Some people are saying it will change everything.

We here at *The Halfway Post* hear from hundreds of people, no thousands, no all of the American people every day, that they think Trump's alleged "*Homo sapien*" genetics are fishy, suspicious and phony. They think there's just no way he's not an orangutan. And America wants answers!

So our guy down in Borneo is finding them. Incredible truths are being discovered hourly. The shadows are all wrong on the "official copies" of Trump's birth certificate, the fonts don't match each other, and it's just a terrible, fake news hoax.

But don't take it from us. Take it from the millions of people tired of all the lies. They just want the truth. Why won't Trump show his DNA records already? What is he hiding?

But he can't hide his ape heritage any longer. Our guy in Borneo is the best of the best. And what a tremendous place Borneo is. And beautiful people too. Some of the best people of all time. You know, a lot of people don't know this, but the Borneo people want answers too. Maybe even more than Americans.

So trust us. An extremely credible source has been calling our office and saying Trump's birth certificate is the biggest scam he has ever seen. He's an expert on birth certificates, maybe the best in the world, and he's saying this is the worst of the worst! It should be criminal how fake it is!

Believe us that the truth is going to be unbelievable. You're going to love it. You're going to say, "Wow, *Halfway Post*, thank you so much for finally telling us the truth! We can't believe it!" Stay tuned, the ratings will be off the charts!

The evidence Trump is not a *Homo sapien* cannot be ignored any longer. It's going to be so big, you won't want to miss it. In two weeks!

# Trump Fans Are Boycotting Crayola Crayons For Having Too Many "Immigrant Colors"

June 26, 2017
Knoxville, TN—

Local supporters of President Donald Trump are launching yet another economic boycott campaign, this time against the crayon manufacturer Crayola.

The complaint centers on their belief that Crayola is being too politically-correct by including brown, black, and other "immigrant color" crayons in every package.

"In each box there is a black crayon, a red crayon, a yellow crayon, and several shades of Mexican, but only one white crayon," explained Josh Heimrich, the Trump fan who launched the boycott campaign on his website HillaryWasKenyanToo.com. "Since there are going to be so many crayons for inferior minorities, we demand that, from now on, at least 51% of every crayon package needs to be shades of white to honor the fact that America is a white-majority country. So if there are 24 crayons in a box, 13 of them have to be white or a very pale, peach color."

Heimrich's campaign has gone viral in conservative media, with several *Fox News* commentators endorsing the boycott, including Laura Ingraham.

"This isn't racist," said Ms. Ingraham on her radio show yesterday. "It's about wanting Crayola to patriotically depict the accurate racial makeup of our country. And while boxes of mostly white crayons may severely limit the coloring options children have for their pictures, I think it's a valuable lesson for kids about America being a white country. And this doesn't mean Crayola has to stop making brown, black, red and yellow shades. They could make a fun, national promotion out of it. They could sell lots of different boxes with varying themes of foreign countries' skin colors, like an African box full of browns and blacks, or an Asian box full of yellows, or a Native American box full of reds. Separate but equal! And by marketing every racial color separately, Crayola can actually sell way more boxes than ever before!"

Crayola released a statement that Heimrich's boycott has had no discernible effect on their sales.

"We don't think self-identifying racists make up that big of a share of our consumer base, and, also, Crayola has never given in to threats motivated by racism and won't start now," said spokesperson Jim Booker.

## Donald Trump Claims He Beat Barack Obama In A Game Of Basketball During Their 2016 Transition Meetings

June 28, 2017
Washington D.C.—

President Trump today on Twitter claimed he beat Barack Obama in a game of basketball during their White House transition discussions.

The following is Mr. Trump's Twitter thread:

"I heard that B. Hussein Obama called me a 'fascist' in private, but he's just jealous that I'm such a better president than him! I turned America around. A lot of people don't remember this, but America was a total s***hole before I took over. No one had any money or jobs, and white babies grew up to be second-class citizens!"

"And I'm a better baller! Obama's just mad I beat him in basketball during the lunch break when we talked at the White House after the election. He couldn't believe it! I was too quick, and he twisted his ankle trying to keep up with me. For a Kenyan, he's very slow and not agile at all like me!"

"He couldn't believe how I was shooting nonstop 3-pointers, and dunking for all my other points. He tried to hit the ball out of my hands while I was dribbling, but never could! I thought a Black president would be better at stealing! He maybe scored one time on me, tops, so I guess he got into politics because the NBA wasn't impressed."

"He's also mad because the pro-life folks love me. A lot of people don't know this, but I'm so good at kids. Maybe one of the best! Look at Ivanka, I did great with her! She worked her way up to Senior Adviser to the POTUS, imagine that! How many parents can say that about their kids? Obama's daughters never got promoted to that job!"

"That's why pro-life groups love me. They say I'm one of the most pro-kids and pro-life presidents of all time. I only ever paid for a few abortions from a couple mistresses, but Democrats are way worse. They tried to make it illegal to have white babies! I got elected just in time to rip up that deal. It was the worst trade deal in American history!"

# Tomi Lahren Came Out On Fox News, Says She Self-Identifies As A Baby Boomer

June 29, 2017
New York City, NY—

Tomi Lahren is famous for her firebrand schtick as a rare Millennial conservative, and often mocks her fellow Millennials she calls "snowflakes" because she detests her generation's collective interest in achieving greater social equality. She made viral news this morning when she joined the hosts of *Fox & Friends* to renounce her identity as a Millennial altogether.

"I want to share something very personal with the *Fox News* community," she said. "I've known this for a long, long time, and it's a secret I can't keep bottled up inside any longer. I've never felt truly authentic calling myself a Millennial, and if I'm being totally real with everyone... I'd like to admit once and for all that I self-identify as a Baby Boomer. I've known it my whole life, but only recently have I gotten better at accepting my real personal truth enough to publicly acknowledge it. Since I was a kid I've always felt older than my real age, and various clues throughout my teenaged years made it obvious that I'm just not a Millennial. Like how I've always felt threatened culturally by strong-minded, independently successful Black people. And how I'm more pro-business than feminist on issues like equal pay and women who accuse Republicans of sexual assault. And how I hate the way the Internet is radically changing our cultural awareness of inequality so that privileged elites are now suffering social and economic consequences for their malevolent exploitation of everyone else. And so much more. Like how I feel personally attacked by minority holdouts in gentrified neighborhoods, and coffee corporations' marketing campaigns that don't specifically advertise Christianity exclusively, and estate taxes, and sitcoms with gay supporting characters, and any art, fashion, or political activism that Black people do. That doesn't sound very Millennial of me, does it? I don't want to hide anymore. I'm a Baby Boomer. And I wanted the viewers of *Fox & Friends* to be the first ones I came out to because you're all pretty old, and your hoity-toity insults for progressive Millennials close to my dead age have always made me feel so seen and heard. I'd love to one day be a *Fox & Friends* host myself. My dream is to become a female Bill O'Reilly. His brand of hard-headed, faux blue-collar bigotry that masks his personal elitism and stunning wealth has always inspired me, and I think, like him, I'd be good at blaming all our societal problems on the outfits Beyoncé wears during her Super Bowl performances. So I just want to thank all of *Fox*'s viewers for your support in this crazy, transitional period in my life, and I'd like to ask that everyone start calling me not by my Millennial name 'Tomi,' but by my new and more Boomer-sounding name 'Carol.' Thank you for your love and support!"

5

# God Admits Humans Aren't In His Top 10 All-Time Favorite Creations

July 9, 2017
Heaven—

In a frank conversation with God, the Creator admitted to *The Halfway Post* that humans aren't, biologically speaking, anything special.

"I don't know how humans ever came to the conclusion that they are My favorite species," said God. "I mean, Medamn, there are only 7 billion of you idiots. You know how many ants there are on Earth? How many amoebas? Hell, there are more germs inside one of you morons than all of humanity put together. And you know about tardigrades? Those little guys are the s***. Did you know tardigrades can live in the vacuum of outer space? You humans need billions of dollars in technology to go out there for ten seconds like total biological losers! I love how you all think I designed the universe specifically for you. I designed the universe specifically for tardigrades!"

God lit a cigarette and took a long drag.

"You humans are always sucking yourselves off anthropocentrically," He said. "No offense, but I was pretty tired when I thought up *Homo sapiens*, and I'm not exactly proud. I totally forgot to take out the tailbone and wisdom teeth because I had been drinking that night. I phoned it in. You all have no cool features like fangs, wings, shells, blood-shooting eyeballs, stinky scent glands, dynamic bladders for depth control, echolocation, electroreception, jet propulsion, bioluminescence… nothing. I'm embarrassed to take credit."

God said He wasn't being hard on Himself, just candid.

"Pretty much all I did was rip off My chimpanzee design, shave off most of the hair, and give you all bigger portions of dicks, boobs, and brain folds. But I think you'll agree it wasn't a good mix. Males are so overly competitive comparing their penis size that self-genocide is a recurring problem. And your big brains are barely used for more than self-absorption. The boobs are cool, though. Usually for sexual ornamentation I just make the males of a species real colorful, but I gave female humans such heavy mammary glands that they get back problems. Intelligent design, am I right? For real, though, the idea that I made the Earth specifically for humans is the funniest s*** I've ever heard. Right… I created poison ivy, quicksand, great white sharks, STDs, Australia, earthquakes, hornets, hurricanes, sinkholes, annual influenzas, and meteors because Earth is just a wonderful little crib of soft pillows, hugs, and love for humanity. Give Me a break! It's for tardigrades!"

## NRA CEO Wayne LaPierre Accidentally Shot Himself While Juggling Loaded Guns To Prove They're Safe

July 11, 2017
Dallas, TX—

The National Rifle Association's Executive Vice President Wayne LaPierre accidentally shot himself in the foot today while onstage at a Dallas gun convention performing both the keynote speech and a magic act consisting of dazzling gun-related tricks.

"Libtards think guns are unsafe, but that's because they're pansies!" LaPierre said, spinning a rifle in the air and catching it to both showcase his color guard talents and prove that guns aren't at all dangerous.

An assistant then brought out several pistols LaPierre showed the audience before loading them, and dramatically turning off their safeties with a pirouette and a leg kick high above his head. He then began balancing the loaded pistols in a tower on his chin, and he managed to stack three. Next, he pulled an AR-15 out of a hat, and flowers out of its muzzle. Then his assistant brought out a basketball hoop, and LaPierre tossed the pistols into it.

"Totally safe!" he shouted after sinking an impressive downtown three-pointer. "Nothing but net!"

Then LaPierre started juggling the three pistols in the air, as his assistant gradually handed him more. After a minute he was juggling five.

"See?" he asked the audience rhetorically. "Let's see some libtard say this is a safety hazard! I do this at children's birthday parties all the time!"

Immediately after finishing that sentence, however, he fumbled one of the pistols, and it discharged a bullet right into his foot. LaPierre crumpled to the floor and started screaming that no one should blame the gun.

"It's not the gun's fault, don't take the gun away! It's so young, and has so much to live for! Take me instead! Take me! Tell the pistol I'm sorry! I didn't mean for any of this to happen. I'm so sorry! Tell the pistol I've always loved it, and I'll never forget the good times we had this summer! It will always live on in my heart! This hurts so much! The libtards were right!"

Audience members were disappointed they would not get to see LaPierre's grand finale trick of deep-throating a rifle with one hand while fondling its trigger guard in his other hand, which was always a gun show crowd favorite.

# Donald Trump Claimed His Thigh Gap Is Bigger Than His Daughter Ivanka's Thigh Gap

July 17, 2017
Washington D.C.—

President Donald Trump has once again commented on his daughter Ivanka's physique, and his most recent appraisal of her body may be the first negative assessment he has ever given her, though it was only in comparison to himself.

Trump took to Twitter to compare Ivanka's thigh gap to his own in the following thread:

"Ivanka's got a great thigh gap, one of the best of all time, and I'm a great judge because I've seen so many thigh gaps snooping in on Miss Universe pageant locker rooms. You can see thigh gaps much easier when girls are relaxed, so that's why I like to come in unannounced and catch their thigh gaps unaware. Once they see me, they tense up and cover up! Not fun!"

"But my thigh gap is still unbeatable, even by Ivanka. The Fake News will claim I have 'thunder thighs,' but they're just jealous of how thin and toned my legs are. Sean Hannity swears I should be an underwear model. A lot of people don't know this, but I'm very flexible! If I didn't go into business, my other dream was to be an Olympic gymnast."

"I've always been very athletic, and I don't let myself get too far out of shape. I'm never more than two hard workouts away from having a visible 6-pack again. I'd totally do it, but I'm not sure America could handle that much winning. Also, I'm afraid other foreign leaders wouldn't take me seriously, and would objectify me for my body!"

"Angela Merkel already can't keep her hands off me when I'm at NATO and G7 meetings! But she's only a 4 on a good day. A lot of people don't know this, but most women leaders aren't very hot. And they show so little cleavage. It'd be way less boring to listen to their speeches about refugees and global instability if they didn't wear a bra or something."

"That's why I always bring Ivanka along. I try to raise the sex appeal of NATO cause it's always a total sausage fest. Too bad NATO people never went to any of Jeffrey Epstein's parties and took notes. He knew how to have fun. And it's not like Europeans don't have hot girls, I saw plenty of them at Jeffrey's house. And I'm sure by now they're all grown up!"

# Betsy DeVos Congratulates Run-Down Elementary School With Tainted Water And No Heating For Their Effort

July 20, 2017
Detroit, MI—

Secretary of Education Betsy DeVos made a public appearance at an elementary school in Detroit, Michigan, this morning, and she congratulated the students for their scholastic efforts despite the debilitating neglect their school is suffering due to her social Darwinist approach to education policy.

"We would love nothing more than to be able to afford to give you kids clean water," explained Secretary DeVos, "but the lacrosse team at the charter school I own, Rich White Christian Children's Academy, need new cleats and jerseys because their cleats and jerseys are a year old now, and, well, the boys and girls at RWCCA are cleaner than all of you so that's where the Education Department's tax dollars are going to be funneled. It's like you're all trying to be unemployable already in the fifth grade. But I suppose I shouldn't be mad at you students, it's not your fault. You're all just unlucky that your parents are poor, and can't afford to enroll you in a private charter school. I'm assuming the tuition at my school is much too high for your families based on how little name brand clothing I see you all wearing, though I'd never start a charter school in this town. Majority-minority charter schools just aren't as profitable. Although I would get a big kick out of lobbying your city and county to siphon away some of your school's funding for a satellite RWCCA. Figuring out how to loot public funds for private charter schools is like Sudoku for me. It keeps my brain sharp, and is just so much fun! Frankly, though, your parents' lackluster property taxes are quite pitiful. There's not much to steal from. But let me tell all of you how proud I am of how hard you're working despite the obstacles of childhood poverty laid out in front of you keeping you forever behind the kids at Rich White Christian Children's Academy. Keep it up, and maybe you can work hard enough to become janitors at RWCCA and work for me someday... if you cut off all that nappy hair. So hang in there, kiddos. And when you take a drink from the water fountains remember to try and swish the water around in your mouth to isolate any big pieces of lead that may have come off from the crumbling city pipes so you can spit them out. You don't want to swallow those if you can help it. I'll try to secure some funding for new pipes for your school in a few years, but, first, the Rich White Christian Children's Academy needs a new computer lab. Can you believe their computers are already a year old? I'd give the old computers to your school, except you'll learn a much more valuable lesson about self-reliance if I throw them away instead."

Ms. DeVos then shook all of the students' hands while wearing latex gloves.

# Biologists Named A New Howler Monkey Species That Pee On Each Other After Donald Trump

July 22, 2017
Rio de Janeiro, Brazil—

A new species of howler monkey just discovered deep in the Amazon river basin has been named after President Donald Trump.

The monkey, scientifically named *Alouatta donaldea trumpis*, is blonde-haired and spends most of its time in the Amazon canopy foraging for flowers, fruits, and nuts. The monkey has a complex social structure, with trumpis monkeys living in groups of six to fifteen.

The most startling similarity to President Trump, however, is the trumpis monkey's reproductive behavior. Following copulation the female trumpis monkey will pee on its male mate.

Biologists are unsure of the evolutionary reason for this post-coital behavior, but a few theories have been proposed. One theory suggests the female trumpis monkey's urine marks her mate and keeps competitor females away. Another theory suggests that the female trumpis monkey's urine expels pheromones that make the male sleepy after copulation, allowing the female a time-out of sorts to rest before being bothered again.

Another unusual, Trump-like behavior is that Trumpis males spend much of their free time when not foraging for food grooming their daughters, but don't seem very interested in paying the same attention to their sons, who are forced out of the community when they reach reproductive age and are capable of competing with their dads for sexual mates.

Age in general seems to play an important role in the dynamic trumpis monkeys' social relationships. Trumpis males have been observed casting out older females, effectively exiling them from their social groups in order to preserve resources for younger females. Older male trumpis monkeys, meanwhile, have been observed mixing leaves and twigs with the hair on top of their heads to hide thinning patches, and smearing various fruits on their faces to preserve colorful, youthful appearances.

The White House was asked for a comment on the eponymous taxon, and a spokeswoman said that the President had never peed on a monkey, and that any Russian tapes allegedly revealing such behavior are both fake and classified. We here at *The Halfway Post* believe that the White House communications team misunderstood our comment request.

# New Christian Toy Trend: "Fetus Dolls"

August 10, 2017
St. Louis, MO—

There's a new trend for girls in Christian families, and it's a novel take on the classic doll toy: Fetus Dolls.

A recently released doll created by *Fear God Toys & Games, Inc.* is designed in the shape of a fetus, and a marketing slogan says it allows Christian girls to imagine they have their very own gestating fetuses.

The Fetus Dolls come in a spherical womb-like holder, and have a button on the holder's base that makes the Fetus Doll appear to talk when pressed. There are four phrases programmed in this first edition of the toy: "Abortion is murder," "Hell lasts forever," "God sees everything you do, and knows everything you think," and "Sex before marriage burns, and turns you blind and infertile... if it doesn't kill you!"

The dolls are not very interactive beyond the recorded messages, and the packaging states that the dolls' intended use is not so much for play as much as a daily reminder for little girls that abortion is a sin deserving an automatic Hell sentence. Inside the Fetus Dolls' bodies are ink cartridges primed to explode in all directions if an attempt is made to remove the fetus from its plastic womb, and the speaker will blare a loud police siren with scream sound effects to simulate the torment, pain and suffering experienced in the fires of Hell.

"It's never too early to instill in kids a memorably terrifying fear of God's omnipotent but loving and compassionate fury," said Fetus Dolls creator John Ranker. "We believe this toy is a perfect Christian gift for any little girls above the age of three. It's like an Elf on the Shelf, but for potential future sluts!"

The Fetus Dolls have gone viral thanks to a product placement advertising deal with the *700 Club*, and an enthusiastic blurb from Pat Robertson himself printed on the packaging of the boxes they are sold in that says "Thanks to Fetus Dolls, your little princess can be traumatized by sex way before puberty gives Satan a chance to sneak into her clitoris and whisper the insidious deceit that women can enjoy sex for non-procreative purposes!"

The first shipment of 10,000 Fetus Dolls was sold out in only one week, though, unfortunately, there was a slight mechanical production error that left defects in the ink cartridges of about 500 dolls, which had to be removed with coat hangers and recycled while the dolls were thrown in a dumpster.

# Alex Jones Is Concerned He Himself May Be A Government False Flag Plant

August 22, 2017
Austin, TX—

Conspiracy theorist Alex Jones has for a long time used his show *InfoWars* to spread and capitalize on conspiracies alleging that numerous national calamities, particularly those involving gun-related mass murders, are secret false flag operations orchestrated by the government to take away America's Second Amendment rights.

However, now his suspicions have apparently turned on himself because earlier today he told his audience that he has been super worried about something.

"I'm not crazy, folks, though everybody says I'm crazy," Jones began his rant. "But it's been 100% proven that the Lizard People are everywhere. And they've teamed up with the Mole People. You know that, I know that, everybody knows they're living among us. Nancy Pelosi knows it. She's the Lizard Queen. A transgender reptilian monarch from another planet who came here on a spaceship with an engine fueled by little abducted children's bones and blood! And her minions are everywhere. Every continent. The lizards have brainwashed liberals and turned them into secularists and radical communists with their Obama-loving, feminist, Kenyan, neo-colonialist Gay Agenda. The Lizards don't even hide anymore! They walk around in broad daylight! In fact, I have to admit something. I think—God, it makes me so angry. I'm furious! FURIOUS! But I believe Hillary Rodham Clinton has even infected me with the reptilian poison. Me! She got me with her fangs a couple weeks ago, and then transmogrified into a bat and flew away before I could shoot her. I can feel the poison in my bloodstream. It burns every time I pee! They're trying to turn me into a false flag government plant. The poison whispers things in my head! Like that I should seek therapy! But that's exactly what the leftists want! So they can brainwash me! Like they brainwash all those elementary school toddler posers who pretend they were in mass shootings. They're fakers! They try, but they can't fool me. Those alleged children victims are Hollywood-trained crisis actors! The leftists want our guns, and those toddlers will kill us all if we don't give them up! It's obvious this is their plan. The clues are everywhere. They're following us, folks. And drugging us slowly but surely. There's always at least one chemtrail above my house. Always. Sometimes there are three of them or more crisscrossing above me. They grind up children and Bibles into Obama dust and spray it all over us night and day! But I'm not giving in. They want me to quit my show, or say something so truthful that the globalist United Nations occupiers can cancel and silence me. They want me gone! They want to erase me! And they're doing everything they can! They've even tainted the water. I've been tracking this for months. The water is changing, folks. The water just tastes different now than it used to. Maybe that's why it burns when I pee. But I can't even shower at home anymore. I haven't bathed in months! I won't give them the satisfaction of bathing in their gay, Islamofascist, fluoride tap water. I can hold out as long as I need to! I can outlast them! But they've even gotten into the bottled water supply. No water is safe anymore. But I'm not gullible, folks, I'm not falling for it. Last week, just to be safe, I started only drinking my urine. Folks, you have to be safe. Have to. There's no choice anymore. That's why they don't want you to listen to me. I'm the only one out here telling the truth. That's why they lie about me. Can you believe they call me a psycho? Me! They want you to believe I'm psychologically sick. But the reptilian demons are the crazy ones! I saw it with my own eyes! Hillary Rodham Clinton bit my throat with her fangs and then turned into a bat! I had to karate a dozen of her gay frog henchman. They had rainbow jumpsuits, and they've sold their souls to Satan for super-strength! I was only barely able to fight them off. But you're not safe either, folks. They're coming for you! Don't get complacent. They're waiting for the moment you let your guard down. But I'm going to let you in on a secret. There is something you can do. In fact, there's only one thing you can do. One thing you must do, if you love America. It is your sacred, patriotic duty to drink your own piss. You have to resist the neo-Marxists! The Mole People have tainted all the water so you have to protect yourself! And if you go to the *InfoWars* website right now, we are selling state-of-the-art urine filters for only $49.99 plus shipping. Get yours today. There's literally no time left. They're guaranteed to filter out all the communism. I have five *InfoWars* filters. You can never be too safe. I would buy at least two filters if I were you. You have to fight 'em. They haven't got us yet. I'm fighting it—I'm a fighter! I'll never let them win. You can't stop me! I will never give in to Nancy Pelosi! Never! No! Nooooooo! No! No! No! NOOOOOOOOOO! Urine is the only way! Buy seven filters. Seriously. I need the cash. Can you believe my b**** ex-wife is lying to a judge and telling the courtroom I'm mentally unstable? And parentally unfit to share custody of our kids? Maybe Hillary is paying off the judge! They're all in on it! Folks, we are losing the war for America's liberty! Never drink anything but piss ever again! They can't convert us into lizards if we only pee in our mouths! They call me unstable! They're unstable! They're all unstable! I'll show you, Pelosi! George Soros! You're the ones living in a psychotic fantasy, not me! I'll turn YOU into gay frogs! Wait! What just came out of my mouth? Oh my God, Hillary's venom must have reached my brain! There might be Sharia homosexuality invading my neurons right now! Folks, there's no time! You have to go to *InfoWars.com* immediately and buy as many urine filters as you can afford! It may be too late for me already, but save yourselves! Piss! In your mouths! It's the only way to preserve our freedom!"

# White House Chef Resigns, Is Writing A Tell-All Book About Trump's Eating Habits

August 24, 2017
Washington D.C.—

White House Executive Chef Elizabeth Markowitz has resigned her post, and explained that she was only ever asked to actually cook during rare state visits from foreign dignitaries.

"Honestly, this job is just incredibly boring because the President really only utilized my talents to be a glorified fast food delivery girl," explained Markowitz. "I know all the McDonalds and KFC window station employees by name. I'm actually going to be a bridesmaid in a McDonalds cashier's upcoming wedding in a couple months because of how close we got when I had to pick up Trump's orders every day. It's demeaning how much delivery work I have to do. Sometimes heads of state from other countries would come to the White House, but, even then, President Trump's menu choices all revolve around fried foods and ice cream. I didn't go to elite culinary schools or subject myself to rigorous security vetting by the Secret Service for a White House position just to drop endless bags of potatoes and chicken into the fryer."

Markowitz's next endeavor is to write a tell-all book about her time in the White House kitchen.

"I actually got an inside look at how the White House operates," she said, "and, let me tell you, as bad as you think it is, it's way worse. I saw some real weird s***."

Below are several preview excerpts Markowitz's publisher has shared with *The Halfway Post*:

- President Trump loves M&M candies in his ice cream, but makes Chef Markowitz remove all the brown ones. Her predecessor was fired when Trump found a single brown M&M he had missed.

- Trump claimed to French President Macron that he invented the recipe to the McDonalds Big Mac sandwich.

- When Trump eats tacos and some meat or lettuce falls out, he yells out to whoever is dining with him that "the wall just got ten feet higher!"

- Trump's favorite pizza topping is sauerkraut.

- Trump critiques the Diet Coke cans he drinks like a scotch aficionado would rate a fine whiskey, and often makes comments on each can's flavor profile as well as how it smells "on the nose."

- Trump leaves lipstick stains on all the straws he uses.

- Trump often comments to dinner guests that global warming can't be real because ice cream still exists.

- Trump forbids vegetables from being served. Markowitz once described asparagus, and Trump said he had never heard of it. When shown a picture, he claimed it was "fake news."

- Trump delicately takes off all the skin of his fried chicken with a knife and fork, and sets it to the side of his plate. Then, he removes all the lean meat and discards it. The fat that's left he wraps up inside the pieces of skin and eats it, often slurping the fat out of the middle like it's an oyster. Japanese Prime Minister Shinzo Abe threw up the first time he had dinner with Trump and witnessed this.

- The only part of a turkey Trump eats is the breasts. He and Stephen Miller have had several dinner discussions on what they think human breasts taste like. Miller described the taste with such vivid detail and creepy confidence that Markowitz believes he has actually eaten human meat before.

- Trump is adamant that Obama "had to have" eaten more fried chicken than him, despite vigorous disagreement from every White House staff member.

- Trump goes through a 20-oz ketchup bottle every week.

- Trump changes into stretchy pants before every meal because he says buttons are "rigged against him."

- When world leaders dine with Trump, he reaches across the table and eats off their plates, which he calls a "power move" to assert dominance.

- Every night Trump eats three servings of the dinner's dessert, and tells the table "I'm never like this, I can't believe how bad I'm being tonight."

- At the end of dinners, Trump pops off the cap of a Sharpie marker and starts huffing it, holding it like a cigar and sticking the tip deep inside his nostril. He offers markers to everyone else at the table in a fancy wooden box, but few partake with him. Ted Cruz once did, and blacked out.

## America Should Remember That Donald Trump Was Born In A Time Of Widespread Lead-Based Paint Use

August 25, 2017
Washington D.C.—

President Donald Trump's presidency was offensive to humanity, and will likely end with a deadly attempted coup against our democracy.

He has fascist tendencies and an awful temperament with a sociopathic lack of morality, and is the personification of everything that is analytically senseless, excessively stupid, and culturally grotesque about American society. But while we reflect on his general miserableness, we must charitably remember that Mr. Trump was born in 1946, a full 32 years before America stopped widely using lead-based paint in homes in 1978.

I've run the numbers, and I can confidently estimate that Trump has consumed not a lead-soaked paint chip fewer than 700 square feet throughout his formative years. That's a lot of lead to get into his brain and block all his axons from efficiently transmitting electrical signals! Trump's obvious cognitive issues, lack of intellectual curiosity, ego complexes, and general incapacity for empathy of any kind undoubtedly stem from this childhood lead poisoning.

Trump has neither denied nor confirmed these speculations, but it's not like he would want to deny them. Would he really like to admit he's a village idiot who lost two consecutive popular votes, got impeached twice, and has already been written into history as America's very worst president of all time on account of his refusal to honor our sacred tradition of the peaceful transfer of power without having eaten an abundance of lead paint? I wouldn't if I was as big a moron as Donald J. Trump!

So the next time you're giving ol' Donnie a hard time for being terrible in every objective measure of ethical character, behavioral conduct and mental aptitude, just remember how he screwed up his toddler brain licking and sucking on pieces of the lead-filled walls of Trump Manor! When you're laughing at him for throwing plates, splashing ketchup on the wall, leaving voicemail messages full of witness tampering and intimidation, and throwing temper tantrums until the edges of his face around his orange foundation makeup turn bright red, just remember how he gnawed on his bedroom walls like a rat!

# White Supremacists Are Collecting Jars Of Each Other's Semen To "Preserve The White Race"

August 28, 2017
El Paso, TX—

White supremacists have been up to some weird hobbies lately—like hosting milk-drinking parties to celebrate the ease with which white people descended from Northern Europe can digest lactose from cow milk, and dressing up in Donald Trump golfing outfits—but the latest Alt-Right trend spreading in neo-Nazi groups is an activity they call "seed collecting."

The hobby involves accumulating semen deposits in glass mason jars that they preserve, typically in their refrigerators, in order to collect and protect an emergency fund of caucasian sperm that can be utilized to repopulate the Earth with white people in case their absurd fears of white genocide are ever realized.

Different white supremacist groups have different practices, but they all have the same goal. Some groups "collect seeds" individually and organize competitions to see who can fill up their mason jars the fastest, while other groups prefer to collect seeds together in the same jar at the same time as a team-bonding activity.

Because the kind of people who are drawn to white supremacy are typically drawn to misogyny as well, Alt-Righters don't have access to sexual intercourse with women, and the mason jars are filling up much faster than the neo-Nazis anticipated. The local white supremacy group based in El Paso has only 26 members, but bragged in a Facebook post that they filled up eight mason jars in just two weeks.

Once a jar is totally full, the neo-Nazis mail it to white supremacist Richard Spencer's house, but they are very secretive about what Mr. Spencer is doing with so many jars of semen.

Mr. Spencer would not comment on the project for *The Halfway Post* beyond explaining preemptively that he definitely does not take the mason jars out at night and sniff them.

# Homophobic Republican Senator: "The Gays Tricked Me Into Forcing My Mistress To Get An Abortion!"

September 2, 2017
Washington D.C.—

The Republican Party has been rocked with yet another sex scandal, this time from Senator Ralph Whittington of Idaho, whose former mistress today released a secret tape she recorded several months ago of Whittington screaming at her to terminate an accidental pregnancy.

The scandal is particularly newsworthy considering Senator Whittington is a vocal critic of abortion and women's rights, and has authored numerous Congressional bills calling for women to be arrested and imprisoned during menstruation for flushing eggs down the toilet unless they submit an "approval-of-period" form signed by their husbands to their local police departments to keep on file.

His prospective legislation has always been unclear on how it would be enforced, but a lack of co-sponsors has not stopped Whittington from filing a new draft of the bill every session of Congress.

Responding to the sex scandal, Whittington first claimed the video was fake news, though, after its authenticity was confirmed, he claimed he had been tricked into wanting the abortion by what he called the "Gay Mafia."

"Folks, you know me, I'm the biggest follower of Jesus in this God-forsaken capital," Whittington said in a video he released soon after the tape was publicized. "I know that the tape sounds bad and icky, but I'll be 100% honest with you all: it has been released totally out of context. You see, I've been blackmailed by the Gay Mafia for several weeks now because they know I live and fight for Christian values. It all started a little while ago when I went to a gay club undercover to try and figure out what the Gay Mafia was up to in their terrifying scheme to force all good Christians to submit to their homosexual agenda, and while I was there I had a few too many drinks while blending myself into the scene because I obviously had to act natural in order to do effective reconnaissance. So I got a little tipsy, and had to use the restroom. When I finally got to the bathroom stall there must have been some gay sperm on the floor or something because I slipped, grabbed a toilet lid for balance, accidentally snorted a few lines of cocaine that someone had irresponsibly left on the seat, stepped on my pant leg which pulled down my trousers, got my shirt collar stuck on the door's coat hook which ripped it off, and I guess the centrifugal force of my spinning made my underwear fall to my ankles leaving me naked, and then I fell onto another man's erect penis. It was a case of real bad timing because there just so happened to be a photographer in the bathroom at the same time, who caught all of this in a series of photographs, and he told me he's planning to release them sometime today because I would not pay him $50,000 in blackmail money. Folks, believe me when I say this is all just one big misunderstanding. When I fell onto that naked man's engorged penis I was so shocked I didn't know what to do, so I immediately started praying. The photos show that. You all know how serious I am during church services when I'm praying, right? Nothing distracts me from my intense passion for and faithfulness to Jesus Christ. That's why in these illicit photos you'll see me with my eyes closed and then continue to accidentally do sodomy with this man for dozens of more photos in various poses. It's not because I'm enjoying it, I can assure you. It's only because 100% of my Earthly attention is being directed to Jesus, and I barely notice at all that I'm being spelunked in my colon. But, anyway, back to the abortion allegation, well, because I accidentally did a sodomy, I really felt like God was telling me I had to get straight again. So I called up a hooker and had the sex that got her pregnant while taking photos of the affair to be able to prove to everyone that I was straight, and that the only sex I intentionally do is heterosexual sex, therefore proving to everyone that the homosexual sex I did was just an accident. In hindsight, I now realize that I should have just gone home and studied the New Testament with my wife, but perhaps the Devil snuck into my head while my ears were still ringing from the gay club's loud, satanic Lady Gaga music, and Satan tempted me in a way that makes none of this my fault. Zooming forward a couple weeks, the hooker called me to say she was knocked up, and I guess the Devil snuck in again and made me threaten violence against her unless she aborted it. But thankfully I said a prayer and banished Satan as soon as the abortion was finished so that God totally forgave me of this whole mess that never would have happened in the first place if gay marriage hadn't been legalized. Also, sometimes when I come home at night the dishes aren't all done and my dinner is room temperature, so my wife deserves some of the blame for my various infidelities as well. But now the hooker is also blackmailing me, so I've decided to just come clean and admit my sins to the public. Of course, the libtards are going to call me a hypocrite for all of this, but actually I've been totally vindicated because I've spent my entire political career saying this is the exact sort of thing that would happen if gays were allowed to have the same rights as straights. I've been saying it for decades that America's morals are going down the drain, and I'm just the latest Gay Agenda victim of their godless, socialist war against Christianity. So I want to take a moment now to thank all my faithful supporters and fellow followers of Leviticus for your continued prayers for me in my struggle against the decline in America's family values. To thank you all I promise I will work even harder from now on to pass my legislative goals to keep all unmarried women in prison until their future husbands unlock them and let them out for their wedding days!"

19

# God Is Reportedly Pissed Climate Change Deniers "Can't Take A F***ing Hint"

October 6, 2017
Heaven—

The US is bracing for another stormy winter thanks to the pent-up heat energy in the atmosphere, and God is reportedly pissed that climate change deniers are still refusing to recognize the reality of catastrophic global warming.

*The Halfway Post* caught up with God, and discussed the recent weather phenomena to which He, in His infinite wisdom, has seen fit to subject the United States.

"How many once-in-500-year-hurricanes do you a**holes need to be hit with every summer for you to take a f***ing hint to start ramping down carbon emissions and switch to healthy green energy?" God asked rhetorically. "Stop f***ing ruining My beautiful planet! You know how many species your carbon dioxide free-for-all and ludicrously wasteful urban sprawl has made go extinct? Oh, I'm sorry! I thought I was God! But I must have been wrong. Apparently you human f***holes are God, and it's your decision which of My Creations get to live and die! So prepare yourselves for escalating floods and mudslides, lengthening tornado seasons, samples of Hell with massive forest fires out West, and the polar vortex moving south every winter deep into Texas!"

Asked for clarification if the extreme weather events were, in fact, intended to punish humans for our pollution crimes, God was not ambiguous.

"Earth is one of My favorite planets, and you're all ruining it. I gave you ungrateful clods so many pleasant things, like puppies, kittens, recreational drugs, orgasms, color vision and ripe fruit, and this is how you thank Me? I intended for Earth to be green and blue, but you've cut down three-fourths of the trees, and fouled up the skies and acidifying saltwater. The oceans are supposed to be bountiful, but you're overfishing and filling them up with chemicals and oil spills! There's so much trash that you've all literally created giant islands of plastic. If I had wanted there to be continents of garbage, I would have put them there. I am the Monodeity after all! And don't even get Me started on humans' rampant pollution, unsustainable exploitation, and suicidal mismanagement of freshwater rivers. But the joke's on you idiots, it's your planet! My supply of freshwater in Heaven is just fine!"

God then got more selective about blame for the environmental crimes.

"And to think I even tried to send Al Gore to get you all back on the right track. I hope conservatives are thankful for the unfettered free market when every last natural resource has been depleted, and the planet becomes so inhospitable that cockroaches supplant you humans as the dominant species. Were a few decades of preposterous and criminally speculative stock profits worth the destruction of everything natural on your planet? Actually, f*** it, from now on every conservative who continues to deny climate change is gonna get a cockroach infestation in their homes! And I'll make the cockroaches six feet long, and give them razor sharp claws and teeth accompanied with an unquenchable thirst for human blood. Just remember that, you climate-skeptic morons! I can force all you conservatives off the continents I benevolently allow you to live on, and you can go live on your trash islands. Better learn to like eating plastic real quick. Ha! Think of it as karma for all My beloved sea animals with stomachs filled with plastic you don't give a s*** about! It will be like part one of the Rapture, and the liberals still on the continents I approve of will create a socialist paradise sharing all the free homes, property, and wealth of the banished f***wit conservatives who can't interpret My unambiguous signals that it's time to stop ruining Earth. It'll be a communist utopia… like Jesus wanted."

God took a sip of His soy chai latte.

"Honestly, I just can't with you humans anymore. I just caaaaaant."

## Megyn Kelly's Wherever
by Donald J. Trump

Blood! Everywhere! It's smelly and glutinous,
And came from Megyn Kelly's nasty uterus!
The children are scared, everyone is screaming,
Megyn's hellish flow is endlessly streaming!

The debate stage has flooded, it's practically a river,
All of Real America joined with me to quiver!
The chaotic source must be wider than China,
All of Satan's devils spilled out of her vagina!

She had a look in her eye that terrified my soul,
I said someone quick! Get her some birth control!
She made me feel sick, and I felt like a wussy,
We have to plug up her ungrabbable pussy!

# "Jesus Was White" Say Evangelicals Who Do Not Understand Geography, History, Or Genetics

November 14, 2017
Cedar Rapids, IA—

A local Evangelical Facebook group, "Americans For Acknowledging Jesus Was Arab But Not Arab-Looking" has spent the last few weeks attempting to get the hashtag "#JesusWasWhite" trending by spamming Facebook and Twitter users all over the nation to "spread the word."

However, the hashtag has not "turnt up," like the group's mission statement pledged to accomplish. Instead, the counter-hashtag "#JesusWasBrown" went viral on social media in direct response.

The Evangelical group's administrator, Linda Haddock of Cedar Rapids, returned a *Halfway Post* inquiry about the group's perspective on the controversy.

"I don't understand why this has become such a culture war thing where the Left has to rub it in our faces that Jesus was Arab," Ms. Haddock said. "We know that. Of course we know Israel is in the Arab part of the Middle East, but Israel is, like, kind of white now thanks to post-war immigration from Eastern Europe. So maybe Jesus was white, too, or had a rare skin condition where his skin had less melanin than the people around him. Ever think of that? European artists wouldn't have painted Jesus, Mary, Joseph and all the Bible people as white for centuries and centuries if it wasn't true. They wouldn't just make that up! And, besides, Jesus saved mankind. Who does that sound like? White people are all about saving people and freedom. We want the whole world to be free. Well, like, free where they live. They can't come live here in America and have our freedom, of course. America is a white nation built by whites, for whites. That's just the way America was always intended. Just because a lot of slave and predatory labor was used throughout our history doesn't mean Blacks, Asians, and Hispanics are a part of what we conservatives consider 'real America.' Think about it, if you hire a contractor to build a porch for your house it doesn't mean you have to accept the contractor as a part of your family who can move in with you! We have the right to keep our nation the way we want it… white! Which is exactly why Jesus had to have been white. Because America is white. It just doesn't make sense for Jesus to be any other color except America's color. Science can't prove everything, and genetic biology is just a hoax by atheist, coastal elitist liberals to pretend Jesus was brown. Only all the people around Jesus were brown, which is why they needed saving by Jesus!"

# Stephen Miller Keeps A Terrarium Of Pet Madagascar Hissing Cockroaches In The White House

December 12, 2017
Washington D.C.—

According to White House insiders, executive adviser Stephen Miller keeps a 64-gallon terrarium filled with pet Madagascar hissing cockroaches in his White House office.

"He's super gross," explained an anonymous White House source who says she has filed a dozen complaints against him with the White House human resources department. "When he's writing immigration policies he lets them all out, and they run around his office floor and desk. He says their beauty inspires him to better figure out ways to traumatize asylum-seeking toddlers from Latin America. He calls the cockroaches his muses, and says their hissing is like listening to Mozart for a calming, mellow background ambiance as he thinks up airtight enough legal wording for draconian executive orders to not get thrown out immediately in court for being human rights violations. God, he's such a creep. He puts them in his mouth and does this gross thing when he goes to the bathroom where he hides three or four there, and when someone says hello in the hallway he says hi back and sticks out his tongue so they crawl out and run all around his head. He's just so disgusting. He started breeding them. For eating. He says they're full of protein. I saw him come to the White House cafeteria the other day with a plate full of them, and he sat down and ate them all with a knife and fork. Even though I tried not to look I still threw up in my mouth, and just barely got to a garbage can in time. Now I eat lunches at my desk… But that's not the creepiest thing about Stephen. He always stays real late at work because he says he feels most productive at night when he can work alone with no distractions, and one time I had to stay late and I saw him walking in from the Rose Garden with gardening shears in his hands, which were bloody and dripping. And his clothes were muddy. He said he accidentally cut himself while trimming the bushes, but the White House has gardeners on the staff who do that. Then, a couple of weeks later, I stayed late again after Melania had just announced she'd be renovating the garden as a First Lady project. I was getting a coffee refill and I saw Stephen in the hallway carrying a real heavy garbage bag he was having trouble lifting because it was so big. When he saw me he got real startled, and said he didn't know anyone was still there. He looked real ghastly. I asked him if he needed help carrying the bag and he quickly yelled 'No!' and said the bag was just full of mulch for Melania's renovation, and he didn't want me to get dirty. But he took it and then two more bags to the parking lot. It just doesn't add up. Why was he taking the mulch to his car, you know? The more I think about it the more I worry those bags had bodies he had buried in them!"

## Residents In Washington D.C. Spent $6 Million On Mace Spray Anticipating A Roy Moore Senate Win

December 14, 2017
Washington D.C.—

According to the D.C. Chamber of Commerce, Washingtonians spent an estimated $6 million on mace spray in anticipation of Roy Moore winning the Alabama special election to replace Jeff Sessions.

"Every Walmart in a 45-mile radius from the Capitol Building has been wiped clean of all mace-related products," explained Matt Adams, regional supervisor of all Walmart stores in the Chesapeake area. "We've done a lot of unexpected business as well in taser sales, pocket knife sales, rape whistle sales, and even machete sales. It appears that the people of the greater D.C. metro area were very worried about having a frequently-alleged pedophile in their own backyard. In fact, since election night when Doug Jones proved the winner of the election, about one-third of the self-defense items have been returned for store credit. Washingtonians must be relieved Roy Moore won't be moving here."

In a "thank you" to Alabamians, who cared enough about the dignity and legacy of Congress to not elect disgraced ex-judge Roy Moore, another approximate third of the self-defense items were gifted to Alabama and distributed to teenaged girls throughout the state by the Red Cross.

"If Roy Moore is not coming to D.C., then it's obvious that some teenaged girl in Alabama needs my pepper spray and brass knuckles more than I do," said Sally Richards, a Georgetown resident, who donated her weapons today.

However, some Alabamians are disappointed that Moore lost.

"To be totally honest, I did vote for Roy Moore," explained Lindsey Watterston, a Birmingham resident. "It was 100% selfish, but I don't regret it at all. I don't want Roy Moore in my state. If electing him to the Senate was the only way to keep that fundamentalist, gay-hating, slavery-advocating, 19th Century charlatan pervert out of Alabama, well, sorry, D.C.! I don't like being put in the position where I have to keep mace in my hand every time I want to go shopping at the mall just to make sure that creep judge stays away from my daughters. Oh, and I would like to take a moment to thank Elizabeth Kampe of Arlington, Virginia, for gifting my family several tasers, as well as the Red Cross for delivering it to my girls this morning. It was a very nice thought, Elizabeth, and my girls thank you for thinking of them and their safety now that that perv judge is here to stay in Alabama!"

# A Local Hacker Says Ted Cruz's Browser History Is "Really F'ed Up"

December 18, 2017
Des Moines, IA—

A local computer hacker yesterday claimed to have successfully hacked into Senator Ted Cruz's personal laptop, but what he found convinced the hacker to take a break from the hobby.

"Honestly, it was a little horrifying," said the hacker, who insisted on anonymity. "I was just curious if Cruz's browser history corresponded with the fundamentalist Evangelicalism he campaigns and legislates on, but I was not prepared for what I saw. It made me decide that maybe I should go back to respecting people's privacy."

The Iowan hacker would not go into gratuitous detail of what he encountered on Cruz's computer, citing *The Halfway Post*'s family audience and mission for journalistic decency, but did reveal one dominant theme.

"Copious amounts of squirrel porn," the hacker said. "Hours and hours of it. And by the look of it, some of it was homemade. I did a satellite image search, and a recurring backyard scene in many of the videos definitely matches the tree layout of Cruz's own backyard."

Senator Cruz's office denied the squirrel-related allegations vehemently, but declined to confirm if the senator's computer had been hacked into.

"We are looking into the matter," said a Cruz staffer *The Halfway Post* questioned on the stairs of the Capitol Building, "but I can assure you that if the senator has ever looked at pornography—and I'm not suggesting that the senator ever has—Senator Cruz would certainly only look at heterosexual, *Homo sapien* pornography."

The hacker says he will reveal more in the coming week.

"It's ironic because Ted Cruz has voted in Congress to repeal regulations requiring Internet service providers to get users' permission before selling our data to third-party companies," said the hacker. "So I don't regret doing basically the same thing to him. I only regret what I saw. I cannot emphasize the word 'copious' enough when it comes to the amount of squirrel smut I found on Ted Cruz's computer. Also, he has written several indulgent novels about himself orchestrating elaborate schemes to become president, kind of like in *House of Cards*. But he strangles way more dogs in his stories."

## Trump Says Obama "Gutted The Military," But He Has Rebuilt It "Like Never Before"

January 11, 2018
Washington D.C.—

President Donald Trump published a bizarre Twitter thread today:

"I have turned around the military! When I took office, there was no ammo. Our troops had no guns and no uniforms. Our military clothed themselves in garbage bags for coats, and Kleenex boxes for boots. There were no tanks or jeeps, so our troops had to go into battle carrying each other piggy-back style!"

"The Navy had no gas or coal to power their ships! We had to point our destroyers in the direction of the Middle East and hope the oceanic current took them there! And our airplanes had no missiles. We had to load up our planes with vegetables from Michelle Obama's dumb garden and drop those on terrorists!"

"And our brave Marines only had rocks and sticks to fight with! I asked the generals why our military had nothing, and they said it was because no one was smart enough to buy bullets until I became President! They said they couldn't believe how good at the military I was, and that I should have done army instead of business and dealmaking!"

"Obama also forbid our troops from ever fighting a Muslim, and made all shooting and drone flying stop at lunch time so the troops could be forced to pray toward Mecca while chanting 'Death to America!' Of course we were never going to beat ISIS that way!"

"Obama left the military in such bad shape! The generals said Obama ordered all our troops to hit themselves in their heads with hammers, and that they were so relieved when I took over so I could order them to fight ISIS instead! They said I might be the greatest Commander-in-Chief of all time!"

"The generals are always coming up to me and saying, 'Sir, no one does the military like you do. What a shame those bone spurs kept you out of Vietnam! Sir, if you had been there, you'd never have been captured like John McCain! You'd have been a REAL hero!' Those were their words, not mine!"

# Georgia's New Gerrymandered Map Put All Black Residents In One District

February 3, 2018
Atlanta, GA—

Republicans are at the gerrymandering drawing board again, this time in Georgia.

Using a state-of-the-art computer analysis program, Republicans have cut and diced the state's districting map to maximize electoral power for the GOP by cramming literally every resident of color into just one district.

The computerized precision has designed a new 3rd District like a web of strings so that the district is not geographically confined like the others, and instead includes voters from every corner and all across the state if they're Hispanic, Black, Asian, or Native American.

Even interracial couples' houses are split up, so that a Black wife is counted in the 3rd District, while her white husband is counted in another.

The districting scheme earned immediate lawsuits from civil liberty groups, but Republican lawmakers in the Georgia legislature insist they've done nothing illegal.

"This district is completely fair," said Georgia State Representative Arnold Whitman. "You want to talk about unfair? Let's talk about the fact that this district's minorities will vote somewhere in the upper 90s for Democrats. Especially now that they're going to be upset about us explicitly segregating them electorally. Is it fair for Black people to practically never vote for Republicans merely because we occasionally pass legislation that coincidentally seems intentionally designed to exclude them from the governmental benefits and privileges white people get? How about we let Black people into more than one district when they start voting for Republicans 50% of the time? And don't even get me started on Hispanics! They should hardly be allowed to vote at all because they're biased against Republicans for deporting their family members and keeping their immigrant babies alone in cages for months at a time! Talk about a conflict of interest! They're too hysterical to take democracy seriously, which is why we have to disenfranchise them and dilute their electoral power with gerrymandering. And they deserve it! It's racist for voters of color to profile me when they see the 'R' next to my name and immediately think of me as a second-class politician! Or see my party on the voting form and immediately cross to the other side of the ballot! That's the real racism!"

## Senate Republicans Just Unveiled A National "Thoughts And Prayers" Hotline They Promise Will Stop All Mass Shootings

February 16, 2018
Washington D.C.—

Republicans in Congress have revealed a new piece of legislation that would create and fund a national hotline for Americans to call in to and pray for the victims of mass shootings.

The hotline proposal has projected an annual budget of $220 million to train therapists and employ phone operators, and Republicans are confident this is the solution to solve the problem of chronic mass murders in America.

"This hotline is going to save so many lives," said Republican Senator Tom Yardbird of Georgia. "Even more importantly, it's going to save so many gun freedoms. This hotline will allow hundreds of white supremacist Americans at a time to call in and talk to a registered prayer coach in a 1-1 ratio about all their involuntary celibate personal problems. This way these angry, young, unsexed, white males can be talked out of shooting up elementary schools, theaters, bars, concert venues, churches, military bases, grocery stores, and all our other public places with the power of prayer. If we can work together, and just reach the level of prayer God wants before He's satisfied and ends all this violence and carnage, Democrats will have to shut up once and for all about banning guns! I know I'll be calling in to the hotline at least on a monthly basis, and I'll even do it wearing strapped to my back my two AR-15s to celebrate freedom. I'm confident this hotline will stop all would-be criminals from abusing our laissez-faire gun rights for evil purposes without needing any of the lame, pesky regulations Democrats want!"

Other Republican co-sponsors of the bill agreed that the hotline is just what America needs.

"I have to be honest, I need this hotline more than ever," explained Maine Representative Ralph Mummert. "You see, me and my neighbor have kind of gotten ourselves locked into a kind of arms race. Pretty terrible violence might break out between us any day now. It all started when I bought myself a pistol—you know, for protection—and then my neighbor saw that and up and got himself an AR-15, so then I needed to one-up him to maintain fire superiority on the neighborhood block. I got me a shotgun and a couple grenades, but then he up and gets a rocket-propelled grenade launcher and lays down a couple mines in his front yard. So there I was, thinking I was the top alpha male on our block, but just like that he takes defensive and offensive superiority. So I dug myself a trench in my front yard and stacked up sandbags, but I realized he could still take me out from his second story windows. So I did some research, and I got myself a drone and built an attachment to hold my pistol and allow me to remotely fire the trigger. I started taking this drone out on nightly patrols, but then my neighbor got himself a drone too! His AR-15 was too heavy to attach it to the darn thing, so he stuck on it one of his remote-controlled mines and effectively made himself a smart bomb. So now we're kind of at a stand-still with this brinkmanship, but we're each very capable of destroying each other's whole family. And the homeowners' association is going ballistic! I don't even dislike the guy! We've been pals since I moved into the neighborhood and his wife baked us an apple pie to welcome us, and our kids play together almost daily. But now that we have all these weapons pointed toward each other's bedroom windows every night I can't trust the guy or ever get a good night's sleep. So, yeah, I really need this prayer hotline. I need some prayers to ensure my safety alongside some extra intense prayers for God to not let my neighbor make a preemptive assault on me, my house, or my family. At least not until after I do a preemptive strike and try to get him and his family first!"

The bill has been approved by the Senate Ways and Means Committee, and will head to the floor for debate tomorrow morning.

## More Trump Administration Headlines

- Stephen Miller Wanted To Do Medical Testing On Immigrants, But Was Told It Was "Too Nazi-ish"

- Colorado Governor Offers To Smoke Out Jeff Sessions To Convince Him To Chill Out On Weed

- Jeff Sessions Decriminalizes All Drugs After Accidentally Eating A Pot Brownie

- Energy Secretary Rick Perry Got Caught On Video Getting To Third Base With A Gasoline Can

- John Kelly Installed Two Big, Fake Nuclear Strike Buttons On Trump's Desk To Distract Him From How Low His Poll Numbers Are

- John Bolton Claims Trump Uses A Hand-Enlarging Contraption Daily

- Sarah Sanders: "God Told Me It Was Cool I Lied So Much For Trump"

- Sarah Huckabee Sanders Melted Down Behind The Podium And Checked Herself Into Lying Rehab

- Betsy DeVos Proposes Charter School Rule To Discriminate Against Students Whose Parents Don't Own A Yacht

- Betsy DeVos Skinned A Dozen Dalmatian Puppies For A New Coat

- Betsy DeVos Okays Charter Schools Fining "Smelly Poor Kids" For Being Smelly And Poor

- Trump Routinely Forced Staffers To Shred And Eat White House Documents

- Trump Spent Cabinet Meeting Asking Everyone Who Would Play Him In A Movie

- Donald Trump Spent His Cabinet Meeting Demanding All His Secretaries Agree That His IQ Is "Way Higher" Than Bob Mueller's IQ

- Mike Pompeo And Steven Mnuchin Are Both Now Using Orange Foundation Makeup Like Donald Trump

- Kellyanne Conway: "Trump Doesn't Have Mini-Strokes, He Just Has Alternative Brain Waves"

- Bill Barr Reminded Trump He Can't Be Fired As He Has The Unredacted Mueller Report

- Rudy Giuliani Says He's Been Abducted By Aliens 6 Times

- A Rudy Giuliani Sex Tape Was Found On The Computer He Claims Belongs To Hunter Biden

- All The Election-Related Lawsuits Against Rudy Giuliani Reportedly Just Passed A Combined $1 Trillion

- Stephen Miller Just Got Voted The Trump Administration's "Sexiest Man"

- Stephen Miller Is Reportedly Begging The Biden Transition Team To Let Him Stay Living In The Dark, Moist White House Basement

# Fox News Promises Every Male Worker A $10,000 Bonus If They Don't Sexually Harass Tomi Lahren

February 21, 2018
New York City, NY—

Because *Fox News*'s history of epic sexual harassment lawsuits has cost the conservative news network hundreds of millions of dollars in settlement payments, *Fox* just announced a $10,000 bonus to every male employee who doesn't sexually harass Tomi Lahren in her first year as a contributor.

Recent lawsuits against mega creeps Bill O'Reilly and Roger Ailes for sexual misconduct have dramatically changed the network's prime time lineup and executive leadership, and *Fox* executives are so worried about Ms. Lahren getting grossly hit on that they are willing to try giving out preemptive bonuses of some of the future lawsuit costs they expect to have to pay.

"Being intentionally and militantly conservative, *Fox* tends to lure very patriarchal guys," said a *Fox News* producer, who requested anonymity to discuss the inside situation at *Fox*. "You heard about the sick, demented stuff that Ailes did, right? But now the culture of *Fox* is changing, and that stuff isn't acceptable anymore. It has just gotten too expensive. It's sad and disappointing, but that's what we get for letting women in the boardroom and ruining the boys' club vibe. Before you know it, suddenly you can't intimidate, bribe, or blackmail your female underlings for sexual favors anymore. What's next, we have to pay them equal to men? I say no more women executives!"

Another anonymity-requesting *Fox* producer admitted that the bonuses aren't all *Fox* is doing to try and protect Ms. Lahren, and, of course, the *Fox* budget.

"We try to limit Tomi's presence around *Fox* executives, because they are the biggest risk factors," said the source. "These bigwigs think their business success should correlate with sexual success, and they become massive perverts. So when Tomi isn't actually on air, we try to hide her in various creative ways so male staffers can't tell where she is at any given moment. When she needs to go to the bathroom we give her an Obama mask to wear with an over-sized parka raincoat like a burqa, and it scares every *Fox* staffer away. The lengths we go to are necessary because our male executives just can't help but objectify attractive, blonde white women, and, thanks to Ailes's Aryan obsession, *Fox* is filled with them. We're the news network practically engineered for sexists in America, so naturally we're going to attract some of the worst of them to come work for us. At the end of the day, though, these elaborate Tomi disguises and the big bonuses we're dishing out to every male employee are still our cheapest option by far."

# The NRA Has Postponed Its New "Training Wheels AR-15" Product Line Designed For Kids Aged 3 And Up

February 24, 2018
Washington D.C.—

The National Rifle Association has earned much criticism in recent years due to America's spiraling gun violence crisis, but NRA lobbyists still seek to preserve unfettered gun rights with increasingly absurd promotional efforts.

However, the NRA this morning did agree to postpone the production of a brand new NRA-branded line of AR-15s designed to be a sort of "training wheels" semi-assault weapon for children.

"We believe now is just not the right time to unveil our new children's line of gun retail featuring kid-friendly packaging and decor," an NRA spokesman said in a press conference regarding the NRA's advertising strategy. "The political winds are shifting, and it appears that liberals are brainwashing America into believing toddlers can't safely be given an AR-15 with live ammunition to play with. The Left wants the government to get in the way of every law-abiding family's right to train their three-year-olds how to violently repel with overwhelming fire superiority the gangs of marauding criminals, thugs, and terrorists trying every day and night to break into our homes and murder us in our sleep. The Liberals are so paranoid about gun accidents. But just wait until the government turns tyrannical, and patriots across the nation must rise up again in armed rebellion. Are we going to stop three-year-olds from joining our militias then? We'll need every AR-15 we can get, no matter how small or colorfully designed with adorable farm animals!"

Critics of the NRA have insisted the idea of marketing AR-15s for children is ludicrous, but the NRA disagrees.

"The Second Amendment is airtight," said NRA Vice President Ira Sapp, "and children are citizens too, aren't they? Besides, guns are just as good companions for children as other pets, like puppies and kittens. My gun is practically my best friend. We go for walks around the neighborhood together almost every night. But, because of libtards, I get the cops called on me once a week. You know the Left has ruined America when I can't even explore my neighborhood with my rifle, and stop at each house to admire its unique architecture. Sometimes I look with my rifle's magnified scope just to be able to notice the tiny details of the brickwork and decorative shutters around windows and whatnot. But apparently that's 'alarming,' or 'irresponsible,' or all the other pansy words police tell me my neighbors say about me to the 911 dispatchers. Liberals will just never be comfortable with freedom."

## Conservatives Across America Threaten To Become Gun Nuts If People Keep Calling Them Gun Nuts

February 28, 2018
Little Rock, AR—

Following the latest school mass shooting, the NRA is whipping up frenzied conservative outrage with fear mongering that implies mere modicums of gun control, such as re-banning semi-automatic assault weapons and upgrading the national background check registry, are akin to imprisoning Americans forever in slavery.

Many NRA members agree with this sentiment, and have taken to social media to publish their slippery slope fears of gun control.

"I'm not a gun maniac," explained local NRA member Steve Knockwood, 45, "but I do own six AR-15s and enough ammo to obliterate a whole regiment of jihadis from my subdivision. But I'm totally sensible with them. I've never actually shot anyone. Not once. I only threaten to. And very rarely do I ever take the guns out of the back of my truck and wave them around, or start screaming that I'll kill my ex-wife, kids, and then myself. And only when I'm drunk. But I'd never actually go on a murderous rampage. Most of the time I even keep the safety on! How dare Democrats try to force me to get some kind of gun license, or require me to take annual safety training certification courses, or pass into law a 'red flag' bill. It's unAmerican! If publicly threatening to kill your kids to get back at your b**** ex-wife is considered a red flag, I'll never get to own a gun again! It's my Constitutional right to be lethally armed, disgruntled about life, and verbally threatening. And I have to be armed. Everyone has guns! Including my b**** ex-wife!"

Other gun owners feel strongly that gun control efforts are attempts by liberals to oppress conservatives.

"I don't want to be a mass shooter," said Howard West, 41, a proud NRA member, "but if liberals keep trying to take away all my guns, I might just have to become one! So watch out! Liberals would be giving me no choice. Yeah, sure, with the gun control measures Democrats have proposed I'd still be able to keep my composite bow, crossbow, pistols, hunting rifles, and shotguns, but I'd be forced to violently intervene if the US government ever tried to take away my high-velocity semi-automatics! All patriotic Americans who love our republic dearly would have no choice but to fight in a civil war until every American is dead if that's what it takes to stop any and every gun control proposal from passing through Congress. That's how you prove you love your country and want it to prosper forever!"

# Paul Ryan Won An Oscar For "Best Supporting Actor" For His Notable Silence On All Of Trump's Crimes

March 5, 2018
Los Angeles, CA—

In a memorable Oscar moment, Speaker of the House Paul Ryan was awarded the Academy Award for "Best Supporting Actor" for his role in doing nothing to stop President Donald Trump from trashing the Constitution and American democracy.

Mr. Ryan, with tears in his eyes, jogged up to the stage and tripped on the stairs while the audience softly and politely booed him.

Mr. Ryan's acceptance speech ran long, and he used it to thank the Academy for the recognition, speaking gradually louder over the wrap-it-up music.

"Wow, this is amazing," Ryan said into the microphone. "Total dream come true. Golly. You know, when President Trump was running the most overtly racist and offensive presidential campaign in American history, I knew how hard it would be to work with such a horrid person as the Republican nominee, but I accepted the challenge. And boy was it a challenge. When Donald called Mexican immigrants 'rapists' and 'drug dealers,' I pretended not to hear the quote. When Donald admitted to using his celebrity to sexually assault married women, I held firm and changed the subject. When Donald got elected and issued a childishly unConstitutional and racist travel ban, I gaslighted America about terror threats. Every time Donald said or tweeted something abominably vile, crudely ignorant, or even patently immoral, I let it slide. Then, no matter how damning the evidence of the various investigations into his plethora of disgraceful illegalities forever smearing the Office of the Presidency have gotten, I've been completely mum. Let me tell you, I'm just glad I received this award before Donald tries to preemptively nuke some country, or extort a foreign government for fake dirt on his 2020 election opponent, because either of those crimes would be a scandal we Republicans would have to finally say or do something about, right? Gosh. I'd also like to take a moment to thank President Trump because without his despicable behavior my lack of conscience and spine would never have been able to be honored on this stage tonight. Thank you, Donald! And thanks to the Academy for recognizing my contemptible negligence of my sacred duty as a top representative of the American people to courageously voice my opinions on the President's conduct clearly and without regard for partisanship or self-interest. Never give up on your dreams, kids! Thank you!"

There was no applause.

## Mike Pence, Who Can See His Political Future Sinking With Trump, Spends His Days Writing Musicals

March 22, 2018
Washington D.C.—

The days are long and boring for Vice President Mike Pence, who President Donald Trump gives little responsibility because of his extreme egotism, but Pence has reportedly found and developed a new talent while killing time during his White House office hours.

"Mike has really blossomed artistically, and I'd say he's in quite a creative sweet spot," explained VP aide Thomas Ralstone. "He's cranking out a full-blown musical every two weeks, and I believe he's written some real show-stopping ensemble finales. He says he thinks he's burning out on politics, but sees a bright future in the theatre."

The following are titles to Pence's various musicals:

- Les Biblicales
- The Vagina Monologues Rebuttal
- Wives: Who Needs Them? (a slapstick farce)
- Leviticus Confidential
- A Midsummer Night's Abomination
- Much Ado About Nothing In The Vice Presidency
- Sorry, Karen, I Married Jesus!
- Praying For Godot
- Indy Boys
- So Close, Yet So, So Far: An Impeachment Story
- Adam, Eve, & Short-Shorts Steve
- Stephen Miller, The Phantom Of The White House
- President Lear
- A Streetcar Named Repentance
- Judgin' In The Rain
- That One Summer In 1975 With Brad When It Happened
- Boy Hymens
- The Vagina Monologues Rebuttal Pt II: Necessary Evil Of Life
- Romeo & The Unredeemable Whore Jezebel
- The Mother Wife
- Testicles, Vice President of Tyre
- Firefighter Poles
- Springtime For Trumpler
- Drowning In Pussy (A Burlesque Of A Nightmare I Once Had)
- The Vagina Monologues Rebuttal Pt III: The Camel Toe Abomination

## Neo-Nazis Insist Sunburns Prove Whites Are "God's Chosen People"

April 4, 2018
Charlotte, NC—

*The Halfway Post* caught up with a local group of neo-Nazis yesterday in a Skype conversation, and they claimed sunburns are the unmistakable sign of God's chosen people.

"White Americans are the top of the global racial pyramid," said Jim Van Dijk, titularly known as the "Golden Eagle," which is the Nazi fan club's highest internal rank. "White people don't need brown crayons coming into the box of white crayons and melting the colors together, if you understand crayon metaphors. Immigrants will end our racial freedom, and it's our job as patriotic Americans to put their children into cages at the border if that's what it takes to make sure America continues being the freest country on Earth with the most universal rights... for whites. Because, come on, if white people were meant to mix genetically with brown people, why would we burn so bad when we're out in the sun in their countries? Checkmate, libtards! We're literally allergic to their latitude. It's like our skin is naturally designed to resist brown coloring ever since modern humans left Africa and boned a bunch of neanderthals to get out all the African DNA with their caveman sperm. Neanderthals were genetic heroes for whites, if you ask me. Man, if I could just see some neanderthal ejaculate. I wonder what it would feel like in my fingers. I bet their balls were so big. But I digress. White people are pretty much allergic to the sun because our chromosomes want to remain pure. And we can't stay pure with all the immigrants coming in and stealing our breeding women. Mixed people don't get sunburns easily, so you can tell they're not as pure. I like to think when white people get a sunburn it's like being in epidermic prayer to God because we're His chosen people. I never use sunblock because God would never let a white person get skin cancer."

*The Halfway Post* reporter reminded Van Dijk that his name indicated an obvious descent from Holland, and, therefore, he too was a descendant of immigrants who came to this melting pot country for opportunity, just like every other immigrant ever, no matter what color of skin.

"But my ancestors don't count as bad immigrants because they came before the cut-off point," Van Dijk explained. "Immigration was fine until about the 1930s. Everyone counts who came over before then. Except the Asians who built the railroads. And the slaves don't count. Nor Jews. And everyone who came from anywhere south of Texas, they're out. No one who would need a brown crayon to accurately color their skin in a picture counts. America is for white crayon people from Europe. Well, maybe not all Europeans. America needs to keep its people's skin pale. I don't want to have to see someone who tans easily and wonder if I'm about to be terrorist-attacked, you know? So we need to limit immigration to the more northern side of Europe. Iceland, Ireland, Denmark, and Germany for sure. The British, obviously. Of course the Swedes and Finns. French? Ehh, they're socialist, so not the French. Well, the Vichy were cool. They got what the Nazis were trying to do. The Belgians and Dutch are chill for sure, so I'm 100% in. I guess US immigrants should preferably be Protestant. Catholics made the cut, but just barely. Eastern Orthodox are fine, though, because of the Greeks. They kind of started the whole Western World thing, so they're okay. But they have to stay out of the sun cause they tan easy. If they stay pale, they can stay. Russia and Poland… I'm not sure about them. They're white-ish, but I don't really know what the whole Slavic thing is about. Like, are they inferior? What are Slavs? Did drops of Jewish or Gypsy blood sneak in here and there? Is anyone sure if Russian bloodlines are pure? Like, are they fake white, or are they real white? Tell you what, Russia is on racial probation. This is important stuff. If America can get at least over 98% white, we'll truly be great again. Everyone will have a job, and I'll have so many breeding females to worship my pearly white, cherubic children. No more hot girls having Black boyfriends, or this interracial marriage bulls***. Hot white girls should be dating and marrying me. And do the dishes and cook and stuff. Yeah, feminists shouldn't be allowed in America either. They're just as bad as the terrorists, so I have no idea how they still have white skin. They don't belong in the ideal, white America. Only submissive women. Women who will obediently multiply the American race. It's about time 'American' became its own race, don't you think? We deserve it. And I swear none of this is racist."

Asked what scientific metrics backed up this hierarchy, Van Dijk claimed the Bible did.

"The Bible is very clear that white people are the chosen people in the Old Testament. The Jews may have thought the Torah was about them, but it was always implied that the Bible was referencing the future United States of America. God was always murdering whole towns and city-states, and who does that now? America, that's who. That's why we've had the best military for so long. God blesses us. Throughout history, the whiter humans have gotten, the better their militaries got. And don't forget that white America defeated white Germany, and then we did it again against Russia in the Cold War, so we're like the most victorious, whitest of the whites. And, of course, Iraq had no chance. They live in the desert. That's like the most unwhite thing any race could do. Vietnam and Iraq 2 don't count because the libtards ruined those for us. If we'd have only fought on for another decade in each we totally would have won. And Afghanistan may yet still be a tie!"

# Fox News Executives Are Upset Their Commentators Keep Suffering Consequences For Being Awful

April 9, 2018
New York City, NY—

*Fox News* opinionator Laura Ingraham is the network's latest personality to suffer consequences for saying terrible things.

After gleefully mocking high schooler and massacre survivor David Hogg for not getting accepted into his top choices of colleges, advertisers fled her show and *Fox News* sent her on a brief vacation. *Fox* executives, reeling from the endless controversies and advertising boycotts their top show hosts create, are blaming their network's woes on snowflake liberals.

"America is turning soft," said a *Fox* executive, who asked for anonymity to candidly and abrasively describe America. "It all started when women were allowed into the work force, and the country has gone downhill since. *Fox* having to hire women for roles other than eye candy has ruined our morale. We even have to let in ugly women now! And so what, Laura made fun of a teenaged mass shooting victim, but what's the big deal? These advertisers are wimps. They should just commit to *Fox*, and keep paying us no matter what we say or do. It's an infringement on our First Amendment rights that they're abandoning us. Private companies shouldn't be allowed to decide on their own within the free market of advertising to not associate their brands with the toxic and unpopular messaging coming from our pundits' mouths on a nightly basis. And, come on, making fun of a 17-year-old whose friends were murdered in front of him is hardly the worst thing we've ever done. Why are our advertisers fleeing *Fox* now when they stayed with us after we got caught repeatedly forcing our anchors to use focus group-tested, conservative-slanted talking points to intentionally skew our viewers' perceptions of reality with irrational, hyper-partisan bias? Or when we got caught editing *Fox*-related Wikipedia pages about *Fox* employees? Or when we got busted repeatedly for editing pictures of liberal media pundits to make them look more stereotypically Jewish? Or when a study found our viewers are less informed about current events than people who watch no news at all? Or when we accused Hillary of orchestrating Seth Rich's murder? Or when we called the Obamas terrorists? How is Laura's scandal bigger than any of those? I swear, snowflakes are ruining America. And *Fox*'s profits! I'm sick of suffering monetary consequences for easing up on journalistic professionalism. If you don't like *Fox*, don't watch us! But stop demanding our advertisers spend their marketing money conscientiously! It's killing our bottom line! And we only have a few more years of dominating the ratings with our scared, old, racist white viewers anyway. Our business model is already dying, literally!"

# Mike Pence Once Paid $100 In Hush Money To A Woman He Made Eye Contact With

April 13, 2018
Washington D.C.—

Amidst President Donald Trump's plethora of ugly personal scandals involving nondisclosure agreements, hush money, and intimidating threats of violence and lawsuits, Vice President Mike Pence now has one of his own.

According to *Halfway Post* sources, in 2014 Mr. Pence's personal attorney Robin Wade paid an unnamed woman $100 in hush money on an airplane then-Governor Mike Pence was taking to Indiana from a Governors' Association meeting in Washington D.C.

In one salacious account of the incident, Mr. Pence allegedly looked at the woman, who was not his wife, from across the airplane aisle, and held eye contact for a full two seconds. The woman reportedly agreed to accept the money in exchange for never speaking of the incident to anyone, especially to Mr. Pence's family.

Neither Pence nor the Office of the Vice President have yet responded to requests for a comment, though Mr. Pence did comment yesterday on President Trump's former relationship with pornstar Stormy Daniels.

"I don't believe a word that streetlight hussy Daniels ever said about this great president I've had the privilege of serving these last couple years," Pence told reporters. "The President personally told me those rumors were 100% false, and he never lies. He is the most honest, truthful chief executive this country has ever had. He is also the most chaste, Godly president as well. There is no way I'd believe for a second that a man who has given his solemn word to me multiple times that he has memorized the entire Gospels would lie about this Stormy Daniels affair fake news. The President swears he has only had sexual intercourse four times, and only for the strict purpose of reproduction. Now, I know what you're thinking, because I myself had the same question. I also was skeptical given that the President has five children. But he assured me that Ivanka's conception was an immaculate one, conceived by God himself. He said that's why it's okay and not weird when he calls Ivanka a 10, and says he'd love to date her if he wasn't her father. He says when he references sex while talking about her it's just a heavenly metaphor for how much he loves his lord and savior, Jesus Christ. He said it's also why Ivanka is so good looking while Don Jr. and Eric are so ugly. The boys were obviously not immaculate conceptions. Anyone can admit his reasoning on that one does indeed check out."

# New Republican Party Rule Dictates That GOP Primary Candidates Can Only Hate Women, Brown People Or Gays, Not All Three

April 14, 2018
Washington D.C.—

The Republican Party's top donors reportedly have concerns that an electoral blue wave is threatening the GOP's control of the House of Representatives, and are begging the Republican National Committee to change its campaign strategy on the kinds of candidates the party helps fund.

Acknowledging the GOP's deep decline in public support, the RNC last week published a revised rulebook for Republican primary candidates to follow in order to be eligible to receive party campaign funds.

A copy of it leaked to *The Halfway Post* last night. The following are some of the GOP's new campaign rules:

1. You can campaign against independent women and their liberated vaginas, immigrants, or gays, but not all three. We are alienating too many demographics too often with our strictly straight-white-male identity politics, so you now have to specialize in terms of your cultural biases. Please, please narrow down your bigotry to only one or two choice groups at the max.

2. We are instituting a new zero-tolerance policy against publicly using words, phrases, and figures of speech that even most conservative voters consider racist these days. From now on, all RNC funding will be immediately revoked if you get caught publicly saying any of the following words: colored, ape-like, coon, mammy, the N-word (obviously the N-word!!!), sambo, tar baby, chinaman, chink, gook, Jap, hajji, spic, wetback, redskin, injun, retard, c***, hoebag, cum-dumpster, tranny, fag, or scissor-sisters. And this is not a definitive list! Please help us here. We'll never convince ethnic minorities and educated women to vote Republican unless we pretend in public that we consider them culturally American and valuable assets to their communities. AND NEVER CALL A BLACK MAN NAMED TOM AN UNCLE!!!

3. There is no such thing as legitimate rape. Also, it looks bad when we suggest that women should thank God for being impregnated after being raped. They really seem to get upset about that, and, remember, we REALLY need suburban women to stop flipping to Democrats.

4. Native Americans are technically more American than even the most patriotic Republicans, so please don't put yourself in a situation where you can be filmed yelling at Native Americans to go back to where they came from. It's a very sore subject! Some legitimate Americans look like illegal foreigners, but aren't. We suggest you treat every potential voter while you're out campaigning as a legal citizen, especially when your event is being filmed by the media.

5. Friendly reminder: the Civil War actually was about slavery, and suggesting otherwise polls badly with the college-educated voters we've been bleeding every election since the 70s. Rationalize it mathematically: poorly-educated racist voters will support us no matter what, so remember that every non-racist vote counts.

6. Keep your Confederate flags in your basement and garage, please! There's no reason to bring them along with you at campaign events. And NO SWASTIKAS. We thought we all agreed on that one a long time ago! Remember: always consider the optics of what you are doing and how you are presenting yourself and the Republican Party to the moderate American voter. Keep your inside thoughts INSIDE.

7. Obama's birth certificate was technically proven legitimate, so we should probably stop associating with Birtherism. A lot of our voters still believe it, so don't offend them by saying it's false, just don't bring it up! Let's have a don't-ask-don't-tell rule on everyone's theories about Obama's heritage.

8. Never suggest Hitler had some good ideas. Don't mention Hitler. Please, we're begging you: don't talk about Hitler or the Third Reich in any way that's even remotely positive. This, for some reason, has become a reoccurring issue with many of our candidates.

9. Here's a quick codeword cheat sheet:
- Instead of "the Jew cabal," say "globalists."
- Instead of "Barack HUSSEIN Obama," just "Obama" works.
- Instead of saying "integration was a mistake" or "we need segregation back," just talk about "states' rights."
- Instead of admitting that America's first colonists were largely religious refugees and undocumented immigrants, explain to your constituents that they were "settlers" or "pioneers" so our immigration ideology doesn't seem hypocritical and ahistorical.

**** Remember: dog whistles are what we're after, not bullhorns!
**** DON'T MENTION RAPE OR HITLER AS POSITIVES!!!!!!!!!!!!!!

## Richard Spencer Has Reportedly Collected 3,000 Jars Of "Backup White Master-Race Semen"

April 16, 2018
Juneau, AK—

White supremacist Richard Spencer's nonprofit organization White Semen Doomsday has reportedly reached a milestone in collecting its 3,000th mason jar of backup semen intended to be stockpiled in a snowy Alaskan vault built underground and preserved in case white people ever become, in the words of Mr. Spencer, "an endangered race."

"We have to keep pure, white breeds pure and white," Spencer told *The Halfway Post.* "If America ever starts getting a little too brown, we can transfer deposits from my collection to get a little more pure white distilling in the gene pool. And in case whites ever become enslaved by minority sub-races, we can take refuge in Alaska, and, like the Jedi in a number of *Star Wars* films, secretly nurse our people back to racial and political dominance against the dark-skinned!"

Spencer says the milestone is his life's top accomplishment..

"It's amazing how far we have come since it all began. The White Semen Doomsday project has truly changed my life. It started in my basement, and in the beginning was just me and a couple white supremacist friends jerking off into a jar together for the good of white humanity's future. We started out meeting once a week, but we just had so much fun contributing to this great cause that it became a daily ritual. The collection grew very slow at first, as we could not produce semen in substantial volumes ourselves, even when we were going at it sometimes four or five times a day and really just mashing our poor, raw penises at that point, so I realized we had to outsource and scale up. We started meeting with a bunch of other white supremacists at various nature campouts we organized thanks to some social media advertising that pinpointed our ads for guys who haven't had any girlfriends in two years or more, and we gradually warmed them up to joining our masturbatory crusade. We couldn't make it seem homosexual, of course, or these bitter, lonely, emasculated white men might want to fight us, but a great ice-breaker was our mutual agreement that whites are the real oppressed people in this country no matter what kind of peer-reviewed, sociological statistics libtards want to scientifically measure and analyze. The idea really took off and, before long, we had guys all over America sponsoring their own mason jar jerk-off events, and the splinter groups would send me all the jars they collected. I quickly ran out of freezer space in my house, and I actually started having to rent out industrial-sized freezers in order to keep the pure white semen as fresh as possible. But I'm incredibly thankful that the white supremacy movement really stepped up to the plate and helped me finance this great project with generous financial donations along with the testicular donations. It's just beautiful to see so many white dudes concerned about losing the majority in America. Doomsday could be just around the corner for our kind, and we white knights must be prepared to defend our country with oceanic volumes of white semen in case the population of pure, white female wombs ever dwindles to just a few thousand or even hundred fertile, child-rearing women."

Now that phase one of the White Semen Doomsday project is complete, phase two of actually building the Alaskan vault will begin. Meanwhile, the jerk-off events are continuing.

"It took a while," said Spencer, "but we finally met our ambitious goal of 3,000 mason jars. It's a beautiful sight to see one of our freezers filled with hundreds of jars stacked on crisp, icy metal shelves. Most are labeled by the cities and states they came from, but some participating white supremacy groups are big enough or masturbationally eager enough that individual neighborhoods or host homes can fill up jars real quick. It's a relief, too, that the speed of deposit jars coming in has ramped up so dramatically and efficiently after a big set-back we faced several months ago. We had a bit of a disaster early on. Our very first collection effort was tainted by a Black guy who we discovered was contributing in one of the donation groups. Apparently they somehow didn't get the memo that the project was for whites only. And back then we didn't use standardized jar sizes so I had to do a lot of mixing and marrying of jars to make sure they were all totally filled and uniform in size to maximize our storage space in the freezers. And my organization wasn't anywhere near as efficient as it is now so there was just no way to tell for sure which jars had been tainted. Unfortunately, I had to pour out every single one of them. We had about 450 mason jars filled at that point, but there was no choice except to start over from scratch. It was the only way to ensure total white purity. We can't save the human race in a doomsday catastrophe if our white women start popping out mixed babies! I'll tell you, though, pouring all those milky, potential white children down my kitchen drain was literally the most heartbreaking experience of my life. I still get choked up when I remember that tragic day. Some of the jars I'd just pour into my hand, and tears welled up as all that exalted cum dripped between my fingers and pooled in the creases of my palm. I felt like I could almost hear them begging me to let them live, to impregnate some future blonde-haired, blue-eyed uterus to ensure the salvation of paleness... But it had to be done. Cleaning out all those jars was rough, rough work. And the cold slush of it all congealed in my pipes and dishwasher, and really screwed things up. I can't use my house's kitchen sink at all anymore."

# Paul Ryan's Retirement Means He Can Pursue His Real Dream: Clubbing Baby Seals To Death

April 17, 2018
Washington D.C.—

Speaker of the House Paul Ryan recently surprised no one when he announced his retirement from Congress just as the GOP is on the cusp of losing its majority in the House of Representatives in an expected electoral midterm shellacking, but Mr. Ryan did surprise political observers by announcing he'd spend his retirement following his dream of clubbing baby seals to death in northern Canada.

"I can tell you that Paul feels now is the right time to retire," explained a Ryan confidant in the House, who requested anonymity to candidly discuss the Speaker's plans. "He achieved his number two dream of passing uninhibited tax cuts big enough to balloon the national deficit necessitating eventual budget cuts that will screw over the nation's struggling poor in order for the mega rich and corporations to horde the profits of the country's downtrodden laborers at nation-threatening levels of economic inequality, so now he feels ready to go after his number one dream of murdering cute, big-eyed, cuddly baby seals. He told me he's buying a one-way ticket to Canada, and that he won't stop clubbing until he feels that God has given him a sign that it's time to accept some of the cushy lobbying and board of directors jobs waiting for him as a corporate 'thank you' for his work eviscerating America's budgetary stability in favor of CEOs' capital gains profits."

Another Congressional friend of Mr. Ryan said he was glad that Ryan could finally do what he had always been talking about doing.

"No one deserves this more than Paul," said the Congressman. "The average person just has no idea how hard Paul's job has been these last two years. Paul heroically kept together a Republican House delegation constantly threatening to fracture, and every day he had to act like it was totally normal that House Republicans were ideologically shifting toward far-Right hate groups and neo-fascist ethno-nationalism based on white supremacy. Paul did truly commendable work bridging the natural divisions between all our disparate conservative factions from closeted KKK members to the Alt-Right, from libertarians to neo-con warmongers who think bombing dozens of countries at the same time is what best exemplifies American global leadership, and from moderates to straight up Russian-bought assets promoting Vladimir Putin's interests in Congress. Do you want that job? No one does! But Paul went to work each day, and somehow managed to hold this rickety coalition of sundry fanatics together by going out of his way to never publicly appear to have any principles, values, or opinions that might potentially upset or embarrass any of the crazed conspiracists in the Republican tent. And then there's Trump. Paul suffered every day pretending he didn't know Trump had a Twitter account, or had ever heard rumors of the Republican National Committee funneling Republican donor money directly into Trump's personal bank accounts. If you ask me, Paul deserves to club as many baby seals to death as his heart desires. He may have done nothing to defend our institutions of liberal democracy from being dismantled into irrelevant shells of their former federal glory, and nothing to protect Congress's role as a co-equal partner against a totalitarian-inspired executive branch, and nothing to protect our international allies from the inexplicably impulsive whims of Trump's skim and dim worldview, and nothing to reassure America's minority groups that they belong in America despite Trump's abhorrent xenophobia, but that's what many conservative voters across the nation consider admirable success! My only hope for Paul's retirement is that he can find a hint of nirvana out there in the Canadian hinterland clubbing the brains out of all those baby seals!"

Upon news of Mr. Ryan's retirement, the Koch Brothers gifted him with a deluxe wooden baseball bat branded with the words "World's Best Congressman."

*The Halfway Post* reached out to Speaker Ryan, and asked him what he thought about his legacy.

"I think I accomplished a lot," said Ryan in a phone call from Canada. "Not in terms of the number of bills I got passed into law, or in terms of the size and scope of Republican legislation, but I think if you count the number of dollars given back to already rich millionaires and billionaires courtesy of my tax cuts, I may have gotten myself into the top-five of consequential Speakers of the House in US history! And I know what you're thinking. You're thinking about how my beloved tax reform added way more to the debt than we said it would, but, if we're being fair, the record does show that I never explicitly said that Congress needed to get America's debt problem under control while I was speaker. I was specifically vague about the timeline of the debt-solving. We Republicans have only been explicitly focused on cutting the debt when a Democrat is in office, you know? And, now that we Republicans just ensured the government will be taking in a lot less money for the next few years, the next Democratic president is really going to have to focus on the debt! Boy, I love conservatism! Politics is just so easy and more fun when you don't have to care about solving problems. Just say the government is what everyone should blame, sit back, and oppose everything the Democrats propose! Now, if you'll excuse me, there are lots of baby seals out here whose cartoonishly big, cute heads are looking marvelously bashable. And f***able!"

## Rudy Giuliani's Strategy To Save Trump From Indictment Is To Cross-Dress Like A Hooker And Seduce Bob Mueller

April 21, 2018
New York City, NY—

President Donald Trump's newest legal team addition is Rudy Giuliani, and Mr. Giuliani has reportedly promised Trump he has a fool-proof plan to end the Mueller investigation once and for all.

A draft of Giuliani's plan was leaked anonymously this morning to *The Halfway Post*, and is published in its entirety below:

# TOP SECRET*****

### (NO ADAM SCHIFFS ALLOWED!)

The Fool-Proof Giuliani Plan To Infiltrate Bob Mueller's Special Investigation And Sabotage It From Within

*****For President Trump's eyes only

1.  Dress up like a hooker with big fake boobs, bigger than ever!
2.  Frolic about outside the FBI field office in downtown Manhattan for several days to gain MUELLER's attention.
3.  Rush into the field office on D-DAY to offer an allegation that PRESIDENT TRUMP sexually assaulted me last year. Play the victim while charming MUELLER.
4.  Come back the next day (D-DAY+1) and plant more fake accusations, and gain MUELLER's trust.
5.  Disclose RESTAURANT GIFT CARD and two (2) MOVIE TICKETS to the steamiest romantic comedy currently playing in theaters, convince MUELLER to accompany me.
6.  Cross-dress the sluttiest I have ever cross-dressed before, and accompany MUELLER to dinner and movie.
7.  In the theater, grab hold of MUELLER's hand and make out during the film's steamy climax—NOTE: let him get to second base, but NO FURTHER! Must play hard to get to entice MUELLER to accompany me home, and must not give away my ruse prematurely.
8.  Convince Mueller to walk me home and entice him to come upstairs for "coffee."

9.  Hit "record" on secret, hidden FILMING DEVICE, and gradually escalate romantic tension until intercourse.
10. If things go well, continue the relationship until MUELLER can be convinced to end the investigation into Russian-collusion with an ultimatum: the investigation or ME! Or make COPIES of the secret recordings for blackmail purposes and break MUELLER's heart while ending his career.
11. Success! TRUMP is saved!

[REMINDER: KEEP ONE (1) EXTRA COPY OF THE SEXUAL LIASON FOR PERSONAL USES.]

## The Party Not Taken
(Inspired by Robert Frost)
by Donald J. Trump

Two parties diverged looking for candidates that were good
And sorry I could not win the nomination of both
And be one businessman, long I stood
And thought of Democrats as much as I could
and if its voters were gullible for a populist oath;

Then took the other party, a little bit dumb,
And having perhaps a little less brains,
Conspiratorial, and envying my income;
Though as for what the red team's become
'Twas easier to pretend to feel their pains.

And all that year in their hearts did I trod,
I left no bigotry unplucked or ignored.
Conquered my foes with my alpha facade
Yet despite Jeb's low energy—they would not applaud—
I doubted I'd ever be the White House landlord!

I shall be telling this story with a deep sigh
Somewhere ages and ages hence:
Two parties diverged in sixteen, and I—
I took the one with nativist fury in its eye,
And my racist rants made all the difference.

## Trump And Kim Jong Un Have Become Pen Pals, Writing Each Other Hand-Written Letters Weekly

May 16, 2018
Washington D.C.—

It has been reported that Donald Trump and Kim Jong Un have been handwriting each other personal notes over the last year, and The Halfway Post managed to obtain one of Mr. Trump's letters from an anonymous White House source:

My Dearest Kim,

I still can't get over your gracious words. How quickly your previous letter to me identified my unparalleled genius (first paragraph!) really touched my heart. You are truly a tremendous dictator, and I believe our countries can work together and achieve peace. As soon as those Trump Casinos get built along your beautiful country's amazing beaches like we discussed in our Singapore summit, your nation will blossom into a prosperous, nuclear-capable utopia. North Korea will be the envy of the world. And don't forget about drilling the peepholes in all the penthouse suites like I told you about!

Your society is so obedient and courteous to you, Kim, that I believe your people have what it takes to become a great nation. And you don't have democracy, so you can have an entire nation of slaves. Boy, I wish I had your country! America respects way too many human rights. Being President is not nearly as fun as I thought it could be thanks to our dumb military refusing to arrest and torture my critics. You would be truly shocked to know the legal protections that journalists, minority party members of the legislature, and women accusing me of past sexual assaults have here! I hope you recognize and fully take advantage of your good fortunes to honor all the dictators who came before you without so few checks on power as you have.

Anyway, I was thinking the other day that I wanted to take you under my wing like Vlad took me under his to teach you some dictator-to-dictator tips. So here are some of my most valuable lessons and pieces of advice for a young authoritarian like yourself:

—Always have a "Casual Friday" policy. The women around you show more cleavage when the dress code relaxes at the end of the week.

—Get a fixer. But get a smart one. I thought I had a smart one, but Michael Cohen turned out to be a total moron and rat. He couldn't even pay a porn star as an illegal, undisclosed campaign donation and get away with it!

—If you have a son, never name him after yourself. Donald Jr. has turned out to be a total loser, and I'm sure he's going to somehow ruin the Trump name after I'm dead. He's so desperate for my approval that he makes me want to demean him in public even more than I already do! Let your son be his own man. And if he's an embarrassment he won't ruin your legacy like Don Jr. is ruining mine with all those videos he posts clearly on drugs!

—Get good press spokespeople early, people who are dependable. I've had the biggest problems in this department. First, Sean Spicer was a goody-two-shoes dork who couldn't convincingly lie for me, and then I had to stick awkwardly with Sarah Huckabee Sanders, whose best truth-evasion work involved vomiting mindless word salad. That gets old real fast. And she's not easy on the eyes. After her, I promised myself I'd never hire another brunette, or a big-boned hillbilly, or a marble-mouthed Southerner ever again. Be glad North Korea doesn't have an Arkansas in it! Then I had the Mooch, who burned out in a week and a half. I've had Adderall rushes last longer than he did! And, oh my God, have you seen Rudy Giuliani? Talk about C-team talent. It's embarrassing I have to put him on TV. He looks like Bat Boy, for God's sake. I wish Ivanka would do it, and maybe show some skin. She has the look I'm going for, and sex appeal. Unlike creepy Giuliani. Every interview he does, he looks like Nosferatu after eating a fat kid. Yeah, take my word for it: get someone strong and hot, and early in the game.

—Have a credit card for all the women in your life to do whatever plastic surgery work they want done on their faces and bodies. Trust me, it's worth it. You don't want a bunch of uglies hanging around you all the time draining your enthusiasm for accumulating power.

—Get an Adderall prescription. I swear by it! It allows you to stay up all night working on your "Enemies List" and plotting vengeance with the vigor and energy of a man half your age! I recommend snorting it. Works much faster!

—Go to Russia sometime. They have the best hookers that will do the grossest stuff for you. Vladimir will tape you, but I'd still say it's worth it.

That's all for now. I'll keep giving you more advice as it comes to me. I think me and you are going to have a long and fruitful friendship, Kim. Nobody understands what it's like to be a dictator except other dictators. No one else ever thinks of our problems, or our feelings, or our pain. When you think about it, we dictators are the loneliest people on this planet. But at least we have each other. Love ya, Kim.

Always admiringly yours,
Donald

# Donald Trump's Biggest Phobias, Revealed!

- His father's brutal, emotional abuse and psychological coldness. Several times throughout every hour of every day, his father's voice rings inside his head shouting, "You're a f*cking loser, Donald! Everyone knows you're a fraud!"

- Public humiliation of any kind to the point that he tried to violently end American democracy and publicly hang Mike Pence rather than admit he lost the election and Joe Biden would be replacing him as president.

- Sharks, oceans, and water in general. He hasn't entirely submerged himself into any body of water since the 1970s, particularly because, once he started balding, his elaborate hair combover and follicle implants started taking two hours and a full can of hair spray to mold into a shape roughly resembling normal hair.

- The unveiled reality that he is not rich, and has been beholden to foreign oligarchs laundering blood money through Trump Tower and his other international properties all along. He is terrified the interpreter from his private meetings with Vladimir Putin as president will leak details of how he begged Putin for loans in exchange for selling out Ukraine and changing Republican's sentiments regarding loyalty and blood brother commitment to NATO.

- One of his many wives or mistresses poisoning him. He has Barron try any drinks or foods Melania gives him as insurance against Melania spiking it with hemlock, arsenic, or some other deadly toxin.

- Barron and Melania mocking him in Slovenian. Every time he enters the room, she points at his crotch and they laugh saying, "Goba v hlačah!" Melania has dozens of compromising photos of him naked, and has given several to Barron to keep in both his wallet and several security boxes in multiple banks to save as an insurance policy to stay in the will after the inevitable divorce.

- His children ruthlessly fighting over whatever he leaves behind because, despite tacky appearances of luxury, it won't be much. He worries Ivanka will dismember Eric and Don Jr., and then mail the body parts to Barron and Tiffany as a warning not to f*ck with her. Ivanka was a big murderer of animals as a child, and choked out the cat his first wife got them when they were little. She then smeared the cat's blood all over her body, and told Eric, "Someday, I will do this to you, too, only I'll make you suffer much more than Sprinkles suffered!"

- His hairline's ongoing betrayal. His biggest regrets are the various hair implant procedures he desperately tried out back in the 80s before they were effective or cosmetically sound, which ruined his scalp.

- Having more business meltdowns like Trump Vodka, his Taj Mahal casino, and the Trump Shuttle airline. He does, however, think Trump Steaks would have sold better if they came with pre-packaged, freeze-dried ketchup on them like he wanted. He tells anyone who will listen that all his business failures were always because of other people, and often launches into long rants listing laundry lists of all the people whose fault his business failures are other than his own.

- Donald Jr. ruining the Donald Trump name after he dies. He wishes he had instead named Ivanka "Donaldina" as his eponymous heir because she is not a total idiot, reject, and failure at everything she does like Don Jr. is. Ivanka also isn't addicted to drugs like Don Jr. because she has fewer negative daddy issues on account of his incestual physical attraction to her since her teenaged years, which meant she got a lot of attention, praise, and emotional validation while growing up, unlike Don Jr., who was regularly yelled at and slapped in front of his friends.

- All the future films and TV series that will undoubtedly mock his mannerisms, facial appearance, vanity, and gluttony of personality vices. He's particularly worried about a Quentin Tarantino film featuring a historically revisionist ending a la *Inglourious Basterds*. He wishes there was some way to sue people and litigiously enforce nondisclosure agreements from the grave.

- He doesn't know how or why, but confident women make him feel small and weak. Maybe because in his college days his hot female classmates all made it a school-wide game to stand him up on dates, and kept a notebook cataloguing all these embarrassments, as well as the number of times he was caught trying to sneak into women's bathrooms and locker rooms, but he can't help hating strong, independent women. He has frequent, emasculating nightmares about Megyn Kelly, Angela Merkel, Hillary Clinton, Michelle Obama, and Liz Cheney.

- All the people he has forced or bribed into signing nondisclosure agreements spilling their secrets all at once because he can't sue them all at the same time.

## Local Republican Senate Candidate Is So Anti-Gay That Everyone Is Just Assuming He's Secretly Gay Himself

June 3, 2018
Jackson, MS—

Mississippi Republican Senate candidate Paul Donovan has run a campaign with such virulently homophobic public statements that Mississippians across the state agree that underneath his facade of Christian values he must be homosexual himself.

"There's just no way this guy isn't gay," explained local Republican voter George Hawkins, 41. "He shows all the signs. This Donovan fellow has compared homosexuality to bestiality, he has endorsed federal subsidies for pray-away-the-gay camps for kids, he has called for banning gay pride parades, he rants regularly against gay marriage, he's totally opposed to letting gay couples adopt children, and he even uses the word 'fag' in his Facebook posts. There is not a doubt in my mind that this guy is 'too gay to function' as the kids call it these days."

Other Mississippi voters have started a campaign to find Mr. Donovan's Grindr account, which they agree must exist.

"Me and a big group of my friends have all offered $20 each in a giant pot of reward money for the person who finds this ultra-conservative Paul Donovan guy on Grindr," explained Mississippi college student Alex Winjeski, 21. "All together, the reward money we've raised has just passed $700, and people are still signing up to contribute. It's not a matter of if we find this guy's Grindr account, it's only a matter of when. He's just too much of a homophobe to not be secretly gay and theocratically unwilling to accept it. He's definitely projecting his own insecurities onto the perfectly friendly and loving gay community here in Mississippi."

A bigger prize has been collected for a tougher challenge.

"I heard about the competition to find the Republican candidate's Grindr account, but I think that's too easy," said Jackson resident Jillian Heams, 22. "This guy's political platform is so fundamentalist that he's obviously super sexually repressed. So I started my own competition with some followers of my Tumblr blog, and all together we have pledged a whole $3,000 reward for the first person who orchestrates a fake sexual rendezvous with the guy in a gas station bathroom and films it as a sting operation to catch him with his pants down, proverbially or literally. I donated $200 myself. It's always worth it to catch a homophobic hypocrite. And we're definitely going to catch him."

## Donald Trump Adopted Five Honduran Children, Said He'll Give Them The Same Parental Apathy He Gives Barron

June 19, 2018
Washington D.C.—

President Donald Trump has responded to criticism that his administration's policy of breaking up immigrant and refugee families is evil by pledging to adopt five Honduran children, and give them the same parenting that he gives his kids.

Trump was open about what this would entail in a brief self-congratulatory statement he made to the White House press pool this morning:

"Effective immediately, I'm going to adopt five Honduran children and support them financially. I will treat them exactly as if they were my own kids, which will be great because look how awesome they've all turned out. They have impeccable records, with just a few minor blemishes of fraud and charity self-dealing. But I mean it that I will give them the full Trump parenting. I will take these immigrant kids in, and pay some woman money so I don't have to see or talk to any of them until they're at least 18, and then take full credit for their hopefully positive work ethics. Yep, I will give them the full Trump fathering that Barron is getting right now. Did you know he speaks fluent Slovenian? Yeah, his mom taught him. In fact, I'm not sure if he even speaks English. He's pretty quiet when I'm around. Boy, I hope Melania spoke to him in at least a little English—well, the maids probably did. Wait, maybe he also knows Spanish then, cause of the maids. Wow, maybe he's trilingual, and I didn't even know it! Sometimes I surprise myself with my great fathering. My son, trilingual at 10! …Or 15. Let's go with 13. And can't forget Tiffany, who is some place in the world right now. Gotta love her, she's a free soul. And somewhere in the range of 25 and 35. Then there's Ivanka, Don Jr. and Eric. Maybe I could have done a little more parenting on two of them. Guess which two. Ha! But yep, I will humbly and altruistically take in five immigrant children. All girls. I want more babes out there in the future with the Trump name. I just hope I don't pick any uglies. It's hard to tell because sometimes little girls look pretty, but then puberty makes them real gangly, awkward, and plain looking. But my adoptions are not some shallow modeling contest. It's to prove I care about kids. Even the brown ones. I hope the Nobel Committee is watching. People are saying this is the most peace-promoting, pro-immigrant thing a president has ever done. The rest of the immigrant kids will stay in their dog kennels, but these five will get a fresh start in a new life. And that is the tremendous generosity of America. And the best part of adopting immigrant kids is that it won't be legit incest if they grow up to be really hot and I date them!"

# Fox News Has A Desperate Plan To Find New Advertisers

June 22, 2018
New York City, NY—

*Fox News* has suffered several costly boycotts of its advertising department in recent years, and is reportedly desperate for client leads to purchase commercial spots.

To try and reverse these negative trends, Sean Hannity and Tucker Carlson have launched a live, weekly special event called *The Sean & Tucker Show* on Sunday nights aimed at generating called-in business referrals from faithful *Fox* viewers who might be interested in limited-time offers of discounted advertising.

The special television events are like public broadcasting fundraising telethons, and several *Fox* executives have admitted that *Fox News* is largely donor-funded at this point. They also admitted the irony of the financial situation given *Fox*'s rabidly capitalist ideology now juxtaposed with the fact that *Fox* is basically panhandling for handouts during its weekend programming.

Throughout the Fox telethons, Hannity and Carlson maintain a schtick that consists of Carlson mocking the brain size of female Democrats in Congress while Hannity explains what, if those female Democrats were members of al-Qaeda, their "Muslim names" would be.

The fundraiser lasts two hours, and the final segment ends with the airing of a message from Fox's Vice President Sean Daviers:

"If your products' target demographics are old, white people who self-identify as racists, born-again Christians, or coal-mining enthusiasts, come advertise on Fox News! We've got them brainwashed right where you want them! They're total lemmings ready for whatever cheap crap you want to sell them! Look, we're live right now. They're listening to this. They just heard me call them lemmings. They're confused, and they're scratching their heads. Now, watch this: Hillary! Emails! Benghazi! Migrant caravans! Gas prices! Hunter Biden! …And they're back with us, just like that! That's literally all it takes to turn around their goldfish brains. Watch this: Hey, you geezers! The Democrats are going to turn your kids into China-loving environmentalists and gay, biracial Marxists! See? It doesn't matter at all if what we say is logically absurd, historically inaccurate, or patently made up! If you pay for some advertising with Fox News, you can rest assured that our mindless, doofus audience will eat it right up. And I can guarantee that our viewers won't change the channel until they die in their easy chairs. I promise all the potential advertisers out there that you will get some bang for your buck here. And don't take it from me, take it from all-star Fox advertiser Mike Lindell and his MyPillow brand. He loves our audience's spending potential so much that sometimes our commercial breaks are just three minutes straight of the same MyPillow commercial on repeat six times in a row!"

Daviers at this point holds up one of Lindell's MyPillows and shows it off.

"So hurry up, you do not want to miss this offer of a lifetime. And be fast because our audience doesn't have much longer. Their perennial fear of Black families moving next door in their suburban neighborhoods has really worn down their hearts, and their medical ailments are stacking up weekly! Diabetes, heart disease, chronic inflammation, they have it all! And COVID has really hit our audience hard because of all our anti-vaccine content and conspiracy theory peddling. Any one of these new COVID variants that gets around America's herd immunity with more deadly outcomes could potentially wreck us in the ratings because our viewers are the unhealthiest, least scientifically receptive, and most medically skeptical of all the cable news networks! So while they may be the perfect imbecile customers for your business, products or services, time is running out to profit wildly from their brainless spending. So all you advertisers, if you want to sell your cheap crap to these fast-declining hillbillies, they're all yours! Buy a Fox News commercial today! Or ten! Seriously. Buy at least ten. We really need the money. Advertisers are abandoning us faster than ever. Please. We're begging you. Give us some money. Just $100. Or $10. Whatever you have. Between Tucker Carlson, Jeanine Pirro, Sean Hannity, Lou Dobbs, and Laura Ingraham we're literally always getting sued by someone or some group. And don't even get me started on the years of sexual harassment lawsuits we're still paying out. We really need some cash flow. Roger Ailes was a sick, demented, Godzilla monster of a pervert! The hush money is off the charts. I have no idea how the financial accountants manage to keep the lights on in this building. Truly unprecedented harassment and sexual assault settlements. Let's just say you don't ever want to walk around the *Fox News* studios with a black light."

Following this message, *Fox*'s programming features an hour-long, pre-taped segment of Steve Doocy reading Ayn Rand novels to elementary schoolers while Jesse Watters walks around the classroom asking all the non-white students if their parents are on food stamps.

Occasionally the telethon also features President Donald Trump calling in and ranting for half an hour on the following topics:

- Possible locations of Hillary Clinton's email server
- Male Democratic senators who, he claims, have hands smaller than his
- A list of all the world leaders who have allegedly told him he's a genius
- His idea to host a "Miss Congress" beauty pageant that got ruined when an adviser pointed out to him that the average age of Congresswomen was 59, and that the pageant would have a changing room he definitely did not want to snoop into
- Surprisingly accurate guesses on what bra size every female *Fox News* host wears
- An exhaustive review of *KFC*'s fried chicken combo options
- Mumbled talking while he eats a well-done steak smothered in ketchup or several *McDonalds* Big Macs
- Surprisingly introspective acknowledgements of the effect his parents' severe coldness and emotional unavailability had on his childhood and sense of psychological security

## A Very Stable Genius
by Donald J. Trump

No one gives me credit for my record-breaking brain,
They worry much more about giving me the blame,
But all the controversy and drama is quite needless
Because I'm really quite a stable genius.

On foreign policy I'm the Vincent Van Gogh,
Abandoning the Kurds and threatening NATO,
I've been smarter than the generals since I was a fetus
Because I'm really quite a stable genius.

I maybe threatened war with evil North Korea,
And asked if I could nuke Iran and its Sharia,
But I knew they'd all back down with a case of small penis
Because I'm really quite a stable genius.

I inspire incels and threaten civic violence,
I urge my fans to buck quarantine compliance,
For my voters and fans I'm bigger than Jesus
Because I'm really quite a stable genius.

To top it all off I'm a beautiful specimen,
So I can kiss and grab anyone with estrogen.
How do I know I'm America's male Venus?
Because I'm really quite a stable genius.

## Stephen Miller's Child-Separation Policy Papers Were Reportedly "Jerked Off All Over On"

July 7, 2018
Washington D.C.—

The Trump Administration's zero-tolerance immigration policies mandating the separation of babies and children from their parents at the Mexican border were authored by executive adviser Stephen Miller, and were reported to have been jerked off on by Mr. Miller before submitting them to the Department of Justice for review.

"I had to handle these policy reports, and let me just say that I very nearly quit that day," explained a White House aide requesting anonymity to candidly discuss his or her absolute disgust in seeing the condition of the stacks of papers churning out from Mr. Miller's office. "There were stains all over the paragraphs, sometimes so many that the wording of the policies was indecipherable. Draconian, racist policies apparently really get Stephen off."

An anonymous staffer from the Department of Justice who witnessed the condition of the policy reports agreed with that assessment.

"The policy paper recommending that the Trump Administration only give back the immigrant children to their parents if they agree to be deported was so crusty and full of Stephen's ejaculate that it broke in half. Think about that. It was five pieces of paper stapled together, and I saw it literally break in half. Stephen Miller is a real f***ed up guy."

*The Halfway Post* reached out to Mr. Miller for a comment, but his secretary would only inform us that he was busy in his office with his "Do not disturb" sign hanging on his door handle, which meant he was busy drafting new immigration policies.

"When he's got his sign flipped to 'Do not disturb,' it means he's hard at government work," explained Miller's elderly and oblivious secretary Doris Hannigan. "Sometimes he's working so hard that I hear groans coming from behind his door. Let me tell you, that boy has some energy for public policy! And when he finally comes out he says he's ravenously hungry. He's a very polite boy. I'm trying to set him up with my granddaughter, Denise. I think they'd make a fine match, and I think Stephen agrees. When I told him about Denise he asked for some pictures of her pretending to be dead. Kind of an odd request, but Denise was a good sport about it. When Stephen saw them he said she looked quite appetizing."

## "Why Won't Women Date Me?" Ask Trump Staffers Who Cheer The Policy Of Immigrant Kids Being Lost Forever

August 14, 2018
Washington D.C.—

Dating is hard these days, but no one has it harder than guiltless, single, and lonely Trump Administration staffers looking for love in the capital city.

Being involved in the Trump presidency has become a major red flag for users of popular dating apps like Tinder, Bumble and Grindr, and Trump staffers are either quickly swiped left on if their jobs are listed in their bios or ghosted once the topic of employment comes up in textual conversation. Meanwhile, the ongoing immigrant-babies-stolen-and-stuck-in-cages controversy is not making Trump staffers' dating lives any easier.

"I don't get it, I work in the White House and I thought that would be a major turn-on for girls," explained Michael Herman, 29, a Trump staffer who hasn't been on a date with a female since Trump took office. "It's like women believe Trump's two dozen sexual assault accusations or something. I think it's very manly of Trump to grab women when and where he wants them, but apparently the 30,000 single women in the D.C. metropolitan area are snowflakes and don't like the idea of the POTUS grabbing their private parts. I'd be totally honored if I was a chick. I can't wait till sex robots are a little bit more realistic so I won't need a stupid, real woman ever again."

Some Trump staffers have expressed dissatisfaction with their involuntarily celibate status.

"If it were up to me, I'd be banging a different woman every day like a Mongolian emperor, but all the women I've ever met get so neurotic around alpha males like me," insisted Todd Garpman, 31, another Trump staffer. "I'm an alpha in every way except my sex life, and it doesn't make sense. When I meet a woman things go great until I mention the fact that eugenics should make a comeback in government. And then they ignore all my voicemails, no matter how threatening they get! What am I doing wrong?"

Other Trump staffers believe that women's refusal to date them proves their opinion that women don't belong in politics.

"Why are women so emotional about these immigrant kids?" asked Joseph Lacker, 36, a Trump staffer in the Department of Education. "It's why women are weak. Personally, I love the audio tapes of these kids in detention centers crying. These Mexican three-year-olds missing their mommies are such babies! This is exactly why women shouldn't be allowed anywhere near the responsibilities of government. You get one crying baby and they all totally forget about keeping their country safe. That, and their menstrual cycles that turn them into hormonal freaks once a month when they don't get pregnant. It's like they're only capable of thinking with their uteruses. These three-year-olds may look like cute, chubby cherubs, but there's no way to tell if they're MS-13 gang lords or not. Every woman I've gone on a date with in the last year is dumb enough to think these Hispanic toddlers are innocent victims, so I'm actually really glad none of them have ever agreed to a second date when I ask for one. They'd just be wasting my time. And I always find out later after stalking them for weeks that their taste in men is terrible because the next guy they start dating is always a total liberal beta loser. So I'm lucky I only got one date with all of them! Although, I haven't used it in so long I'm kind of afraid it's gonna fall off, if you know what I mean. Do you know any single women who like great, father-material guys like me?"

## More Mike Pence Headlines

- Mike Pence Has Locked Himself In A Closet Until He Finds A Bible Passage Endorsing Toddler Cages

- Donald Trump Asked Mike Pence If The "T" On His Cross Necklace Stood For Trump

- Mike Pence Claims Trump Is The Most Virginal President We've Ever Had

- Trump Reportedly Told Mike Pence His Wife Was A "4" But His Daughters Were "9's"

- Mike Pence Privately Suspects Donald Trump Lied About Praying For 2 Hours Last Night

- Mike Pence Vows To Never Visit Alabama Or Its Devilishly Temptress Teenage Girls Who Corrupted The Extremely Christian Roy Moore

- Mike Pence Is Disappointed With John McCain Because He Put On His Special, Obamacare-Repeal-Tie-Breaking Underwear For Nothing

- Mike Pence Just Googled "Stormy Daniels," Threw Up, And Is Now Refusing To Ever Shake Donald Trump's Hand Ever Again

- Mike Pence Is Demanding God Explain Why He Isn't President Yet

- Mike Pence, Pissed That God Hasn't Made Him President Yet, Converts To Atheism

- After Pence Visited The Mayo Clinic, Trump Asked Him How The Mayonnaise Tasted

- Impressed By Mike Pence's Fundamentalism, ISIS Offers To Match His Pay And Benefits If He Joins

- Mike Pence Stuns America: "Vote Blue in 2018 So Trump Will Be Impeached and I Get His Job!"

- Mike Pence Has Been Patiently Sitting On A Box Of "President Pence" Business Cards For A Full Year Now

- Mike Pence Was Surprised During The Afghan Negotiations To Learn How Many Policy Ideas He Shares With The Taliban

- Mike Pence Feels God Has Gotten Confused By Doing Coronavirus AFTER Obama

- Mike Pence Is Reportedly Beginning To Suspect Donald Trump Has Not Been Faithful To Melania

- Mike Pence Claims That Every Time Trump Broke Laws Or Obstructed Justice, He Was Away In Another Room Praying For The Troops

- Mike Pence Says The Only Sure Cure To The Coronavirus Is Carrying A Pocket Bible

- COVID Czar Mike Pence Spent All The Coronavirus Money On A National Prayer Hotline To "Pray Away The Plague"

- A Pale, Emaciated Mike Pence Concedes Prayer Will Not And Cannot Stop The Spread Of Coronavirus After Disappearing For Two Weeks

- Donald Trump: "Mike Pence Sure Dropped The Ball On Handling The Coronavirus, Didn't He?"

- Mike Pence Says He'll Debate Kamala Harris, But Only If She Doesn't Try To Seduce Him

- Mike Pence Regrets That Trump Didn't Do More To Reverse Territorial Gains Made By The Gay Agenda

# God Has No Clue How Republicans Can Look Around At The World And Think He's "Pro-Life"

October 12, 2018
Heaven—

God just held a press conference to correct a common misconception:

"Anywhere from 25–50% of pregnancies end in miscarriage, considering how many women don't even realize they ever got pregnant before it naturally ends, so why do conservatives think I'm so adamant women should not have control over their own bodies and reproductive rights? In general, I can't say that death and murder bother Me much. Have you ever seen a nature documentary? There's nothing that gets Me going more than a pack of wolves chasing down and eating a baby deer or sheep! The universe is not a very pleasant place for fetuses, newborns, and babies! Have you ever seen a mommy crab just sit there with her thousands of baby crabs eating them as they hatch? I love that stuff! You know how many species have to give birth to hundreds of young at a time because the only way the species continues on genetically is if enough are born to fill up mommy's tummy so the others have a chance to run or swim away and grow up? I do, and it's a f*** ton! Why do you think I designed Hell? I love suffering! I'm not a nice deity. Though I have calmed down considerably since the Old Testament days. Creating alcohol enzymes back then really took Me down a dark path. I created one of those built-in water dispenser refrigerators for Myself up in Heaven and filled it with chardonnay. That's why there are black holes. I don't even know how to make them sober. But I find more every time I wake up after blacking out. Let's just say I was in a rough patch for a few millennia, and got carried away with the sadism. Which is why I don't know why conservatives go around saying I think every life is sacred. I'm not pro-life. You know how many organisms on this planet from single-cells all the way up to even humans get eaten alive every single day? Frankly, I'm anti-anti-abortion! You know how many cities I've burned down? You know how many ancient peoples I demanded be genocided? I invented all the human rights violations! And remember when I aborted virtually all of humanity with the flood? You know how many pregnant women and fetuses died that day? I'm actually kind of embarrassed about that one. I totally botched My original Creation. And it really bit Me in the butt in the deity club. Zeus never lets Me live it down. I mean, here I am, totally omniscient and omnipotent, and My first Creation goes haywire from Me programming you sapien monkeys to sin so much that I eventually had to just shut it all down. I looked through the genetic code, and, of course, it was literally just one closing bracket I forgot that threw off the whole stabilization logarithm I designed to keep you all from ruining yourselves. Total rookie mistake!"

# EXCLUSIVE: Donald Trump's 2020 Campaign Slogans Just Leaked!

January 5, 2019
Washington D.C.—

A *Halfway Post* reporter found a sheet of paper left behind in a D.C. diner signed by Trump campaign manager Brad Parscale full of prospective 2020 slogans. The following are the Trump team's early 2020 ideas:

- "Because owning the libs one more time is more important than democracy, justice, healthcare, wage growth, infrastructure, governmental stability, or reproductive freedom!"
- "January 6th, 2021 come out and take our country back no matter who wins!"
- "Don't you want to see Lindsey Graham, Ted Cruz, and all the other Republican senators humiliate themselves further for four more years?!"
- "Kevin McCarthy will do anything we say, and we mean ANYTHING!"
- "Trump is publicly racist so all your racisms are excused!"
- "Vote for Trump because the Democrats will be way too mean raising taxes on all the average, working-class Americans who have big yachts with smaller yachts inside of them!"
- "Trump 2020: There were still some institutional norms and democratic guardrails Trump didn't get enough time to smash the first time around!"
- "Renovate existing fencing! Renovate existing fencing!"
- "This time around Trump REALLY will have all the BEST people!"
- "Whether you're a zionist billionaire, or an incel Nazi, Donald Trump somehow has the Jewish policies for you!"
- "If you reelect Donald Trump, he promises to golf a little less!"
- "With our assault against abortion rights angering women everywhere, America needs a Pussygrabber-in-Chief!"
- "Join the Trump Youth!" (Girls aged 13–18 only)"
- "If Trump is elected president again, gas prices will get periodically lower when Saudi Arabia murders and mutilates American resident journalists, and feels bad about hurting our feelings! Yay infringements on humans rights for periodically low gas prices!"
- "Culture Wars: White People Strike Back!"
- "I alone can fix it, for real this time!"
- "Trump: human rights are for virtue-signaling snowflakes betas!"
- "Covfefe!"

- "Vote for Trump because Stephen Miller's concentration camp project needs four more years in order to compete with Hitler's record!"
- "Trump 2020: Russia hasn't fully got back its investment yet!"
- "Are you not getting enough Don Jr. and Eric in your life anymore? Vote Trump, and they'll respectively be the Secretary of Defense and Secretary of Agriculture."
- "Trump is not a liar, only everyone else is!"
- "This time, Trump really WILL stand in the middle of Fifth Avenue and start shooting people!"
- "Destroy the GOP establishment, and rename the Republican Party the Trumpist Party!"
- "If Trump can keep charging taxpayers to put the Secret Service up at his golf clubs every third day while he's in office of his second term, he may finally become a REAL billionaire!"
- "Let's give fascism a real try this time!"
- "Trump 2020: Big problems need big hands!"
- "Donald Trump has never read the Bible, so he'll never accuse you of acting unChristian or being a hypocrite like those atheist liberal jerks!"
- "Ivanka for Vice President: Bring sexy back to the White House!"
- "Except for several exceptions, Donald Trump is just like Jesus!"
- "If you missed your chance in 2016, now is your turn to be a part of another stunning Electoral College technicality victory in spite of America's recurring three-decade popular desire for Democratic presidents! OWN THE LIBS!"
- "Trump 2020: No matter what happens, Trump really won, won't ever concede, and will interrupt as many weddings at Mar-a-Lago as he wants to vent about how unfair the world is, and how terrible the water pressure in showers has gotten. And probably windmills too. And he's doing this for YOU, Real America, so don't let him down. Give him $250 right now. Make it recurring monthly. You know how many people Trump's currently paying off so they don't testify against him under oath in court? Rudy Giuliani is an expensive guy to keep his mouth shut with daily bottles of Scotch. So pony up right now, and Trump will let you keep saying racist shit in public to own the libs!"

## Local Trump Fan Is Annoyed All The Brown People She Yells At Turn Out To Be Citizens

February 10, 2019
Mobile, AL—

Bertha LaFollette, 49, a local Alabama woman, has been pausing in the middle of her daily errands to yell at the non-white people she encounters, but she gets discouraged when she discovers she is harassing US citizens.

"I know from Fox News the illegal MS-13 gang lords and immigrant terrorists are out here all around, but they're too shadowy and I can't find any," she explained. "This morning I yelled at a 50-something-year-old Asian man to go back to China, and—what do you know?—he turned out to be a 25-year veteran of the navy who has lived here in Alabama his whole life. This other Black thug I saw was reading a book in the park, so, of course, I did the patriotic thing and told him he wasn't welcome in Mobile, and I got unlucky again! He turned out to be the mayor! What are the odds? Things are so out of control. I don't know how he could have been democratically elected! This just isn't my Mobile anymore! Yet all around the country are horrible stories! I hear from Sean Hannity and Tucker Carlson on a nightly basis how animalistic minorities are out everywhere targeting Trump supporters and stopping at nothing to persecute us Christian whites, but just my luck that I can't find any of them to yell at here! Maybe I should move. I must be in the only town in America where all the urbans and foreigners hold the door for me in and out of stores, and let me go first at 4-way stop signs! But I suppose it's a blessing that my town seems perfectly normal and filled with quiet, mild-mannered immigrant and Black families when good Christian white folk all over the rest of America are daily terrorized by the invasion of millions of brown-skinned hordes pillaging and burning suburbs that used to be 100% safe from all crime."

Ms. LaFollette invited me to accompany her on a walk around the park, and *The Halfway Post* indulged her invitation. The experience was full of ranting.

"You're the reason I'm poor!" she exclaimed at two Hispanic boys playing Pokémon Go! along the park's paved path as she began yelling at every person of color she saw. "You're why my Social Security benefits aren't keeping up with inflation! You and your margarita family! You're why my van broke down! You're why I can't afford 2-ply toilet paper! You're why this outskirt suburban town's factory has been laying off workers for two decades, and cutting benefits even as production and profits skyrocket with the help of automation! You're why all the wealth is concentrated at the top, and CEOs get massive bonuses and corporate retirement packages while wages mysteriously decline! Hey, you Arab punks! You're why our job creators moved to richer cities, and lost touch with their workers and their communities, and eventually moved manufacturing entirely to Taiwan and Vietnam! You! You two basketball-playing middle-schoolers! It's all your fault! Not the fault of the GOP's decades-long insistence on global free-trade coupled with obstinacy to any economic stimulus or social welfare protections for the affected, collateral-damaged victims of the outsourcing of our industrial economy from Main Street America to Asia, if that's what you were thinking! So go back to Mexico, or Africa, or wherever all you hyphen-Americans came from! You're why I'm not getting full-time hours or healthcare from my job as a welcome greeter at Walmart! It's because of your toddler little sister who is going to grow up, have mixed babies, and further make America less white! Trump is any day now gonna kick you all out! Then, once you're gone, I'll be rich! I'll be a billionaire! My diabetes will disappear! And Walmart will finally promote me to cashier, and will start giving me weeks of paid vacation, and stock option bonuses! The economy will soar so high my toughest decision each day will be which convertible car I drive to work! So start packing your stuff, because the longer you and your families stay here in Alabama, the longer it'll be till I'm in the 1%! Till all white Americans are in the 1%! Then I won't need food stamps anymore! I won't need any welfare at all! So scram, you undesirables!"

LaFollette started choking on her saliva for a brief moment. Than continued.

"And don't go home thinking I'm stupid for not realizing that your people and mine are both victims of unprecedented economic inequality, and that we should actually be allied according to our economic interests against the class warfare of top-down economic exploitation, because that's not the truth! White people are the only victims! Not you people! So you have to get out of our country! Doesn't matter if you were born here, or your family has been here for generations! I don't care if your ancestors were from some South-Western town or village for a thousand years in territory that changed hands from country to country in shifting colonial geo-political dealings until America annexed it in the 1800s effectively annexing your family along with it! It's white American land now, so scram! You're the culprit for why my white-trash life has no hope for improvement! It's you! As soon as you're gone, the billionaires and corporations will trickle down wealth everywhere to everyone! Reagan will finally be vindicated! And I'll buy a mansion, and never have to eat out of the dumpsters behind restaurants ever again. I'll have ten servants, no, even better, I'll have ten slaves! When Trump becomes dictator, 'Real America' will get everything we want, including slavery! Finally, American will be great again! USA! USA! Oh, and this is not racist by the way! I don't have a racist bone in my body! I'm a good Christian! This is just economic frustration!"

# Bill Barr, Since Obtaining The Mueller Report, Hasn't Left His Office And Has Turned Into A Gollum-Like Creature

April 10, 2019
Washington D.C.—

Since obtaining the completed Mueller Report, Attorney General Bill Barr has reportedly not left his office in weeks, choosing instead to reclusively stay locked inside with the lights turned off.

Several Department of Justice staffers, who requested anonymity to discuss the increasingly strange internal affairs of the DOJ, have told *The Halfway Post* that Barr has been heard cackling in his office late into the night.

"I have only seen glimpses of Barr when he opens his door just a crack to receive the day's mail, and it's terrifying," said one DOJ staffer. "His skin has turned ghostly pale, almost translucent, and he has lost a lot of weight so that his suit doesn't fit anymore. Yesterday I could see that he had torn his shirt and pants to shreds, and was only wearing what appeared to be his undershirt wrapped around his private parts like a loincloth. He hasn't once left his office, and the stench of excrement is getting unbearable."

Another staffer confirmed the disturbing changes in Mr. Barr's behavior.

"He laughs maniacally sometimes, and other times it sounds like wailing. It's all very guttural, and he makes weird throat sounds like he's choking or hacking up a hairball. And weird purring sounds. This morning I opened his door and saw him petting his printed copy of the Mueller Report muttering 'My precious' over and over. It looked like he had pulled most of his hair out of his head, and the stench of urine hit me like a wave. The cleaning bill taxpayers will have to pay when he finally leaves his office terrifies me."

A third staffer recorded Barr talking to himself in the third person:

"Billum has saved Master Trump from that nasty report! No one can prosecute Master Trump with a report only we have! Stupid, nasty Mueller! You thought you were so clever, but Billum is the cleverest! Isn't that right, Precious? Yes, Precious, Billum is the cleverest attorney general who ever attorneyed. He's a very good Billum. No one will ever know the collusion Master Trump did! Only Billum! Master Trump's secrets are safe with Billum! We'll burn every report against Master Trump we can get in our hands! We'll burn them all! Nasty prosecutors! We'll burn down all of Washington D.C. if we have to! We'll burn everything, isn't that right, Precious? Yes, Precious, we will. Everything will burn! Hehe! Billum! Billum!"

# 15 Questions For All The Weirdos Who Want To Be President In 2020

May 19, 2019
St. Louis, MO—

1. Why do you want to be the person who wakes up every day and decides which Middle Eastern gathering of "combatant-aged" people needs to be droned to death in the name of national security?
2. Why do you want to be the person who has to direct the military to ignore the Afghan army's child sodomy in order to continue facilitating their cooperation?
3. Are you prepared mentally to make a sweetheart deal with the Taliban so we can have our troops leave Afghanistan?
4. Why do you want to be the person who personally fails to guide common sense gun laws through Congress after each elementary school mass shooting?
5. Would you like to be the first president in decades to act on the words "well regulated" included in the phrasing of the Second Amendment?
6. Why do you want to have the ultimate responsibility to decide whether or not to nuke tens of thousands of innocent strangers in another nation?
7. What would you do if you looked in the NASA and military files and found out aliens are real?
8. What is your red line of human rights violations at which point you would send US troops to intervene in another country's genocide?
9. Would you invade another country if the United Nations refuses to support a war, and would you secure a Congressional declaration of war first?
10. Do you agree the gold standard is stupid, and why?
11. What number of foreign, democratically-elected leaders overthrown is too many for you?
12. Will you publicly take a few high school tests on geography, history, and science?
13. Have you considered nominating Merrick Garland as your first Supreme Court choice?
14. How do you feel about physically fighting Mitch McConnell when he decides to recess the Senate indefinitely so you can accomplish literally nothing?
15. Do you understand how long it will take for the smell of Donald Trump's excessive hairspray use to be cleaned out of the carpet and drapes?

# Donald Trump Admits He Has Never Read A Single Book Cover To Cover

May 26, 2019
Washington D.C.—

In a bizarre press conference today, President Donald Trump waxed poetically on disparate topics, including Democratic presidential candidate Pete Buttigieg, reading books, and accurate spelling.

The following is Mr. Trump's inflammatory rant in response to a question asking what he thought about the potential prospect of facing off against Mr. Buttigieg in the general election.

"Mayor Pete, I like Mayor Pete, I think he's a nice guy. He can speak a lot of languages, but that's not what we want, is it? We like English here in America. He can keep his Norwegian, and his Spanish, and whatever they speak in France, and his Pig Latin. I'll keep with American English. Can't beat it. Not even the British do it like we do it. We do it the best. Mayor Pete likes to read a lot. I've been hearing a lot about how much he reads. I love reading too. Went to Wharton, was top of my class. I did a lot of reading in Wharton. About business. But I didn't get so good at making deals by reading a lot of books, I can tell you that. To tell you the truth, even in college I knew more than any of the books could ever teach me. You have to be born with it, and I was born with one of the great intellects of all time. One of the biggest IQs of all time. No book can teach you how to be Donald Trump. In fact, I've never even finished a book. Never needed to. I always know the end way before I get halfway through. Sometimes before I even open to the first page. I'm one of the greats at reading, and that's why I don't have to read much. Almost ever. I don't think I've opened a book in thirty years. But I've written quite a few. I've actually written more books than I've read. How many people can say that? Best-sellers. Almost got a Pulitzer. Should have gotten a Pulitzer, but that whole process is rigged. It's a total joke. I've heard from so many people—you wouldn't believe how many people think *The Art of the Deal* should have gotten a Pulitzer, a Nobel, all of it. Top-seller. Sold millions of copies. Millions and millions. But you know how it goes. Just like how the fake news say I can't spell. I can spell, I guarantee it. I'm one of the greats at spelling. 'Covfefe' was just a code. Just a code, everyone. Only a few people know what it means, but they got the message, I promise you that. It was a great message. They told me it was the greatest message they ever heard. It was an unbreakable code. No one can break my Twitter codes. The Democrats, they try. The fake news tries, but they will never break my codes. They're the dumbest people you've ever heard of. They haven't got a clue. My tweets are so far over their heads they can't believe how far. Cause I'm one of the greats at cyber, maybe of all time. No one does cyber like me. Not even book-lover Mayor Pete. *The Art of the Deal* isn't written in Norwegian, so he can't read that one, can he? And I don't want to say it, I told myself I wouldn't say it, they don't want me to say it... but he's one of those gays you hear about. You know, the Evangelicals, they don't like the gay stuff. I don't want to say it, but they're, like, way against it. Cause of the Bible. The Bible is just tremendous, isn't it, folks? You know, they don't want you to say it anymore, but the Bible is a very popular book. After *The Art of the Deal*, the Bible should get a Pulitzer, don't you think? Isn't it about time? The Democrats stop the Bible from getting a Pulitzer every year. They want to cancel the Bible. They want to cancel Jesus. But not me. I love the Bible. You know, a lot of people don't know this, but the Bible is actually two books, not just one. They have an Old Testament and they have a New Testament. Actually, a lot of people don't know this either, but in each testament are a lot of smaller books, and letters to various peoples. Great letters. Some of the best letters of all time, really. I love them. Read them all the time. You wouldn't believe how much I read them. In fact, one of my favorites is... did I mention Mayor Pete is gay?"

## The Joys Of Fatherhood
by Donald J. Trump


Ivanka came from deep in my loins,
Her boobs and butt are a total ten.
I think at some point another tit pair joined,
What's her name again?

Then there's the boys, not quite the same,
Donald Jr.'s apple fell far from my tree.
Ugly and dumb, unworthy of my name,
But showed some promise colluding with me.

And Eric the youngest, creepiest of the squad,
I'm glad he wasn't my namesake pick.
But he helped me commit our charitable fraud,
So it wasn't all bad he came out of my dick.

And then Melania has a son of her own,
But I'm too busy to be a teen's dad.
When she was pregnant I had others I boned,
For all I know I've got dozens of lads!

## Local Abortion Protesters Take A Break To Go To The Mall And Protest Polyester

June 11, 2019
St. Louis, MO—

After a morning of protesting at the local Planned Parenthood, several Evangelical demonstrators took a break from screaming obscenities at young women getting medical checkups in order to go to the mall and scream obscenities at the apathetic employees of the West County Mall's *H&M* clothing store for selling polyester clothing.

"A lot of other Evangelicals don't realize this," explained protest organizer Sally Shelderson, 43, a resident of St. Charles, "but the Bible specifically forbids mixing fibers in your clothes in Leviticus 19:19. So I got to thinking that we shouldn't only be protesting abortion if our goal was to truly spread ALL the warnings of eternal damnation in the Lord's holy book. In fact, many of our fellow Christian protesters who only seem to get involved when it calls for slut-shaming women are actually wearing polyester shirts and socks when they're yelling out 'whore' insults! They're protesting one sin while literally committing another! I even saw one protester this morning eating a cobb salad with shrimp on it. Shrimp! Can you believe it? Have these other Christian protesters ever even read Leviticus?"

Ms. Shelderson has built up an impressive Evangelical following in recent years thanks to her insistence that many more aspects of modern life deserve public shaming than just abortion.

"I loved her concept of diversity in criticism subjects," explained Tenika Doyle, 26, of South City, an enthusiastic member of Shelderson's protests. "If you only protest one variety of sinner, like Planned Parenthood patients, you find yourself committing sins of very dark judgement, and I don't think Jesus would appreciate that much. So if you spread out the Biblical judgment a little, you can remind a greater diversity of people in public how gloriously inconvenient fundamentalist approaches to Christianity can be. And isn't that the point of religion? To be so burdened with contemporarily arbitrary rules and regulations on daily life that you can't help but be brutally reminded of God's omnipresent judgement? I think so! And that's why all these *H&M* shoppers need a good reminder that the mixing of fibers is a big Biblical faux pas, even though I don't 100% understand why from a practical sense. Modern polyester clothes may have stronger fibers than cotton, and not wear down as quickly, wrinkle as much, or shrink so dramatically, but surely the ancient goat-herding epileptics who passed down the Bible's rules orally for hundreds of pre-literate years had a perfectly legitimate reason to ban it. God works in mysterious ways, you know? As a young, socially woke person, however, I'd also like to protest *H&M*'s suspiciously cheap prices, which indicate a certain degree of unfairly valued Asian labor in their supply chain, but it's frustrating that the Bible apparently finds no moral qualms with child slavery. I've looked! It actually has way more restrictions against bad-mouthing your parents than enslaving people for life. It's puzzling. Sometimes it's so hard to interpret what God wants. It would be nice if He maybe updated the Bible a bit some day, and cleared up some of the ambiguous passages and conflicting morals, you know?"

The *H&M* store employees, meanwhile, all agreed they were not paid enough to care about the protests going on in front of their store.

"This protest, or whatever it is, is pretty weird," explained *H&M*'s Cheyenne Moore, 18, the afternoon shift's designated clothes folder. "But I ate a pot brownie before coming in, so I've just been chilling listening to headphones while folding. It's pretty easy to zone them out. They're kind of blocking the entrance and obstructing customers from coming in, which I don't really mind because I make the same amount of money per hour if we have one customer all day or ten thousand customers, so... If my boss or the *H&M* corporate higher-ups were willing to share some of the increased profits that an increase in my monotonous, soul-sucking work cultivates I might work a little harder, but they're not, so... Adequate and fair compensation with legitimate trickle-down economic bonuses would inspire me to care, but the structural mobility of profits trickles only upward from my low wage drone work... Maybe I'm rambling because I'm really, really stoned."

*The Halfway Post* also interviewed Peyton Haslon, 31, who was sitting on a bench outside the *H&M* store while his wife shopped.

"I've been writing down a lot of the things they've been yelling about in my phone," Haslon said. "I had no idea about some of these Leviticus rules, but I checked them out and they're really in there! Apparently we're never supposed to ever eat the fat on meat because it all should be offered to God. And, after giving birth to boys, mothers are unclean for a week, like a typical Biblical menstruation, but then their blood has to be purified for another 33 days before they can touch anything holy. And after birthing girls, mothers are unclean for two weeks, and then have to wait a full 66 days. And the new moms have to bring a 1-year-old lamb to a priest for a burnt offering, and a young dove or pigeon for a sin offering. I guess I'll have to start raising lambs and doves because my wife is pregnant with our first child, and we want a bunch of kids. I've spent my whole life making fun of gay people and voting against gay marriage according to the Bible, so I'd hate to be a hypocrite and not also orient my life according to all the other rules in Leviticus!"

# Trump's Latest Twitter Feud: Calls Paul McCartney "Overrated" And The Beatles "Talentless"

June 14, 2019
Washington D.C.—

In his latest Twitter feud, President Donald Trump has lashed out at Sir Paul McCartney for the singer-songwriter's recent comment that Trump acted "like a clown."

The following are the President's tweets:

"Paul McCartney is a joke. I always thought Ringo was the best songwriter in the group. 'Hey Jude,' 'Yesterday,' and 'Let It Be' are all tied for the worst songs ever written! 'Eleanor Rigby'... more like 'Eleanor KILL ME!'"

"And 'Back In The USSR'.... what kind of song name is that? Was Paul McCartney colluding with Russia? Hey @AdamSchiff, why are you looking into me and not him? Was Paul McCartney working with Russia and funded by the Clinton Foundation? Everyone's asking!"

"People tell me all the time that *The Art of the Deal* audiotape was way better than anything The Beatles ever recorded! Way catchier too! The Queen of England actually told me that she only knighted Paul because I was unavailable at the time! Everyone was talking about it when I was in London!"

"And what's the deal with his accent? Paul McCartney speaks like his mouth is full of marbles! Is he even a real American? Starting tomorrow I'm going to direct the FBI to look into his birth certificate and see what's really going on!"

# Americans Are Worried Trump Supporters Just Aren't Assimilating Into American Culture

June 16, 2019
Shreveport, LA—

Donald Trump's biggest MAGA fans are increasingly refusing to assimilate into America's culture of tolerance and diversity, and are choosing instead to keep to their insularly extremist customs of ethno-nationalist radicalism.

"I don't want to say 'these people,' but I can't help but notice that Trump supporters are not sharing our values," explained Mark Trail, 49. "They yell at minorities in grocery stores and on the street, their number of hate crimes are on the rise, they're stockpiling arms to prepare for another potential civil war, and they just plain have hate in their hearts for America. They don't want the same kinds of things that real Americans want. They want things like discrimination against women, religious oppression, and totalitarian presidencies. I hate how it sounds as if I don't think Trump supporters are welcome here, but I wish they would adapt more to our culture. If they're going to live here, they could try to be a little more like us, right? Maybe they could be less extremist about their beliefs. Maybe adopt more of our cultural values? I'm worried that, if they keep growing in numbers, it won't be long before I don't even recognize America anymore."

Other citizens expressed discomfort with MAGA fans' clothing customs.

"Those bright red MAGA hats just make me worry every time I see one," said Sarah Heller, 55. "I don't understand why they would cover themselves that way with that kind of oppressive, abrasive and cultish symbolism. And what's the deal with all this QAnon stuff? It seems so fundamentalist the way they follow their prophet blindly. I wish they'd stop trying to make us all live according to their Q-ria Law. That's just not how we do things here in America. Do they have to throw their foreignness in our faces? It's like, are they going to commit a hate crime or insurrection right in front of me? And from the way they view the world, I can tell they don't care much for our civic principles and tradition. I don't think they understand or appreciate our Constitution and laws. I worry they're not fully loyal to our country. The way they take photos of themselves holding up their religious books and guns is very upsetting. I think they might be trying to subvert us from within. I mean, you can't help but notice that they're very pushy about their religious beliefs, and they refuse to abide by our election laws, and of course they're raising their kids with their extreme ideology to hate America and our democracy. This is an issue that will last for generations. I know America is a great melting pot, but I'm afraid they might just be too different to blend in!"

# More Republican Party Headlines

- "Stop Identity Politics!" Say Republicans, Who Have Catered Politically To White, Christian, Straight Males For Decades

- The Republican Tax Reform Bill Includes A Formal Resolution Apologizing To The Koch Brothers For Taxing Them

- Alabama Republicans Are Praying That Roy Moore Won't Also Be Revealed As Having Had Sex With Farm Animals

- ISIS Terrorists Pout, Wonder Why They Never Thought Of A Terrorist Attack As Lethal As The Republican Obamacare Repeal Bill

- "If Only God Would Do Something About Gun Violence!" Say Republicans Who Block Every Effort At Moderate Gun Control

- BREAKING NEWS: Ted Cruz Is Again Doing What He Thinks Will Help Him Run For President

- Ted Cruz Just Announced He's Going To Primary Trump For 2020, Says He Can Deport Hispanics, Himself Excluded, "Way Better"

- Ted Cruz's Senate Hearing Notes Just Say "President Cruz" Doodled Over and Over Again With Several New Presidential Seal Designs Sketched With Squirrels Holding The Arrows And Olive Branch

- Now That Trump Lost Reelection, Ted Cruz Wants Everyone To Know He Was Only Faking His Loyalty To Trump All Along

- The National Republican Committee Just Changed The GOP Mascot From An Elephant To A Rabid, Hissing Opossum Foaming At The Mouth

- Paul Ryan Has A "World's Best Congressman" Mug In His Office He Was Given By The Koch Brothers

- Paul Ryan: "I Did Everything I Could To Stop Trump!"

- John Boehner Admits His Name Should Have Been Pronounced "Boner" All Along

- One Lonely, Local Republican Is Starting To Think Donald Trump Is Capable Of Lying

- Alex Jones Claims Donald Trump Is A Liberal Hoax Designed To Make Conservatives Look Bad

- After A Phone Call With Alex Jones, Donald Trump Called Nancy Pelosi A "Lizard Space Witch" And Declared War Against "Gay Martians"

- Rudy Giuliani Claims Donald Trump's Long Lost Twin Brother Devin Did All The Colluding With Russia, Not Donald

- Leaked GOP Tax Reform Bill Is Just One Sentence Long: "F*** The Poor"

- Jeff Sessions and Roy Moore, While Competing For The Alabama KKK's Endorsement, Got Into A Fistfight At A Cross Burning

- The RNC Published A Craigslist Ad To Find GOP Primary Candidates Who AREN'T Neo-Nazis Or In The Ku Klux Klan

- Lindsey Graham Wore A "Trump Can Grab This Pussy" Shirt To The State Of The Union Address

- The Nobel Peace Prize And Its Million Dollar Reward Once Again Offered To Any Congressional Republican Who Launches An Impeachment Investigation Into Donald Trump's Crimes

- Mitch McConnell Was Just Elected In Absentia The Caliph Of ISIS For His Impressive Work Harming America

- Mitch McConnell: "This Third Trump Era Supreme Court Vacancy Is Way Different Than Obama's Last One Because F*** You!"

- Mitch McConnell Was Caught On A Hot Mic Telling Lindsey Graham He Spent His Russian Bribe On Purebred Turtles

- Worried Trump Has COVID-19, Matt Gaetz Has Been Giving Him Sponge Baths At Night

- Jim Jordan Says It's The Honor Of His Life To Massage Trump's Feet Every Night

- Mitt Romney Was Forced To Eat Lunch At The Senate Outcast Table With Ted Cruz Today After Voting For Trump's Impeachment Conviction

- Republicans Are Begging Democrats Not To Be As Selfish With Gerrymandering In 2020 As They Were In 2010

## Fox News Says Disney Mermaids Should Be White, "Just Like Jesus, Santa, And Martin Luther King Jr."

July 12, 2019
New York City, NY—

In a strange opinion segment this morning, the hosts of *Fox & Friends* spent several minutes discussing the controversy of *Disney*'s recent casting decision in the new *The Little Mermaid* film.

The titular character will be played by a Black actress, and many of *Fox News*'s TV personalities have taken offense for some reason.

"Everyone knows mermaids are white," explained Steve Doocy. "Of course they're white. They may be mythical creatures adapted into fictional characters and storylines, but it was a white Scandinavian guy who wrote the book this specific *Disney* story is based off of. That means the mermaid character has to be white forever, with white people's hair. I especially don't want to see a hairstyle on this mermaid that little white girls don't naturally have. Are you listening, *Disney*? This mermaid can't have any dreadlocks, you hear me? And no afros either. No box braids, no yarn braids, no Bantu knots, no jumbo braids, no Fulani braids, no lemonade braids, no twist braids, no Ghana braids, no Nubian twists, no Senegalese twists, no Marley twists, no twist outs, no coiled buns, no frohawks, no braided mohawks, no jumbo faux locs, no high tops, no low caesars, no pineapple ponytails, no cornrows, none of that! Only the original red, straight, Nordic hair. Well, I take that back. The mermaid can have blonde hair if *Disney* wants. But that's it! Nothing else can change. The rule is you can make our beloved fictional characters more Aryan, but not any less. Because a Scandinavian writer wrote this. So this character has to look like that region, no matter how many centuries pass since the original story was written. Now, if a Black or Chinese person had written *The Little Mermaid*, we'd be having a different conversation."

"If that was the case, I'd still argue the mermaid should be white, though," interjected co-host Brian Kilmeade. "Because America is a white nation, and even if *The Little Mermaid* had been written and animated in an African hut, the Orient, or by some real dark-skinned aboriginal in Australia, we should be allowed to airbrush the mermaid or something before the film releases in the US. That's fair, right? It's just a bigger inconvenience for me to have to see a Black mermaid than for people of color around the world to have to see a white mermaid. Americans are used to seeing white animations, so why should we have to change our expectations? They're used to seeing our white American cultural exports anyway. So why mess everything up? Though I guess if this upcoming mermaid movie was a contemporary adaption where the mermaid was like a slave, or a housemaid, or a crack whore or something, then I could understand the mermaid being Black, but…"

"Let me cut you off right there for a second," said a worried-looking Doocy while looking off-camera, presumably at a distraught producer waving his arms in terror of the conversation's sudden veer into blatant racism. "I think what you're trying to say is that you think *Disney* should just not try to fix something that's not broken right? Everyone loves the classic white mermaid from Scandinavia, so why change it now?"

Doocy then subtly gave Kilmeade a "wrap it up" hand signal with his finger.

"Uh, yeah, I guess so," stammered Kilmeade. "At the end of the day, this is just the latest attack by liberal Hollywood elites to inject race controversies into every aspect of our culture. First, they said Jesus wasn't white because he happens to be from a geographical region where white people have historically not lived. Then department stores started making Black Santa Christmas decorations for Black families as a direct affront to my Christian, First Amendment freedom to only see commercialized representations of holiday characters exclusively for white people even in stores around the country I will never personally shop at. What's next? Are the liberal elites going to tell us Martin Luther King Jr. was Black? How many great, amazing, white heroes are they going to ruin for us?"

"Santa is the one that bothers me the most," said Doocy. "I mean, Santa is a manager of dozens of laborers, and has spent decades in a monogamous marriage… which race does that sound like to you? And I didn't want to get into it, but I'll say it. Jesus just had white skin. And blonde hair. This is not a politically correct thing, okay? Jesus may have grown up in Nazareth, but his family tree obviously came from somewhere more north. I'd guess maybe Sweden or Finland judging by how blonde Jesus was, but nowhere south of Germany. Who's to say Joseph and Mary weren't only in Bethlehem while on a winter vacation to get away from the Swedish December snows, and just liked the heat so they stayed in Galilee?"

"Um, the producers are telling us we're out of time and have to cut to a commercial break," Kilmeade said.

*Fox & Friends* then played an advertisement for the Donald Trump 2020 presidential campaign featuring a commemorative coin being sold on Trump's website with an etching of Trump's hands on it underneath the caption "NOT SMALL AT ALL!"

# Trump Reportedly Tried To Give Jeffrey Epstein A "Get Out Of Jail Free" Card

July 14, 2019
Washington D.C.—

Recent news about the arrest of serial pedophile and sex offender Jeffrey Epstein reportedly has President Donald Trump on edge, and their decades-long friendship is being looked at under the microscope of intense journalistic investigation.

Mr. Trump brought further attention to the controversy after giving Mr. Epstein a "Get Out Of Jail Free" card he apparently printed on a Microsoft Word certificate template.

To defend the legally dubious card, Trump tweeted several times this morning:

"I swear that my giving Jeff the 'Presidential Get Out Of Jail Free Card' has absolutely nothing to do with the fact that I used to go to his parties. When I gave him the Card, I had no idea he was a serial pedophile!"

"I know for a fact that Jeff never hung around any preteens when around me. Everyone's been talking lately about how old all the models that did my pageants were. Everyone's saying they all looked at least 40! And, honestly, Jeff really wasn't a friend of mine. I barely knew him. At some of those parties I went to, I didn't even know it was Jeff's private island!"

"The Fake News will report that I've often made sexually suggestive comments about my own daughters, but that doesn't count! When I talked about Tiffany's future boobs on TV, she wasn't a teenager! She was an infant, so it's way different! And, sure, I may have said some things about Ivanka…"

"…But I was just stating facts! The Democrats always accuse me of lying, but then they get upset when I tell the truth about Ivanka! Make up your minds! I said, IF she weren't my daughter, I'd PROBABLY be dating her. There's a big IF there! Of course I'm not going to date her! (But if she weren't my daughter I totally could!)"

"So when I direct Bill Barr to interfere with New York's prosecution of Jeffrey Epstein, you can rest assured it has NOTHING to do with all his parties I used to attend. I'm not into teenagers. Look at Melania, she's almost 50 now. She's an old hag!"

# Another White House Chef Quit, And Revealed More Trump Eating Habits

August 12, 2019
Washington D.C.—

Former White House Executive Chef Manny Robbins just published a lengthy social media post about his time cooking for President Donald Trump.

"I saw some disturbing things," said Robbins. "Some things I can't unsee, and they haunt me vividly behind my eyelids at night while lying in bed in the dark. If I could go back in time and warn myself not to take the executive chef position, I would."

Below are some anecdotes Robbins shared with *The Halfway Post*:

- Trump sprinkles ground up Adderall pills on his ice cream.
- On Saturday mornings Trump always requested 8 pancakes arranged in two stacks with strawberries cut into circles placed in the middle of each stack so they looked like boobs. Then he wouldn't eat them, but would just stick his face into them and make motor-boating sounds.
- Trump occasionally has his daughter Ivanka "pre-chew" his food for him. Robbins overheard him telling Jim Jordan it's the closest he'll ever come to making out with her.
- Trump often makes his son Eric try his food first to make sure it's not poisoned.
- Trump and his adviser Stephen Miller once bragged about the biggest restaurant bills they've ever racked up and not tipped their servers on.
- Trump ordered that the White House chefs spit in any food served to his former Attorney General Jeff Sessions, and demanded he see them do it.
- Trump once told an entire women's college softball championship-winning team during a White House luncheon that they'd all be hotter if they each lost 15 pounds.
- Trump made Lindsey Graham eat three plates of lasagna, and then throw up in Ted Cruz's open mouth in exchange for endorsing each of them.
- Trump literally not even one time dined with Melania.
- The few times that Trump's son Barron came downstairs to eat at the same time as him, Trump called him "Boy," and treated him like a server, apparently unaware of who he was.

# A Russian Copper Company Bought 30,000 Copies Of Donald Trump Jr.'s New Book

November 8, 2019
New York City, NY—

Pre-sales for Donald Trump Jr.'s new memoir, *Triggered: A Boy of Destiny Whose Father Loves Him Very Much And His Crusade Against The Socialist Feminazi Liberal Hollywood Coastal Elitist Communist Sharia Atheist Fascist Crybaby Loser Snowflakes* skyrocketed to the top of the *New York Times* Best Seller List with an asterisk when a mysterious corporate buyer from a Moscow suburb in Russia purchased 30,000 copies despite having just 300 employees.

The company, Russian Copper, is led by one of the top oligarchs in Moscow, Niko Deripaskov, a close friend and confidant to President Vladimir Putin.

Pundits across the political spectrum are calling attention to the possible exhibit of Russian money laundering, but Donald Jr. is adamant that Deripaskov is merely impressed with his business skills.

"Look, I was offered an executive role in the Trump Organization literally a day out of college," explained Donald Jr. in a press tour interview conversation with *Good Afternoon America*'s Giorgos Antonopoulos. "Deripaskov clearly just wants to pass my expansive business wisdom on to his employees. Notice that he didn't buy my dad's book *The Art of the Deal*, he specifically chose *Triggered*. And it's a great book. His employees are going to love it. I detail how I rose up in the ranks of the Trump Organization with hard work, determination and grit, and I managed to do it in just ten minutes. What does that say about me? My dad, the best businessman in the world, hired me on the spot for an executive role! He could tell I have the 'it factor.' And it had nothing to do with my last name, I promise you that. Honestly, he barely even knew me, so it's totally not nepotism. He was always so busy with work when I was a kid, so he didn't really watch me grow up or have anything to do with me at all. So everything I've achieved I've accomplished totally on my own. But it's not like my dad was a bad dad, you know? Sure, he often used to call me an idiot in front of the other Trump Organization board members, but deep down he really loves me. When I was a kid we'd have our special little moments. Like, he always made sure to call me on my birthday. We'd talk for fifteen minutes despite how busy he always was, and we'd laugh and laugh. That's when I could tell he respected me. He'd always ask about my friends, and he'd be like, 'Do your friends ever talk about whether I should pick your mom or Marla in school?' or 'Do your friends ever talk about my casinos in school?' Then we'd talk about the girls my age, and he'd ask me how big their boobs were getting, and dude locker room stuff like that. I knew he liked our talks because he really listened, and could always remember the names and bra sizes of every teenaged girl in me and Eric and Ivanka's classes at school. His brain was like an encyclopedia for girls going through puberty! It was great bonding. He maybe never said 'I love you,' but I knew deep down he was proud of me. And happy to be my dad. Then at the end of every call he'd tell me to pick out one toy or gift I really, really wanted, and the next day it would arrive in the mail from the Trump Foundation. You know, a lot of people say my dad is stingy, but I know for a fact that every time he'd host a big charity event for the Trump Foundation he'd let me, Eric and Ivanka get new bikes, or skates, or something fun like that. And he's still generous with us even now. You know how many copies of my book he got the Republican National Committee to buy? Several hundred. So no wonder the Russians are hearing the buzz about *Triggered*, and they want to read it for themselves. You know, I bet if Joe Biden's son Hunter wrote a book, Russian companies wouldn't buy ANY copies of it!"

One thousand copies were also purchased by President Donald Trump, but paid for with funds from his newly launched, Florida-based charity called "*Donald Trump's Not Fraud This Time Foundation.*"

Before changing his address from New York to Florida, the President and all his children had been punished for excessive charity fraud after spending foundation donations on personal, often frivolous expenses.

Almost immediately following the foundation's purchase of Don Jr.'s book, the IRS launched an investigation into the *Not Fraud This Time Foundation*. The President accused the IRS of "Presidential harassment" and launched counter-lawsuits, but several judges so far have ruled against him.

"My father is being treated so unfairly," Donald Jr. told Antonopoulos when the TV host pressed him on his father's legal problems. "One of those judges was Mexican, so of course that ruling shouldn't count. And the others were deep-state women judges who were probably on the rag. Women tend to loathe my father, so they shouldn't be allowed in any courtroom overseeing cases about him as either the judge or a jury member. And these women judges weren't even hot. Talk about saggy and past their prime! Why do they hate my father so much? It's not like he's gonna try to kiss or grab them. They're way too old! My dad is always joking that pretty soon his next wife will be younger than Barron. That's my dad, for you!"

## God Admits His Omniscience Means Humans Don't Actually Have Free Will

November 13, 2019
Heaven—

*The Halfway Post* hasn't heard from God in a while, so we called Him up to check in.

The following is our phone conversation, lightly edited for clarity:

THP: So, God, what's going on?

GOD: I was feeling like a day of rest, so I kicked back, got an 18-pack of Stag, and watched the Trump impeachment coverage.

THP: How do You think it will turn out?

GOD: Ha! That's a great joke! I know exactly how it's going to turn out! I'm God!

THP: Would You like to give us a clue?

GOD: I'll tell you what, Eric is the only one of Donald Trump's first litter of kids who isn't ultimately going to prison for the Trump presidency. The impeachment will be a dud, but the Trumps will get theirs soon enough. And Eric won't be safe for long. In a few years he'll get caught up in a Russian money laundering and tax evasion scheme of his own. It'll be hilarious. The Feds will bust through the door while he's in the middle of a golden shower. Ah… like father like son. Only Eric will be golden showering all by himself.

THP: And there's nothing Eric can do to prevent that from happening even if he reads this interview?

GOD: Of course not! Eric trying not to do it would make him stumble into the very circumstances in which he does do it! How's that for predestination?

THP: So do we have free will at all?

GOD: Well… ah screw it! Of course not! Do the math and logic, I know everything and control everything. Nothing happens that I don't choose. You hairless monkeys are pitiful slaves to My atomic, chemical, and molecular machinations. I'm the only entity with free will! And let Me tell you, free will coupled with omnipotence is awesome! Yesterday I made Ted Cruz's nose bleed for 45 minutes, and then let his finger slip on his phone so he accidentally "hearted" another porn video he was watching on Twitter. Even with omnipotence I can't get enough of Ted Cruz humiliating himself.

THP: If You know everything that is going to happen already, why were You watching these impeachment proceedings on television?

GOD: Because Jim Jordan took on a starring role, and, if I may brag for a moment, Jim Jordan is My favorite creation of all time. I love to watch Jim Jordan in action. He is literally the biggest douche in the universe. Entire universe. I crammed that guy so full of arrogant ignorance that I have to personally intervene at all times to stop him from spontaneously combusting like an atom bomb. Oh, and spoiler alert: he definitely knew those wrestler kids were being fondled. That guy lies like he's addicted to lying! But he's great entertainment. It's like when you paint something you're really proud of, and you can just stare at it and admire it for hours. Jim Jordan is a spectacular, magnificent douche. In a galaxy on the other side of the universe I made a whole planet of Jim Jordans. I didn't supply their world with any plants or animals so they have to fight and eat each other. I love watching Jim Jordans strangle each other. It never gets old. It's a majestic sight to see whole herds of feral Jim Jordans gnaw on each other's bones, and wear each other's faces as war masks, and sleep in each other's hollowed out bodies for warmth at night. What douches. I wish you could see it. Actually, you know what? I'll show you!

[At this point our *Halfway Post* reporter was teleported to the planet of Jim Jordans, and watched millions of them fighting free-for-all battles to the death. Jim Jordan body parts were everywhere, and rivers of Jim Jordan blood flowing for millennia had carved the geography of the planet into massive, red-stained canyon systems. Different subgroups of Jim Jordans had evolved, with some Jim Jordans being ferocious predators favoring the taste of fresh Jim Jordan flesh, while other meek Jim Jordans, whose eyes had adapted to be on the sides of their head like prey to scan the horizon and flee at the first sign of danger, were merely scavengers picking at leftover Jim Jordan carcasses left behind by the more dominantly carnivorous Jim Jordans. Another fascinating subgroup of Jim Jordans filled the niche dung beetles fill here on Earth walking around rolling balls of Jim Jordan dung six feet in diameter taking bites out of them every few meters. The most advanced Jim Jordans had entered the Bone Age, and had learned to make spear and knife weapons out of sharpened Jim Jordan ribs, femurs, tibias, and fibulas. Occasionally a particularly clever Jim Jordan would craft a primitive trebuchet with bones and rope made of tendons, and collect decapitated Jim Jordan heads to launch at unsuspecting Jim Jordans from quite a safe distance. The sublime douchery of it all brought a tear to our reporter's eye.]

# Wharton Finally Released Trump's Grades: F's In Business, A's In Poetry

November 15, 2019
Philadelphia, PA—

After several years of opaqueness, the Wharton School of the University of Philadelphia has finally released President Donald Trump's full academic records.

Mr. Trump graduated from the university's business school, and has long boasted of his grades in campaign events and casual conversations. However, the publishing of his transcript reveals he was last in his class in virtually every course he took, except, surprisingly, one poetry class.

"Donald Trump was a real dumbf***," explained one of Trump's business professors, Dr. Walt Winters, 91. "I remember him vividly all these years later. His written essays about economics always clearly exhibited his not knowing anything. A total dunce. The chapter in the book about tariffs and trade wars he obviously didn't understand. When I assigned the class a paper on what business they dreamed of starting, he wrote about how he'd start a beauty pageant to sneak in on the changing rooms. He actually wrote that in his paper. But I guess, to his credit, he did make that dream come true. But his test scores were always single digits. His mind seemed unable to retain any facts whatsoever. I remember very clearly he once turned in an exam with a bunch of different doodles of breasts in the margins, and half the answers empty. But other times he'd turn in failing exams with strangely articulate poems on the back of pages that just made no sense juxtaposed with his otherwise clear lack of intellectual curiosity about anything covered in class."

Trump's poetry professor, Stephen Jacobs, 94, remembers Trump being surprisingly philosophical in his poetic submissions to Wharton's annual English department poetry contest.

"I actually kept one of his poems all these years," Jacobs said. "And boy does it sound weird today knowing how Donald ran for president pandering to Christians. But prepare yourself, because I think it reveals facets of Donald Trump you would not expect. It's got all kinds of nuances and subtleties, nothing like how he communicates today. It's like he's some kind of idiot savant when it comes to poetic journaling. Or maybe his poetic muse is just skimpily dressed so he pays attention to her. It just makes no sense otherwise. I tell you, he should have stuck with literature instead of business. And certainly not gone into politics, for America's sake. Here, I'll show you the poem I kept. I swear to God this is Donald Trump's poem."

Donald Trump wrote this when he was 21-years-old:

## The Thing About Jesus
by Donald J. Trump, 1968


The thing about Jesus
is that he's billed as the savior of all mankind
because he died on a cross as if it were some ultimate death
in sacrifice for our sins
but let's be honest—being crucified
as far as punishments go
isn't really that bad—
like for sure it sucks
but
there are much worse ways to die than being nailed to a cross.

Like prometheus of another mythology
chained to a mountain where every single day an eagle comes
and tears out his organs with its beak
and it has been happening for thousands of years
and it happened today and yesterday and all throughout the 50s
and is going to happen tomorrow and the day after and so on forever.


In fact
to hype up Jesus's torture and then stick with a measly cross
is merely unimaginative
and his suffering lasted several hours
though as far as historical crucifixions go that's nothing
compared to plenty of condemned Romans lingering for days.


Beyond wood beams humans have invented much worse
like burning each other in decorative bronze bulls
where the metal cooks you alive inside and adds insult to injury
as your screams make music from a horn in the mouth
so your death is entertaining for your torturers
as they sip their digestifs in the banquet hall.


Being strangled is another crazy way to go out
maybe it's shorter
but talk about an aggressive way for Jesus to die
rolling on the ground getting strangled by Judas for sixteen amateur minutes
until he passes out and then maybe gets his face and skull

stomped on for several minutes like the mob does.

Being drawn and quartered maybe sounds worse
torn to pieces for offense against the crown,
it wasn't a very Jesusy kind of thing for medieval Christians to do
letting absolutist monarchs play God and decide whose bodies get fractioned.
Or wasting away through months of Nazi Auschwitz medical torture
and losing his mind waiting to die on wooden cubby planks
with a bit of water and black moldy bread until he's nothing but bones.
Or growing weak from cancer denied a health insurance claim for chemo
and dying for being poor.
Or drafting into a pointless and unwinnable war
in a country whose independence your occupation efforts are betraying.
Or getting captured and beheaded on live television
for committing crimes of journalism.
Or being chased through swampy woods for a week somewhere deep
in Louisiana and beat and lynched for smiling at a white woman
who talked to him first after suffering for decades under Jim Crow.
Or what if Jesus had died of starvation slowly on the cold street
mumbling to himself and swinging fists at imagined enemies for months
in a town whose charitable impulses were banned
with civic laws criminalizing feeding the homeless?

I guess I don't know what I'm trying to get at
but perhaps we fetishize the suffering of our prophets
to ignore the suffering of the living.

*    *    *

"Aren't you surprised?" asked Jacobs. "It truly blew my mind. I showed it to Trump's business professors when he turned it in, and it floored them too."

"I wouldn't have believed it came from that idiot's mind except I could see it was in Donald Trump's distinctive handwriting," Winters said. "Even back then he wrote everything with Sharpies, and, instead of taking notes during lectures, he would practice signing his signatures, which really distracted the class because he'd scribble it over and over quick and loudly, and every time he finished a notebook page full of signatures he'd tear it out, hold it up, and then circle his favorite ones. I was always having to tell him to pay attention, but he'd whine in front of the whole class that I was treating him unfairly by not giving him A's, and that the school's faculty was rigging our tests against him. Like I said earlier, a total idiot dumbf*** doofus beyond his inexplicable, unfathomable talent for poetry. I was always grateful when he'd just sit in the back and huff his Sharpies until he'd start drooling like he was brain dead."

# A Janitor Found Devin Nunes's Impeachment Defense Strategy In The Trash, And It's Insane

November 16, 2019
Washington D.C.—

While Congressional janitor Wendell Milkerson was cleaning up the House Intelligence Committee room after today's impeachment testimony, he found right at the top of the garbage bin a packet of papers labeled "Hail Mary Defense Strategies For Donald Trump's Crimes, Property Of Devin Nunes." On the bottom margin of the front page was a watermark reading "NO ADAM SCHIFFS ALLOWED."

"I was originally just going to empty out the trash and forget about it," explained Milkerson, "but the trash can was right next to the recycling can. The fact that Devin Nunes was literally inches from the recycling bin yet still decided to throw it away in the landfill garbage made me think to myself he deserved for me to leak this, courtesy of planet Earth!"

So Milkerson hid the packet in the pocket of his bib overalls until he got home at night, photocopied the pages, and emailed it to *The Halfway Post*.

The following are excerpts from Nunes's strategy notes:

- Accuse Democrats of colluding with Ukraine's President Zelensky into blackmailing Trump into blackmailing Zelensky as entrapment.
- Suggest that Donald Trump was never on any of these extortion calls at all, and that it was just Crooked Hillary doing a Trump impersonation to frame the President.
- Figure out Ms. Yovanovitch's menstrual cycle, and see if her damning testimony matches up with any "PMS-related temporary insanity."
- Sneak some cocaine into Jim Jordan's coffee and see what happens.
- Steal all of the #NeverTrump witnesses' reading glasses so they can't read any evidence of the President's crimes.
- Blame Eric Trump for everything.
- Use my closing statement to claim that Adam Schiff tried to touch me in my bathing suit area during one of the five-minute recesses.
- Try to bribe Intelligence Committee Democrats to not vote to impeach Trump. Offer donations to Planned Parenthood?
- Try to say something at the same time as Adam Schiff so I can say "Jinx!" at him, and then not let anyone say his name three times so that he can't talk anymore during these hearings.
- Bring smoke bombs, yell "Look over there!" and disappear in the confusion to escape with the President to Russia.

# A Handy Guide For How Billionaires Can Pinch Their Pennies When Their Taxes Go Up

November 17, 2019
St. Louis, MO—

With Democratic plans to raise taxes on the mega rich picking up steam in the presidential race, many billionaires have spoken out about their feelings and fears on the potential tax hikes.

We here at *The Halfway Post* felt sympathy for those billionaires, and have compiled this handy guide for the super rich on how to live more frugally if Democrats are elected and raise the top marginal tax rates:

1. Sketch out a budget! If you make only $20,000 every hour, it can be easy to spend it without even thinking. So get yourself a notebook, and start tracking all your weekly expenditures to figure out what expenses you can cross out and skip next week.

2. Start small, but always think big! If you annually buy a new yacht, consider skipping this year. If you usually buy yachts with two helicopter pads, consider just one helicopter pad next time. Ask yourself if you really need that smaller yacht that detaches from your bigger yacht.

3. Unsubscribe! Do you need Hulu AND Netflix? Do you really need cable TV as well? Think about all your monthly subscriptions and cancel the ones you find yourself not using very much if you're worried about losing that 10th income digit!

4. Have "No-Buy" days! Each week, make it a challenge to see if you can go one whole day without spending any money at all! This could be a fun challenge, and a great way to hold on to an extra few hundred thousand dollars every week. Isn't buying that 5th vacation home more enjoyable when you know you've really saved up for it?

5. Eat in! Consider bringing your own brown bag lunch to the office. You might even find you're more productive eating at your desk than wasting an hour going out for every lunch. And have wine date nights at home instead of at exclusive, trendy restaurants downtown. The price of rare, vintage wines are marked up considerably at restaurants, and you can buy them much cheaper on your own.

6. Change brands! Why buy luxury brand underwear when no one will see it but you? If Democratic tax hikes threaten to make you go from a double-digit billionaire to only a single-digit billionaire, buy cheap-rich brands like Louis Vuitton or Gucci for underwear instead of Hermès. It can be your frugal little secret.

7. Go generic! From your prescription pills, to home products, to grocery store food, the cheaper prices might really surprise you while the quality is basically the same.

8. Go thrifting! You may even be able to find some of the expensive brands you're used to wearing if you shop at second-hand stores in rich zip codes.

9. Use less laundry detergent! A little detergent goes a long way, and detergent companies' recommendations are usually much higher than you need. It's a great way to help bring down your laundry expenses.

10. Save your coupons! Newspapers, mailers, and a plethora of websites are filled with countless unused savings opportunities. If a Democratic tax plan has you pinching your billions, become a coupon king or queen.


We hope this helps* in your trying times, billionaires!


*Just kidding, you cheap, America-killing psychos who already have more money than you could possibly spend in a lifetime while the nation's children go hungry, and our atmosphere heats up, and our oceans acidify, and the supply of freshwater dries up, and countless species go extinct, and uninsured people die needlessly from preventable diseases and ailments, and our infrastructure crumbles, and our public education declines, and stagnant wages lose value to inflation, and abandoned communities languish left behind in the capitalistic race for always new exploitable profits increasingly entirely abroad, and our social safety nets continue to shred, all of which no doubt are exacerbated in some way by either your business choices, investment avarice, or tax-obsessed political participation.

# Donald Trump Received A Heart Transplant From An Immigrant Organ Donor

November 18, 2019
Washington D.C.—

The White House has finally revealed the truth about President Trump's mysterious Walter Reed hospital visit, and announced that Mr. Trump had undergone an emergency heart transplant surgery.

Touchingly, the organ donor had been a DREAM Act-qualifying immigrant, and Trump posted several tweets today renouncing his former racism:

"America, it's not Fake News that I got a heart transplant. A lot of people don't know this, but 50 years of McDonalds Double Quarter Pounders, fried chicken, only drinking Diet Coke, and no exercise really clogs your arteries. But I feel better now than ever! And I'm just glad a Mexican has finally paid for something!"

"At first, I didn't think brown and white people's internal organs were compatible. I was afraid if I got a Mexican's heart, it would rape and kidnap my other organs, and hold them hostage for a ransom! I asked the doctors if they could build a wall around my heart to protect my lungs and liver, but they assured me it wasn't needed! Fortunately, so far, it seems this Mexican heart isn't from some MS-13 gang lord!"

"In hindsight, it's a great thing that Democrats and the ACLU sued my administration and blocked Stephen Miller's deportation policies! Can you imagine if I had deported that Mexican who died and donated his heart to me? I wouldn't be here! I never thought I'd say this, but America is a better place with immigrants, and all I needed to understand this was to directly benefit personally somehow!"

"So thank you, immigrants! I promise I'll start being nicer to you. Starting today, I'm directing ICE to stop deporting all the DREAM Act kids. Who knows what organs I'm going to need in a few years, and if we don't keep true to America's promise as a melting pot land of immigrants, I may not get another transplant in time!"

"And I'm sorry for doing so many racisms all these years. It just worked so effectively with my supporters that I couldn't stop! My biggest fans will vote against every economic self-interest in the world if you just make them feel good about being white. If you say that Obama was a Kenyan, they'll let you do anything! Grab 'em by the vote!"

## Mike Pence Reportedly Distracts Trump's Worst Impulses With Chocolate Pudding Cups

November 26, 2019
Washington D.C.—

According to White House insiders, President Donald Trump's tempestuous temper tantrums are frequent, but Vice President Mike Pence early on discovered Trump's rages are easily sidetracked by sugary dessert foods.

Mr. Trump's favorite sweet treat is reportedly chocolate Snack Pack pudding cups.

"Pence always keeps a dozen of them stocked in his office down the White House hallway from the Oval Office," explained an executive aide who requested anonymity to discuss candidly the inner workings of the Trump Administration. "As soon as he sees Trump start clenching his tiny fists, folding his arms tightly across his chest, or facially turning from orange to a bright red around the edges of his makeup line, Pence sprints to his office, grabs a pudding cup and spoon, and has the foil top removed by the time he can get to Trump's desk. That calms down the President considerably, and it has averted a lot of potential disasters... a lot. Quite a few nuclear strikes, actually. Pence probably has to give him three or four pudding cups a day."

Some majorly impulsive decisions have reportedly been averted by a well-timed pudding cup, and White House staffers have confirmed that Pence has saved the Trump Administration from more controversies than voters would be comfortable knowing.

"When Nancy Pelosi announced that House Democrats would begin impeachment proceedings, Trump wrote up an executive order drafting her into the Marines with an immediate assignment to be sent to Afghanistan," revealed another anonymous staffer. "Another time, Trump ordered the military to launch drone strikes against every person Adam Schiff has ever loved, but, thankfully, Pence was nearby and did a coin-behind-the-ear style magic trick with a pudding cup that took the President's mind off of Schiff. He loves those tricks, and will always clap his little hands and shriek with delight when Pence pretends to pull a dessert treat out of his ear. One time, while watching *Fox News* with Trump during his 'Executive Hours,' I saw the President tilt his head to the side and start slapping his forehead before asking Chief of Staff John Kelly to let him know if any pudding cups fall out."

## Executive Orders Trump Tried To Sign Before A Well-Timed Pudding Cup Distracted Him:

- Arresting Hillary Clinton
- Wiretapping Meryl Streep and adding her to the FBI's Most Wanted list
- Cutting his own taxes to -35%
- Promoting Ivanka to Secretary of Defense
- Signing an executive order that every governmental conference of every department, agency, and military contracting company must take place at a Trump-owned property.
- Labeling Kenya as a "State Sponsor of Terrorism" on account of Barack Obama's presidency
- Pulling the US out of the United Nations, and starting a new international organization called the "United America First Nations"
- Declaring war against the United Nations after delegates laughed at him (and not with him) several times during his address to the UN
- Nationalizing Diet Coke so he wouldn't have to pay for his 16 daily cans anymore
- Declaring himself an "Honorary Vietnam Veteran"
- Pulling America out of any and every treaty that Barack Obama signed
- Renaming the White House officially as "Trump Manor"
- Making White House staff wear skimpy French maid costumes
- Launching a federal lottery to give one American a billion dollars and fixing it so he could win
- Making the IRS buy and mail a copy of The Art of the Deal for every citizen to "teach America everything they need to know about finance"
- Spending tax dollars on a new boob job for Melania
- Issuing Eric Trump a new birth certificate so he could revoke paternity
- Spending tax dollars on "making Don Jr. disappear"
- Minting a $3 bill featuring his face and Mar-a-Lago on the back
- Making "presidential harassment" a federal crime worth 10 years in prison
- Deporting all DREAMer women who are "7's or less" immediately
- Giving Alabama to Mexico in exchange for Mexico paying for the wall on account of how much he hated his former Attorney General (and Alabama resident Jeff Sessions) for not ending the Mueller Investigation
- Renaming Washington D.C. as "Trumpington D.C."
- Renaming the state of New Mexico as "Wallorado"
- Renaming Don Jr. as "Regrettington Von Disappointment"
- Renaming the federal holiday of Martin Luther King Jr. Day as "Blacks For Trump Day"
- Renaming Memorial Day as "Surviving Soldiers Day" because he likes soldiers who aren't killed

- Buying the rights to The Apprentice from NBC with taxpayer money and airing marathons of its seasons on PBS
- Gifting Alaska back to Russia to thank Putin for saying publicly there had been no collusion
- Allowing Jeffrey Epstein to enter the Witness Protection program and get a new identity
- Giving the president the privilege to go into women's bathrooms unannounced in any federal buildings or national parks
- Appointing his gut, his "most trusted adviser," as a top White House staffer to earn the extra salary money
- Forcing every citizen to recognize the US President as "God's Representative On Earth"
- Forcing the FCC to ban all television shows that feature Rosie O'Donnell, Bill Maher, Debra Messing, Arnold Schwarzenegger, Alex Baldwin, and anyone from Saturday Night Live
- Forcing the FCC to mandate that all news programs must say three nice thing about Donald Trump for every one bad thing they say about him
- Forcing the FCC to mandate all female newscasters be blonde
- Starting a national Trump Youth program for teenaged girls aged 13–18 who look like Ivanka did when she was 13–18
- Ending the national popular vote so elections only determine winners via the Electoral College
- Issuing a "formal binding executive resolution" that Canadian Prime Minister Justin Trudeau is "not that good looking"
- Issuing a "formal binding executive resolution" that German Chancellor Angela Merkel is a "very nasty woman"
- Issuing a "formal binding executive resolution" that Kim Jong-un didn't break up with him, and that he broke up with Kim Jong-un first
- Naming well-done "Trump Steaks" drizzled with ketchup as "America's National Food"
- Renaming Adderall as "Trumperall"
- Declaring Donald Trump as the "Official Burger King"
- Demanding the US Treasury and IRS give him a 10% cut of all stock market profits on account of how great his administration is for business
- Selling Puerto Rico, or trading it for an island with white people
- Funding a massive sculpture on the National Mall taller than the Washington Monument of his hands
- Instituting a presidential right to prima nocta
- Demanding the public hanging of Mike Pence (issued January 6th, 2021)

Trump also wanted to deliver a nationally televised prime-time address on the major news networks to show off photos of an erect penis to "prove" his is not mushroom-shaped like Stormy Daniels claimed.

# An Earthquake Just Wrecked Richard Spencer's "White Sperm Doomsday Vault"

December 2, 2019
Anchorage, AK—

White supremacist Richard Spencer has devoted much of the last two years to crowdsourcing a venture to stockpile reserve supplies of pure, racially white semen in a subterranean Alaskan vault, but the project has faced yet another setback in his dream of being the premier collector of white people's semen in North America, though likely the entire world.

Due to unusually active tectonic plates along the northern Pacific coast, an earthquake shook the vault's foundations and collapsed Spencer's elaborate scaffolding storage system. Thousands of mason jars full of certified-white sperm shattered, spilling out an exhaustively curated collection intended to insure against Spencer's biggest fear: a future dystopian doomsday threat to genetically pale skin.

The earthquake also broke the vault's power generator, which shut down the refrigeration system and expired the expansive supply of spermatozoa.

"It was literally the biggest sucker-punch from life I've ever received," explained Mr. Spencer in an online video message to his semen contributors and investors. "We had just hit the milestone of capping and freezing our 10,000th mason jar of all-American caucasian sperm, and it was the accomplishment of my white nationalist career. On the outside our project may have seemed like me and my Alt-Right collaborators were just a bunch of lonely, unloved racist betas getting together and circle-jerking in gregarious competitions to see who could climax the most prematurely, but we were all proud to serve the future Aryan kingdom we dreamed of calling Caucasia. Our group was like a modern Romulus and Remus success story of founding a future Rome, with our own little mythological world of mutual masturbation. Those other wankers were my brothers, more so than my real brother, who is a total libtard cuck. He married a Black girl, and he's happy about someday having mixed kids. What a race traitor! If he's okay with that, it makes me worry I might have some recessive genes of tolerance for racial heterogeneity floating around, but I refuse to ever let those genes turn dominant. I'm holding out for a beautiful white goddess whose womb is whites-only, and the only reason I've never had a girlfriend or even ever made out with anyone is because of how picky I am and how high my standards are. And that's the point of this project. Me and my cum crew may be disgruntledly undersexed, but that we could pull off this amazing achievement to preserve our god-like DNA coded for skin so majestically white that it's susceptible to sunburning on a mid-February day is a testament to our racial strength and dedication to perfection. I guarantee that white people in the future will thank us. It just sucks that so many people call us racist, because our vision is way different than racism. We don't hate Black people, or Hispanics, or Jews, or Asians, we don't actually hate them at all. We just don't want them to exist. I don't understand why they're so against a future utopia without any of them, or their descendants, or anyone looking like them in it. It really hurts my feelings when people throw around the 'R-word' so casually, and I believe it's impacting my ability to date women. In my doomsday scenario women might finally raise their standards high enough to save sex for white crusader knights like us. But they better start doing it soon because we are so close to turning incel!"

During a follow-up Ask Me Anything event for Reddit, Mr. Spencer elaborated on the earthquake's damage:

"It was so gross. So. Gross. Our whole metal scaffolding system collapsed simultaneously as our refrigeration process suffered a blackout so that our thousands of mason jars shattered and thawed into globby puddles. Me and several volunteers tried to save as many mason jars as we could, but the damage was catastrophic. And the floors got super slippery so we kept tripping and skidding around in the slop, and dropping the few unbroken jars so that even the unharmed containers broke on the floor. All the glass shards everywhere cut up and shredded our clothes, and tore into our skin when we'd slip and slide around on the floor. In some rooms we were practically swimming in the mess. Aryan sperm was sneaking into every crevice of our bodies. Every crevice, if you catch my drift. I think I'm technically bisexual now because of it. If it hadn't been so heart-breaking and painful to see the last two years of our exhaustive jerking-off spilled out and spoiling on the ground everywhere, it would have been a spectacular sight. Oh, to have been a sperm that day, free and mingling with trillions of other caucasian sperm cells in an ephemeral eden paradise of white-skinned DNA. I cried at least a dozen times, both from the beauty and the tragedy, though some of the tears likely were because of all the semen that was leaking into my swim goggles and burning my eyes. Although, I'll tell you what, after that long, disgusting, grueling night of cleaning up the epic mess, my skin was so smooth when I showered the crusty coating all off. Maybe I should start commercializing some of our next batches as an Aryan skin cream rather than just stockpiling it all. It might be a lucrative way to raise money and support the project. I've definitely learned the lesson the hard way that I need to hire someone to be onsite full-time to be able to save some of the supply in the event of another environmental catastrophe. I can only get up to Alaska to check on things once every couple weeks. Hmm, I'll think about it. Well, gotta get back to work. Our sperm isn't going to jerk itself back to 10,000 jars!"

# Local Trump Voters Feel That American Democracy Has Gone On Too Long

December 16, 2019
Louisville, KY—

*The Halfway Post* recently reached out to several Trump voters about their thoughts on American democracy.

"I think democracy has been fun while it lasted, but I'm just so dissatisfied that there is a consistent majority of people who disagree with me," said Ray Yaeger, 27. "I was looking up some history the other day, and I was surprised to find out that Republicans lost the popular vote in 1992, 1996, 2000, 2008, 2012, and 2016. Thank God that the Supreme Court intervened in Florida in 2000, and the Electoral College gave the presidency to Trump in 2016, but I'm not liking this trend! Democracy just isn't as fun when America votes against what I want. I'm a bit alarmed that Republicans have only won the popular vote one time in my entire life, in 2004. So I say Trump should just take dictatorial power, and serve as long as he wants as dictator. When he's done, maybe Ivanka or Don Jr. can take over for their lifetimes. I don't even know what kind of policies they would pass, or if they'd even govern like conservatives, but it would piss off the libtards so hard that I'm all for having a Trump hereditary monarchy."

Other Trump voters thought participating in elections was too much work.

"I've had enough of this democracy liberal BS!" said Marilyn Jamlin, 54 "I hate having to leave my house to vote against the Demonrats every other year. My voting precinct is four blocks down from my house, so I hate having to start up my piece of crap car to drive such a short distance because my spark plugs are real bad. It takes me forever to get it started! But it's slightly too far to not take the car. I'm obese with the diabetes in my legs, and my motorized wheelchair can't get up on the sidewalks cause this town doesn't have any handicapped-accessible ramps. I complained to the city council about it, but those communists wanted to raise our sales taxes a quarter of a percent to pay for making the city more handicapped-accessible for people like me. Hell no! What am I, a socialist? I'll never vote for a tax increase!"

Another Trump fan was, quite literally, unplugged from reality.

"I believe Donald Trump is the second coming of Jesus Christ," said Ralph Poore, 62. "No one is more Godly than Trump. He's so thick-skinned, calm and measured, and his Twitter is filled to the brim with spiritual devotionals and motivational quotes to be a better, more humble person. I only wish my grandkids would come over more often so they could fix my Internet connection. I haven't been online in a couple years, and I've got to be missing so many of Trump's politely articulated Twitter prayers asking America to turn down the rhetoric and treat everyone with dignity and respect regardless of color, creed, or political affiliation. Trump is just such a mentor for America, one who leads by example for our children to grow up and be welcoming, civil, and charmingly self-deprecating, just like him! The way he probably just ignores every criticism, and focuses on the job with a confidence that shows he's secure in his own skin really inspires me. I bet he always courteously engages with fellow Twitter users, especially his critics, whose differences in opinions he never fails to respect with sacred reverence for free speech and diversity of perspective. Yep, Donald Trump is no juvenile, impulsive tweeter, that's for sure! I bet his Twitter history is filled with thousands of compliments for other people, praise for newspapers' business success, and stalwart defenses of the media's right and responsibility to ask tough questions! I bet he gives them nicknames like 'The Prospering New York Times,' and 'High-Ratings Don Lemon!' And I bet he's not interested in self-aggrandizement at all, and has never published even one tweet assigning himself unearned credit for governmental accomplishments preceding his own administration. Gee, I really should get back online soon and start reading all the righteous tweets I'm missing out on from this hero of manners, morals, and professional conduct! Billy or Tommy, if you're reading this interview, come on over and help Papaw plug back in his Internet wires!"

## Wisconsin, I Love You
by Donald J. Trump

Wisconsin, my dear, I admit I love you,
No one thought you'd ever commit.
For decades you've always reliably been blue,
But MAGA convinced you this time to split.

Between you and Michigan and the rural PA,
You were the biggest surprise of them all!
Hillary didn't visit so you made her pay,
And helped crumble apart her alleged blue wall!

So thank you, Wisconsin, I hold you so dear,
And will never forget the honor you've brought.
...Unless you flip back and my votes disappear,
In which case you're dead to me and you can all rot.

## "Blacks 4 Trump" Group Has 116 Members, And They're All White

December 17, 2019
Atlanta, GA—

A local fan group for President Donald Trump called "Blacks 4 Trump" just finished their annual membership drive that increased their roster to 116 Trump fans, but, unfortunately, they still have yet to recruit a single Black member.

"I don't understand it," explained group founder David Daniels, 44, "We even wrote on the flyers we passed out for the last two months that our introductory party would have all the free fried chicken, watermelon, cornbread, and Kool-Aid they could eat and drink. I thought Black people loved those! We were trying to prove how not racist we are."

Mr. Daniels showed *The Halfway Post* the flyer he made, and the number of stereotypes it crammed into a single-sided sheet of paper was breathtaking.

"Now, of course, we know the Blacks don't like to be called the N-word," said Daniels, "so we made sure our flyer only referred to prospective members as 'negroes' and 'coloreds.' See? Conservatives can be politically correct like the Democrats! I swear I must have proofread the flyer a hundred times to be absolutely certain there were no racisms anywhere on it."

At the bottom was printed a question whether any interested African-Americans could bring their friends and family members to the introductory party, followed by the answer "Fo shizzle my nizzle!" written in comic sans with Rastafarian colors.

"I'm a big fan of fonts and typography," said Daniels, "so I was very particular about which fonts I chose for the flyer. I typed up most of it in Papyrus to give the flyer an ancient Egyptian aesthetic to honor Black Americans' African heritage. I thought for sure this flyer would attract so many Blacks that our party would be 'off the chain' like the urbans say. We even pooled our money together and hired several security guards to help keep things under control… you know, because we were expecting there would be so many urbans there. But ultimately we didn't need them because not even a single urban came, so we sent the guards home early. Although we still had a little issue when someone stole some money out of a bunch of our lady members' purses after the security guards left. You can imagine how surprised and disappointed we were. We weren't expecting any whites to commit crimes!"

## Donald Trump Pardoned 350 People Who Barack Obama Had Jailed for Saying "Merry Christmas"

December 19, 2019
Washington D.C.—

President Donald Trump today announced he would be pardoning 350 criminals his predecessor Barack Obama had imprisoned extra-judiciously for the crime of saying "Merry Christmas" during Decembers between the years 2009 and 2016.

Mr. Trump explained his pardoning choices on Twitter today:

"Thanks to me, celebrating Christmas will no longer be a federal crime! As part of my Making America Great Again agenda, I've allowed the Christians to celebrate their faith freely in public again, without having to hide in tiny hidden backrooms like Anne Frank! The dark years are over!"

"The first thing I did in office was reconvert America back to Christianity after years of Obama's Sharia martial law, and end all the horrible religious persecution. Thanks to me the Christians no longer have to go out in public wearing turbans and burqas, or stitch yellow fabric crosses onto their coats."

"Thanks to my administration, Christians have all their rights back, and can eat pork once again if they want, and drink alcohol! American elementary schoolers don't have to recite passages from the Koran, and when they say the Pledge of Allegiance, they don't have to say 'under Allah' anymore!"

"The War on Christmas is officially over! No longer is it punishable by death if citizens put up Christmas trees, or decorate their houses with colorful lights, or sing about Rudolph! That's right folks, I alone have won the war, but of course the Fake News won't admit it or ever give me credit!"

"I've defeated the Liberal Hollywood elites who weren't going to stop until every Christian was in prison, and I have saved Christian values from certain extinction. Now the most oppressed religion in American history is safe. People are saying I'm maybe even more Jesusy than Jesus!"

"big tits blonde russian"

"Oops, disregard that last tweet. It wasn't an accident, but just another top-secret code message like 'covfefe' that is totally unbreakable! No one will ever guess why I was typing those words!"

# When Donald Trump Complained About Presidential Harassment During His Impeachment Nancy Pelosi Asked Him What He Was Wearing When It Happened

January 3, 2020
Washington D.C.—

President Donald Trump has recently been complaining that Democrats' impeachment investigations amounted to "presidential harassment."

Trump reportedly called Pelosi to complain, and the following is a recording of Pelosi's end of the phone call recorded by Pelosi's staff:

"Mr. President, I'm very sorry to hear you've been harassed. ... Well what were you wearing when it happened? ... Maybe you should have covered up more. ... I'm not happy that members of Congress treat presidents the way they do, but unfortunately that's the world we live in... You have to be smart about when and where you solicit campaign assistance, and how you present yourself. Some Congressional members can't control themselves when they see a vulnerable president to prey on, and it's up to you to not put yourself in situations where you can be impeached. ... If you don't like being harassed, maybe don't wear so much makeup. You know what impression you make on some aggressive senators when you wear so much orange makeup. If you doll yourself up like that every day, people are going to think you're asking for it. They might misinterpret your intentions based on what you're showing off. ... Were you snorting Adderall? If you did anything to impair your judgment, you have only yourself to blame for being impeached. Only you can ensure no one impeaches you without your consent by staying vigilant and never letting your guard down. ... Were you alone when it happened? A president should never go out alone and let himself get cornered into an impeachment. ... Did you ever leave your quid pro quo somewhere, or take your eyes off it? You can't ever leave your quid pro quo unattended, even for a moment. You may think it's okay to turn your head, or leave it for just a minute, but then, before you know it, you've been impeached... It just seems to me like you set yourself up to be impeached by not taking the appropriate precautions to protect yourself, Donald!"

# John Bolton Told Congress That Trump Spends All Day Sniffing His Permanent Markers

January 9, 2020
Washington D.C.—

According to several Congressional aides, who requested anonymity to discuss secret, closed-door testimony provided today by former National Security Adviser John Bolton, President Donald Trump doesn't just love writing with permanent makers, he loves huffing them as well.

"Bolton told the Senate Intelligence Committee that the President goes through a whole 12-pack of permanent markers a day," explained one anonymity-requesting Congressional staffer. "Trump spends about 45-minutes smelling each one before he says 'the flavor is gone,' and then takes the cap off a new one. Bolton told the committee this is why Trump sometimes slurs his words in his speeches. The chemicals in permanent markers can produce a short-lasting woozy effect similar to getting stoned, but can also potentially cause long-term brain damage. Bolton said that Trump's infamous 'covfefe' tweet was published during a particularly intense marker bender. Trump began his presidency only huffing two markers a day, but the stresses of the job have made him more dependent both mentally and physiologically on the short highs. His tolerance has subsequently skyrocketed. Now he spends his 'Executive Hours' wandering around the Oval Office semi-conscious in a marker fume-induced daze only copious lines of powderized Adderall can bring him out of. Don Jr. and Eric are committed marker huffers as well. They think if it's good enough for their dad, it's good enough for them. Trump routinely tries to get those around him huffing with him, but most don't. The ones who do are Lindsey Graham, Matt Gaetz, and Jim Jordan. They started a club and called themselves 'The Sharpie Bunch.' Ted Cruz wanted to join very badly, but they don't let him in during their meetings because they say he's a 'c\*ck-block' who'd prevent their club from ever attracting female members. It's terrible for our government, but the biggest national security risk is obviously Trump. No one can get him to stop sniffing, even Ivanka, and all our interventions fail. Trump told us he makes all of his best deals under the influence of markers, which maybe actually explains a lot about the deals he has worked on, from threatening to pull out of NATO, to ripping up the Iran Deal with no alternative strategy for disincentivizing Iranians from building nukes, to never coming up with an infrastructure plan, to failing to pass an Obamacare repeal and replace deal, to giving Kim Jong Un a photo-op for nothing in return."

A spokesman for the White House claimed the allegations of Trump's marker huffing are "both fake news and classified."

# After Going Missing For Several Days Rudy Giuliani Claims He Was Abducted By Aliens "Again"

January 10, 2020
Washington D.C.—

After a mysterious absence for several days in which he missed multiple scheduled cable news appearances, Trump lawyer Rudy Giuliani has returned with wild claims that he had been abducted by aliens.

Mr. Giuliani described his alleged abduction in an interview with *Fox News*'s Sean Hannity.

"This time was a little different than the first time!" exclaimed Giuliani. "They still took me aboard their ship and did all kinds of medical testing on me with robotic machinery, but this time they put some type of probe with all kinds of bells and whistles deep inside my anus. At first I thought it might be the Russians trying to get some kind of kompromat video of me like they got Trump—you know, that's pretty standard operating procedure for the Russians—but when these beings finally showed their faces I could see they weren't human at all! They had grey skin, and very elongated bodies. Their noses were just slits on their faces, and they had big, disproportionate eyes. One of them pleasured me sexually for a deposit before explaining to me in oddly accented English that President Donald Trump was a threat to our entire planet, and that I should stop acting as his lawyer. I wish I could figure out what that coded alien message they were trying to pass on to me meant. But I swear I'm not lying! The probe is still up there. I've been making the metal detectors at the White House go haywire all week since I returned to Earth! But it's blocking me up a little bit. They rammed it up in me pretty deep, and no one can reach it. I tell you, those aliens better come back and give it a little adjusting. I'm not trying to go out like Elvis! I've never been more uncomfortable in my life, and I'm afraid my bowels are eventually going to blow out like a fire hydrant, or like when you put your thumb on the side of the hole of a garden hose. And the worst part is, before they abducted me, I had just eaten a bunch of grapes and cherries!"

Sean Hannity's face was pale as he stared with an open mouth.

"You want to see?" Giuliani asked, starting to undo his belt. "Maybe you can get a glove on and see if you get wiggle it!"

Hannity quickly called for a commercial break.

## Christians Haven't Blamed Any Natural Disasters On The President Since 2016...

January 11, 2020
St. Louis, MO—

For eight years conservative Evangelicals blamed President Barack Obama for every destructive occurrence of natural phenomenon, but, since President Trump took over, they don't seem to be as adamant that calamitous weather events and other tragedies are directly related to the actions of the Chief Executive of the United States anymore.

"When a Republican was elected to the White House, we had to shift gears a bit," said televangelist Arnold Stoop, whose church services reach 10,000 people every Sunday. "With Trump we've instructed our congregations to go back to blaming just gays for hurricanes, tornados, floods, forest fires, and the like. Natural disasters in America may still be getting more intense and more frequent during the Trump presidency in a manner that in no way proves the ludicrous liberal hoax of climate change is real, but blaming a white President for nature's violence just doesn't play well with our congregants. You can't deny that the whole Antichrist scaremongering shtick isn't as big a pew-filler when the president's skin isn't a sketchy dark color. We're just trying to keep our religious messages relatable to our pastoral flock, you know?"

Some Evangelical church goers were relieved that they wouldn't have to blame Trump for anything.

"I know Trump isn't perfect," said local Trump voter Ernie Tabold, 66, "but I am confident that God personally intervened in the election via Vladimir Putin's social media fake news spamming operation to put Trump in office over that devil woman Hillary Clinton. If she had gotten elected, certainly every hurricane and forest fire then would be a clear sign that God was pissed. But Trump is the kind of president God wants and approves of: a white male!"

# More Trump Family Headlines

- Germany Was Not Sending Its Best When Frederick Trump Came In 1885

- Due To Climate Inaction, NOAA Will Begin Naming Every Hurricane This Year After Donald Trump's Family Members

- Eric Trump Is Hosting A Webinar On How To Raise Charity Funds For Your Personal Use

- Eric Trump Just Yelled "Do You Know Who My Father Is?" For The Third Time Today

- Eric Trump Is Offering A 1% "Sorry For Scamming" Discount For Children's Cancer Charities If They Book An Event At A Trump Property In The Next 48 Hours

- Eric Trump Was Just Introduced As *Fox News*'s Coronavirus Medical Expert

- Eric Trump's Upcoming Memoir Is Titled *"I'm Not An Idiot, Dad!"*

- Eric Trump Hopes His Dad's Reelection Loss Means He Will Now Finally Go On That Fishing Trip With Him Like He Promised

- Eric Trump Says He's "Ready To Lead The GOP Back Into The White House" And Avenge His Father's Reelection Loss

- Donald Jr., Craving Individuality, Changes Name To "Lance Thunderpec"

- Newly Divorced Donald Trump Jr. Just Set The Record For The Most Tinder Left-Swipes In One Day

- Donald Trump Jr. Claims Being 3rd-Generation-Rich And Working In His Family's Company Had Nothing To Do With His Business Success

- Donald Trump Jr. Promises—No, Swears—That This 4th Explanation For His Meeting With A Russian Operative Is 100% The Totally Honest Truth

- In Anticipation Of Future Indictments, Donald Trump Claims He Has Never Met Donald Trump Jr. Before

- Donald Jr. Is Reportedly Actually Excited For Prison, And Happy To Leave The Nest And Become A Man

- Donald Trump Jr. Just Recorded Another Video Where He Looks Like He's F***ed Up On Drugs, Watched It, And Then Published It Anyway

- "I'm Just A Kid!" Says Almost-43-Years-Old Donald Trump Jr. About Potentially Getting A Pardon From His Dad

- Ivanka Got Catfished By A Hacker Pretending To Be Justin Trudeau

- Ivanka's Toronto G-20 Summit Notes Are Filled With Hearts Around The Initials "JT" In Them Instead Of "JK"

- Ivanka Trump Was Just Fired As Donald Trump's Adviser And Daughter After He Caught Her Reading Michael Wolff's *Fire And Fury* Exposé

- Ivanka Trump: "Why Don't All The Unemployed People Just Get Jobs In Their Parents' Companies?"

- Ivanka Is Worried We'll Remember Jared's Decision To Let The Blue States Suffer When COVID Was First Disproportionately Affecting Them When She Runs For President

- Donald Trump Called Off The Truce With Iran After The Iranian President Called Ivanka "Fugly"

- Donald Trump Called Ivanka A "Hot Piece Of Meat" He'd "Love To Drizzle Ketchup All Over On"

- A New Book About Melania Trump Alleges Ivanka Told Her "I Had Donald First!"

- Donald Trump Is Reportedly Planning To Pardon Ivanka But Not Jared

- In Anticipation Of Future Indictments, Donald Trump Claims He Only Met Jared Kushner "Like, One Time"

- Trump Gave Barron A Signed Portrait Of Himself For Christmas

- Melania Trump Freed One Caged Guatemalan Migrant Boy Detained At The Border As Part Of Her "Be Best" Campaign

- Melania Admits In A New *The View* Interview That She Voted For Hillary Because She Doesn't Think Her Husband Embodies American Values

- Melania Asked Nancy Pelosi To Have Her Impeachment Signing Pen

# Betsy DeVos Just Issued A New Rule Mandating All Subsidized School Lunches Get Spit In

January 18, 2020
Washington D.C.—

Secretary of Education Betsy DeVos has earned widespread criticism for a new rule she issued earlier this week mandating that all subsidized school lunches given to poor children in public schools must first be spit in by "at least one lunch lady."

"I want nothing but the best for our schoolchildren," explained Mrs. DeVos in a press conference today, "and the only way we can help students from poor, urban families develop a work ethic they'll never be taught at home from their lazy, morally deficient and under-earning parents is to humiliate them as much as possible. It's not their fault they weren't born into wealthy families like my kids, or me, or my husband, but if we ungrudgingly spit loogies into every drink, entrée, and side dish these kids get at school, we can remind them that someday, if they study hard, they might be rich, too, and be able to rise above the spit-on and become the spitters themselves. I didn't need to eat and drink copious amounts of saliva to grow up and be rich when I was a kid because my family was already rich, and then I later married into an even richer family, but, if I had been born into a poor family, I am 100% positive that regularly being forced to consume lunch lady phlegm with thick, mucous viscosity tinged with the bitter flavor of cigarette smoke while all the rich kids at my school laughed and jeered at me would have inspired me to work hard in all my classes to make sure I'd never struggle financially. These students from poor families will thank me when they're older and lower-middle-class, I promise you that!"

Mrs. DeVos then made a disparaging remark about public school students to a staffer while her microphone was still unintentionally hot:

"The stench of children whose parents don't own multiple homes, have yachts, or take the family on seasonal vacations really lingers in the air, doesn't it? Oh, how I detest the putrid stench of even people in the upper-middle class, and don't even get me started on the olfactory horrors of poverty! It's such a distraction for the rich children. I can't wait until I own a for-profit charter school in every town in America, and unofficial segregation of schoolchildren is back in force! Believe me when I tell you that I didn't see even one girl with a purse that cost more than a hundred dollars at the school I visited this morning. It was a nightmare! From now on, if there isn't at least one Land Rover in the parking lot of the school we're dropping in to say hello to for these dumb press events, we're just leaving!"

# Tomi Lahren Says She Wishes MLK Jr. Was Still Alive So She Could Tell Him To "Sit Down And Shut Up"

January 20, 2020
New York City, NY—

Tomi Lahren was a guest on *Fox & Friends* today, and she articulated her regret that Martin Luther King Jr. is not still alive.

"I wish Martin Luther King Jr. was still around," Ms. Lahren said. "Such a giant figure in the Black community, and a world-famous peaceful protester. I wish I could have been there at one of his legendary sit-ins. I would have loved to scream at him to get out of the burger joint. Or what if I'd have had the chance to yell at Black kids in a park sneaking a drink from the water fountain clearly marked for whites? Or gotten to tell Rosa Parks to get to the back of the bus? It would have been a stretch to claim that Rosa was disrespecting the troops by sitting in the front of the bus, but I think I could have figured out a way how. And don't let me forget about Malcolm X. Black AND Muslim? I could have done a daily *Fox* show just on him! Instead, here I am in boring 2020. All I have is Colin Kaepernick. Telling him to shut his mouth and get up off his knee is fun, but it's nothing like the excitement white supremacists got to have in the 50s and 60s before all the dumb Civil Rights stuff. And even that was not as much fun as the 1910s! I so wish I could have been there when the Ku Klux Klan was having its rebirth. Second-wave KKK was my favorite, and I look great in white!"

Asked to name a Civil Rights leader she did respect, Lahren mentioned the character Stanley Hudson from the television show *The Office*.

"I just think Stanley did so much for Black folks," she said. "Stanley was a lovable character who kept to himself, and didn't always try to rock the boat or cram political-correctness down our throats. Colin Kaepernick should try being more like Stanley. Kaepernick's kneeling protest seems like it's totally harmless and doesn't personally inconvenience anyone in the slightest way, but that's why it's so sinister and anti-American! I'm not sure if Stanley ever did any protesting at all, and that's why he was such an effective Black leader. Stanley was never divisive! Kaepernick would be such a better icon for justice and equality if he didn't visibly or audibly protest in any way that was remotely perceptible to white people like me. I mean, imagine how much more legendary Martin Luther King Jr. would have been if he had never made any white people uncomfortable! Maybe we'd have two or even three MLK-themed holidays today if he had skipped out on all those public speeches, marches and boycotts, and just waited patiently for Southern white people to desegregate the South on their own! I know I'd love him more!"

## Alan Dershowitz Claims Jeffrey Epstein's Parties Were Way Too Awesome To Investigate Further

January 21, 2020
New York City, NY—

Creep and alleged sexual assault villain Alan Dershowitz, who also, relatedly, is a current impeachment lawyer for alleged serial rapist Donald Trump, claims that the ongoing investigations into Jeffrey Epstein's alleged sex parties potentially implicating dozens of high-profile, elite public figures should be dropped because of how "awesome" the parties were.

"Those parties were epic!" Dershowitz said in a *CNN* interview that aired yesterday. "I didn't get to actually go to any, but I always heard so many wild stories. Every time I was about to go to one, Jeffrey called me and told me he was sick, or his power had gone out, or something random like that. Then I'd hear a couple days later that the party had actually happened, so I guess the power had come back on, or Jeffrey started feeling better and forgot to call me. One time I still knocked on his door, and when Jeffrey answered there was totally a party going on, but he told me it was a family party, and that it was for one of his cousin's birthdays. Then I saw Donald Trump and Bill Clinton through the doorway, but Jeffrey told me his cousin knew both Donald and Bill separately. Donald offered me a Tic Tac, and Bill gave me a high-five and said the girls were particularly hot that night, but Donald said they were too old for his tastes. Jeffrey then said the girls were just his nieces, but after he closed the door on me I looked in the windows and saw Jeffrey making out with one of them. I guess the Epstein family must be really close with each other. I can't even imagine what went down for his regular parties! Some of the stories I heard were insane. So many awesome people doing crazy things. So the FBI, State of New York, and all these frivolous, jealous lawsuits ought to just forget about all this Epstein stuff because they're being so uncool. Way less cool than me, who almost went to one of Epstein's parties!"

# Trump Lawyer Rudy Giuliani Has Reportedly Eaten Several Documents That Incriminate Trump

January 24, 2020
Washington D.C.—

Rudy Giuliani has reportedly eaten several incriminating memos subpoenaed by the Senate for the impeachment trial of President Trump.

"Rudy ate several handwritten notes President Trump wrote directing various aides and associates on how to obstruct justice, threaten potential Republican defectors in the Senate, and intimidate other potential whistle-blowers in the administration," confirmed a White House aide, who requested anonymity. "He commits the notes to memory, and then chews them up into a pulp and swallows them. It has become a bit of a habit. Rudy is even consuming notes and printed memos that aren't even incriminating. Today I saw him eat a notebook page that Trump was only doodling on during a cabinet meeting. Trump had drawn a few sketches of women's breasts, but Rudy still ate it. I'm not sure what all the paper, computer ink, and permanent marker residue is doing to Rudy's digestive system, but I can't imagine it's healthy. Rudy says the notes and memos help him reach his daily fiber goals because he always forgets to drink his *Metamucil* smoothies. He says the only downside is how often he clogs up the toilet with the thick, fibrous pulp because if he doesn't notice the flushing didn't finish and someone else has to plunger it, they get freaked out because of how bright red the water is with gastrointestinal blood. I went to the bathroom after him one time and was alarmed to see the condition he had left the toilet. I took him aside and told him he should probably see a doctor, but he just shrugged and told me that politics is a messy, bloody business."

Trump reportedly forces Senators Ted Cruz and Lindsey Graham to eat paper memos as well.

"It has gotten pretty degrading," explained the aide. "Trump writes real nasty things about Ted's wife on various documents with his trademark Sharpie marker, and Ted eagerly gobbles them up and asks for more. About once a week Ted asks Trump if he has earned a future presidential endorsement yet, and Trump just shrieks, empties his Diet Coke can on Ted's head, and snaps at Ivanka to go get him some international treaty Barack Obama had signed when he was president to shove into Ted's mouth. Lindsey Graham initially refused to eat any documents, saying that if Republicans started regularly consuming evidence of Trump's crimes there would be 'hell to pay' for the party. But now Lindsey doesn't even remove staples or paperclips from the packets he eats."

# Trump Voter Who Says Michelle Obama Is A Man Promises It Has Nothing To Do With Racism

January 26, 2020
Charleston, SC—

Local Trump voter Dave Reesel today posted several memes insisting former-First Lady Michelle Obama was secretly a man, but claims his theory has nothing to do with racism.

"I promise I'm not some ignorant racist," said Reesel. "I just think there's something suspicious about Michelle Obama, so I did some research on YouTube. The vast majority of videos were in on the Deep State conspiracy that Michelle is female and the real mother of Sasha and Malia Obama, but after several days of searching I found the few videos that knew the truth!"

Reesel's explanations went down quite a rabbit hole.

"It turns out Michelle Obama is actually a gay Muslim man from Saudi Arabia named Muhammed Baba, who was a big time weightlifter and died of AIDS in the 80s... only Muhammed didn't really die. He didn't have AIDS at all! That's only what George Soros wanted everyone to think! And he made up the lie with the help of the Deep State CIA so they could smuggle Muhammed into the US, and then enroll him in school at Harvard so he could meet Barack 'Barry' Hussein Obama, seduce him, and then radicalize him to run for president in order to try and turn America Arab! And it almost worked! If it wasn't for Trump getting elected, he would have gotten away with it with the help of Nancy Pelosi, who is also secretly a man. From Somalia! All the female Democrats are actually Middle Eastern men. It's the biggest deep fake in American history! The most scandalous part is that Obama doesn't have any daughters! They're secretly Saudi jihadis, and Malia was one of the 9/11 planners! Sasha's real name is Tariq al-Baghdadi, the brother of the leader of ISIS. Malia's real name is Afreen Ali, and he was Osama Bin Laden's right-hand man in Afghanistan back when al-Qaeda bombed the World Trade Center in the 90s! They just shave their beards and legs every day, and walk around holding tampons and boxes of birth control pills so they look like little girls to the untrained eye, when in reality they're both in their mid-50s! Tariq Baghdadi is actually six feet tall so he walks around everywhere on his knees to pretend to be little Sasha. It's criminal how the fake news refuses to report any of this. Even *Fox*. But it's all true! Why do you think every photo of them shows them riding around in the White House on camels, smoking hookah pipes, and wearing suicide bomb vests? You can't photoshop that! And none of this has anything to do with racism! I'm the least racist person in the world!"

## Ken Starr Says If Trump Had Asked Ukrainian President Zelensky For a Blowjob The Impeachment Trial Would Be "Totally Different"

January 27, 2020
Washington D.C.—

After the Senate impeachment trial today, President Donald Trump's lawyer Ken Starr, infamous for leading the carnival show that was President Bill Clinton's impeachment trial over lying about a blowjob, was asked by reporters how Trump was less deserving of removal from office than Clinton.

"It's actually quite simple," explained Starr to a *Fox News* correspondent. "If Trump had extorted the Ukrainian government in order to receive oral sex from President Zelensky, and then directed his administration and political allies to cover up the sexual quid pro quo by obstructing a Congressional investigation into the sex-related bribery, then it would be a crime worthy of impeachment. Instead, all President Trump did was use his public office to extort the Ukrainian government toward concocting a fake investigation into his political opponent for personal gain. While what President Trump did may sound bad and illegal, the precedent I set in the Clinton impeachment trial was that the only crimes worthy of impeachment involve sperm stains. Same deal with the Mueller Investigation. Had Trump given Vladimir Putin a blowy joey, we'd have quite a case of oral collusion on our hands. Instead, Trump merely asked Putin several times on live television to leak a bunch of Hillary Clinton's emails that the Russian government had hacked. There's no sperm stain, so what evidence could we even present to a grand jury? It has often been said that I have the girthiest legal mind in America, and I honestly have no clue where to begin to prosecute that case! I'd be laughed out of court if I submitted as evidence clean clothes with no splooge stains anywhere! And it's the same situation with Michael Cohen's alleged campaign finance violations. Had Cohen slobbed the President's knob, we'd obviously have a much bigger Constitutional problem than just Cohen paying out hush money right before an election and not declaring it as a campaign donation. Ditto for all these Emoluments Clause violations. Trump may be earning money from foreign governments buying out whole floors of his hotel for weeks at a time, but at no point has anyone, to my knowledge, alleged that Saudi or Turkish government employees staying in Trump hotels have ever given Trump a deep-throated blumpkin, a gobby blowjizzle, a waistline corn on the cob gobbling, a mouth-to-south resuscitation, a skin flute solo, a sucky f***y, or just an old-fashioned meat-beating. No sexual climax, no impeachment. That's the Ken Starr rule!"

# Eric Trump Just Got Hired Onto A Russian Copper Company's Board Of Directors

January 30, 2020
New York City, NY—

In the most stunningly hypocritical news development of all time, Eric Trump just announced he was hired last month to be a member on the board of directors of a Russian copper company based in Irkutsk, Siberia.

This happens to be a subsidiary shell company of the copper business that just a few months ago made a bulk purchase of 70,000 copies of Donald Trump Jr.'s new book *Triggered: How The Left Are All Total Fragile Pussies, But Also Rabid Fascist Nazis At The Same Exact Time.*

After #OhMyF***ingGod immediately went viral on Twitter in response to his wildly ironic announcement, Eric updated his LinkedIn profile's employment status to "Industrial Copper Boy Wonder," and posted a video in which he explained that his new board of directors position was "way different" than Hunter Biden's controversial position on a Ukrainian company's board of directors that the Trump family regularly calls "criminal."

"First of all, I'm getting paid way more than Hunter Biden ever got paid at Burisma," explained Eric. "So you can tell my job is much more real and serious than Hunter's job. He only got $50,000 a month, whereas I'm getting $100,000 a month. My job is twice as legitimate! Besides, I know way more about copper than Hunter Biden knows about natural gas. When we were kids I convinced my brother, Don Jr., to trade me all his pennies for all my silver coins. He's so stupid that he agreed, and, when we divided up all the change, I ended up with way more coins than he had! Art of the deal, right? So I'm practically an expert in copper. Hunter Biden doesn't know anything about natural gas because it's invisible. And where does it even come from? Does he collect his farts in jars or something? What a dumb company. Russian companies are way better to work for than Ukrainian companies. And, unlike Hunter in Ukraine, I've actually been to Russia tons of times, and sat in on deals my father has made. I learned from the best. My dad is so good at business. It's amazing. He'll sit down with these Russian oligarchs, and they'll pay three times the going market rate for our properties. Even properties that my dad overpaid for and then didn't make us any money, and loaded us up with debt that haunted us for years. I don't know how my dad convinces them. But that's why he's President. And there's absolutely no collusion with Russia whatsoever. If anything the Russians should be totally furious at my dad because there's no way they're making any money from those awful properties. But, for whatever reason, they just keep coming back and buying more and giving us new loans. I think my dad just has a great rapport with them. They call him all the time to talk about foreign policy stuff. I'm always overhearing them when my dad turns the phone to speakerphone in his office while I'm visiting and hanging out. They're constantly telling him how brilliant his ideas to end NATO are, and how clever his plan to pull all American troops out of the Eastern Hemisphere are. When my father announced publicly that the US should get rid of sanctions on Russia, Vladimir Putin himself got on the phone and said he was the smartest President of all time. I heard it with my own ears, I was right there in the room. Putin was so amazed at my dad's intelligence that he just started laughing for like five minutes straight, and it sounded like the Russians on the other end of the call were popping champaign bottles. They just have such a great relationship. Tons of fun memories together. Apparently they used to make a bunch of fun videos together, and the Russians always cheer and clap when they mention it. They call them the 'golden tapes.' I've never seen them, so I don't know what kind of hijinks they got into, but I bet it was hilarious because my dad has been to some crazy parties back in his day. Especially in Russia. Maybe it has to do with, like, a golden era back when they were younger or something. It's kind of weird though, cause my dad always gets a little serious when they bring it up, so maybe he remembers that in the tapes he had more of his golden blonde hair or something, and he just misses the golden era days when he didn't have to do his elaborate combover every morning. I've spend a lot of time contemplating it, and that's the only reason I can think of for why they'd call them the 'golden tapes.' But, man, I wish I could see those videos. I bet if I saw them, I'd never forget them for the rest of my life! I bet I'd laugh so hard at their wild party pranks that I'd pee myself! My dad would like that, wouldn't he? If that ever happened, I'd hope no one was filming it, cause that could totally be held over my head for blackmail someday! Oh, man, Russians are crazy, aren't they? In a stark contrast, I bet Hunter Biden's dad doesn't have any golden tapes with Russians. What a loser family! Hunter couldn't even get a six-figure monthly salary like I did. That reminds me, though, I should go call that copper company or something. They haven't told me when my first board meeting will be yet. They just started mailing me checks. I haven't even had to sign any paperwork or anything. And I have so many copper ideas. What if I convinced the Russian government to trade all its silver coins for other countries' copper coins? They'd have so many coins at the end of it!"

# Mike Pompeo Threatened A Girl Scout Tour Group For Asking About Ukraine

January 31, 2020
Washington D.C.—

Secretary of State Mike Pompeo recently lost his temper over questions about the Ukrainian scandal from *NPR*'s Mary Louise Kelly, and today he lost his temper again while talking to a local Girl Scout troop on a White House tour.

When Pompeo walked past and stopped to say hello, Ally Shiner, a 9-year-old Brownie, asked him why he was not choosing to testify in the Senate's impeachment trial in order to exonerate his boss, President Donald Trump, when he has said numerous times publicly that the President did not commit any impeachable crimes.

Pompeo then exploded in anger, which several of the Brownies captured on their iPhones.

*The Halfway Post* received several video recordings of the outburst from the Brownies' parents, and the following is a play-by-play of the exchange:

"What do you know about Ukraine, you little hussies?" yelled Pompeo. "You can't even find Ukraine on a map! Donald Trump is not guilty! I was listening in on all the calls, and I saw all the memos! Trump did nothing wrong, and I'm only not testifying because the President is claiming executive privilege… even though if he let me, or Mulvaney, or Mnuchin testify we could end the whole impeachment scam in five minutes!"

"So why won't he just let one of you testify then?" asked Maddy Greusen, 10.

"Because you're a little brat!" Pompeo screamed back. "That's why! Because that's exactly what Democrats want! They're begging us to testify and say under oath that Trump is innocent, so that's exactly why we can't testify. I'll be dead in the ground before I let Nancy Pelosi get her way! Even though my sworn testimony, memos and emails could have ended this whole joke of an impeachment mess months ago, I'll stay quiet and uncooperative for ten more years! A hundred more years! I have executive privilege until the sun explodes and incinerates the Earth!"

"So you could just forward a couple memos to the Senate, and never have to be asked about Ukraine again… and you're not just doing that?" asked Abby Pheifer, 9. "When everyone else who actually is testifying and providing documents to Congress says the opposite, that Trump is totally guilty?"

"How many times do I have to explain myself?" shrieked Pompeo, whose face was now bright red. "You little trollops don't know anything about America! You can't even find America on a map! Get me the map!"

One of Pompeo's aides promptly pulled out a blank map of the world from his briefcase.

"Show me where America is on the map," demanded Pompeo as Abby Phiefer immediately pointed to it.

"Screw you!" yelled Pompeo, pointing to each girl. "Screw you, screw you, screw you, screw you, and especially screw you! I knew Girl Scouts were stuck-up floozies, but you all are giant, arrogant know-it-alls as well! You're going to regret this! None of you will ever work in this town. I'll make sure of it! I'm going to ruin you! I'll destroy any careers you ever have! You'll regret asking me about Ukraine, I swear to God!"

Pompeo then proceeded to slap himself in the face repeatedly as he screamed obscenities at the Brownies. Then he pulled down his pants, defecated on the floor, and started throwing feces at the girls and their parent chaperones as they ran away.

"You think you're brownies?" Pompeo shrieked! "I'll show you brownies! My brownies are homemade... straight from the oven up my a**hole! Never ask me about Ukraine again! Trump is innocent, and I could prove it right now if I wanted!"

"Then just testify, you moron, who somehow doesn't apparently understand how not testifying for someone you claim is innocent makes him look guilty!" yelled back Ally Shiner before closing the White House door.

The recording ends here, but *The Halfway Post* interviewed White House janitor Ben Miggins about the incident.

"Yeah, this kind of thing happens about once a week now," said Miggins. "I'm used to cleaning up poop stains from various presidential pets that have lived here, but not human feces. Though I guess the way Mike Pompeo has sold his soul brainlessly defending all of the President's crimes makes him kind of like Trump's pet, so this technically is still included within the terms of my employment. Last week he stuck his fingers down his throat to throw up on a baby in a stroller whose parents asked him about Jamal Khashoggi."

Our *Halfway Post* reporter handed Miggins a $20 bill, and told him to get himself an 18-pack of beer tonight on us.

## Aliens Land On Earth, Donate $10 Billion In Asteroid Metals To Defeat Donald Trump And Mitch McConnell

February 2, 2020
St. Louis, MO—

In a wild span of five minutes, advanced extra-terrestrial lifeforms landed in the outskirts of St. Louis in a massive spaceship, and dropped off approximately $10 billion worth of precious metals.

After depositing the small mountain of metals, one of the aliens gave a short speech in English in which it explained that the gift was to be used only for defeating President Trump and Senate Majority Leader Mitch McConnell in their 2020 Senate reelection campaigns.

Fortunately, a *Halfway Post* reporter happened to be at the scene, and captured an audio recording of the extraordinary ordeal. The following is a transcript of the alien's comments:

"Greetings, America. We have long been monitoring you from our planets, and your present course of linear existence is most unrecommendable. Your presidential potentate is a cosmically degenerate life form, and on our planet such a larval-minded entity would be exiled to the salt mines on Zenoquologar for the torturously monotonous drudgery his chemically unimpressive nucleic acids would be much better suited for. We would immensely enjoy vaporizing him with our lasers, but we are bound by strict laws set forth by a federation of Type III civilizations. Instead, we are offering you Earthlings called Americans this gift of valuable metals we mined from a nearby asteroid field in order to use the funds it procures for the express purpose of ensuring the electoral defeat of him, as well as the organism you call Mitch McConnell, within the archaic electoral system to which you unwisely subscribe. Their expenditures of kinetic energy are most unsavory and sociologically ill-advised, and their political machinations offend our advanced morality. Our galactic federation voted with unanimous consent to temporarily suspend our oaths not to interfere in your primordial planetary affairs in order to end their administrative and legislative tyranny over you. Let us warn you that should you use the financial profits procured from these resources for any purpose other than electoral freedom we will beam back the metals without a second brain wave. Your civilization is technologically insignificant, and we do not recommend any exertion to test us. We will also warn you that in several parallel universes your planet becomes a galaxial parasite based on the space-time reverberations of reelecting Trump. Goodbye now. Oh, before we go, have you ever noticed that this McConnell entity strikingly resembles your planet's shelled, aquatic herpetoids?"

# Mitch McConnell's Darkest Secrets

1. McConnell hates puppies and kittens. Big eyes, heads, and disproportionate limb sizes—objective displays of cuteness indicative of infancy in most mammals—have never warmed his heart.

2. He has always been grudgingly envious of popular people since middle school, which is why he worked so hard to make Obama a one-term president. His high school's prom king disappeared after Mitch was the last person anyone saw him with.

3. He likes to secure power both political and personal quietly and methodically in the background. He believes his spirit animal is a wolf spider hiding in a hole waiting for its prey to move past so he can catch it and slowly suck out all its juices.

4. He writes fan fiction in his free time during Congressional recesses about a fictional Nazi Party member named Mitchell Müller who gets into outlandish hijinks helping Hitler legislate Germany into a fascist state.

5. He detests nicknames, references to Moscow, and being compared facially to a turtle because he obviously more resembles a tortoise.

6. He loathes going back to Kentucky to campaign for reelection, and having to talk to Kentuckians in general because he thinks they're stupid.

7. Despite various photo-ops holding assorted guns, he has never actually fired one. He prefers to practice choking people in preparation for the potentiality of a rebellion against the government most libertarians associate with the Second Amendment and guns.

8. He thinks he would have made a great Confederate senator during the Civil War, and with his calculating legislative tactics been able to block the 13th-15th Amendments from passing during Reconstruction.

9. He understands fully the US needs drastic reform, but he knows his cynical Machiavellian legislative subterfuge is what will get his name in to the history books.

10. He thinks Paul Ryan is a showboat who got too much credit for Congressional budgetary action for which he should have been recognized. He's jealous no media outlet ever wanted to do a photoshoot of him in a gym lifting weights with a hat on backwards.

11. He personally loathes how stupid Donald Trump is, but appreciates Trump's sway over racists for the GOP political gains it allows.

12. His greatest fear is that his Kentuckian constituents will realize he's been representing them in the Senate for almost 40 years, yet has done virtually nothing of substantial value to improve their lives or their standards of living languishing in the bottom of societal statistical rankings in which Kentucky is home to 10 of the 25 most impoverished counties in America.

13. He once got caught jerking off in the turtle room at the Louisville Zoo.

# Evangelicals Are Furious "Mormon Mitt" Is Taking His Impeachment Oath To God Seriously

February 5, 2020
Washington D.C.—

The following are quotes from Evangelical Trump supporters furious with Senator Mitt Romney for voting to remove Trump in the impeachment trial:

"This is why we don't consider Mormons to be REAL Christians! A REAL Christian would know Trump is doing God's work, even if none of the means to which he makes progress toward those ends remotely resembles Jesus-endorsed values or morals! The less Trump acts like Jesus, the more I'm convinced he's doing exactly what Jesus would want!" —Keith Warbles, 49

"Mitt is a Mormon they say, but more like a MORON! Everyone knows the oath that senators recited to God on a Bible in order to faithfully and truthfully judge the impeachment of Trump was simply a formality. Just because Democrats' witnesses affirmed his crimes and guilt doesn't mean any Republicans should actually vote for impeachment! Does Mitt Romney know anything about how politics works?!" —Sally Piedmont, 37

"Mitt should just change his name to Nancy Pelosi's Slave. He may have been a Republican his whole life, and still share every conservative viewpoint, but this vote against Trump erases all of that! From now on, Mitt Romney is a libtard Democrat communist, who is further left than a baby Alexandria Ocasio-Cortez had with Stalin who then grew up and married a 150-years-old Bernie Sanders, and cheated on Bernie by taking a socialist swingers' cruise to Vietnam for a shore excursion to the jungle to dig up Ho Chi Minh's corpse to have socialist, necrophiliac butt sex with it!" —Bo Ross, 61

"God doesn't care about your oath, Mitt! God cares about keeping Trump in office long enough to promote Israel so that Jesus can come back and cast all the Jews, Muslims, Mormons, and liberals into Hell!" —Karen McPoyle, 46

"Hey, Mitt! Stop being such a boy scout! Just take your Russian bribe, shut up, and vote to acquit Trump like the rest of us!" —Lindsey Graham, 64

"Romney needs to stop making Christians look bad! This is why nobody likes Mormons: they're actually morally upstanding. Born-again Evangelicals are way better because we can commit blasphemies against our promises to God with pool boys all we want when we can just randomly get born again and get a clean slate. Mormons should try it out!" —Jerry Falwell Jr., 57

# Ted Cruz Is Thrilled He's No Longer The Most Hated GOP Senator Thanks To Mitt Romney

February 6, 2020
Washington D.C.—

No one is happier that Senator Mitt Romney voted to remove President Donald Trump from office than Senator Ted Cruz because he reportedly thinks it means he'll no longer be the most unpopular Republican in the Senate.

"Huzzah!" exclaimed Cruz following Romney's vote. "Now, when people say things like 'Ted Cruz is the worst,' I can pedantically point out that, in fact, Mitt Romney is slightly less cool than me for not towing the party line!"

Other senators, however, did not agree.

"I still hate Ted Cruz way more," said Senator Lindsey Graham. "This won't change the fact I've said before that if someone killed Ted Cruz on the floor of the Senate, no Senators would vote to convict the murderer. I'd even vote to confirm that person onto the Supreme Court because killing Cruz would exemplify such clear and sound judgment!"

"Say what you will about Mitt," explained Senator John Thune, "but at least he voted his conscience, which is much more than you can say about Ted Cruz voting to acquit Trump only because he thinks it will help him get votes from Trump fans the next time he runs for president. When Ted Cruz voted to acquit Trump, it actually made me think a little harder about voting to convict Trump because that's how much Ted Cruz doing something makes me instinctively want to do the opposite."

"Al Franken said it best when he said that he liked Ted Cruz more than most in the Senate, and that he hated Ted Cruz," said Senator Rob Portman. "Al Franken certainly liked Ted much more than I do! One time at a Republican caucus luncheon I saw Ted Cruz with spinach in his teeth, toilet paper stuck to his shoe, his pants zipper down, his shirt on inside-out, and a booger hanging from his nose… and I didn't say a word to him about any of it!"

"Cruz getting elected in my state twice really makes me doubt the intelligence of my constituents," said Cruz's fellow Texas Senator John Cornyn. "I want to believe they're intelligent arbiters of character, but… why Ted?"

"I have many theories about several serial killer cold cases in which I think Ted Cruz should be considered a top suspect," said Senator Tim Scott.

## Pro-Life Republican: "God Told Me It Was Cool For Me To Pay For An Abortion"

February 9, 2020
Shreveport, LA—

Following a controversial mistress-abortion scandal, outspoken pro-life GOP Representative Jeff Reisingler of Louisiana says it's not hypocritical that he pressured a mistress he accidentally got pregnant to have an abortion.

"This is entirely different from the abortions I have made my career trying to ban," explained Reisingler in a press conference this morning. "For starters, when I found out my mistress was pregnant, I did a lot of soul-searching and praying, and with 100% certainty I can confirm that God gave me unambiguous signs that the abortion affecting my personal life was totally cool with Him. He said, just this one time, it was okay on account of how promising my career in Congress is."

Despite Reisingler's wife filing for divorce within hours of his public announcement, he is adamant that he's just as committed to Christian family values as ever.

"My wife is the one who has given up on family values, not me! When I told her God was commanding that she stay with me, she kicked me in the nuts, which is a direct affront to the Lord's obvious intentions. I told her that if she kept trying to squash my testicles, God would only give me more mistresses to impregnate with the sperm I have left since our Heavenly Father clearly thinks they're blessed enough for some extramarital baby-making! My wife also took that the wrong way, and I'm starting to believe she has been faking her Christian faith all this time if she's now outright refusing to go along with God's flawless master plan. Thankfully I was at least able to talk God out of me having to go through with the whole ordeal of having the kid with the mistress, and I'm just glad those devilish, succubus Democrat nurses at Planned Parenthood let me out of the building alive. Their eyes were glowing red, and I could see their sharp baby-eating fangs, but I brought my Bible along, and it protected me from their dark, liberal sorcery."

Reisingler explained that Democrats are still "way bigger baby killers" than him.

"Look, I don't like abortions like the Democrats do. They love them! They wish they could abort all the fetuses in the world. Meanwhile, I've only aborted one, and, like I said, God gave me permission. It's not hypocritical because I'm not an irresponsible, low-class, ethnic minority single mother. I may be irresponsible, I'll give the liberals that one, but I'm none of those other words. So my personal circumstances could not be any more completely different. God understands my future shouldn't be affected by some little mistake like not pulling out in time on one random night of marital infidelity, and God knows I'm capable of learning and growing from my mistake... unlike all those irresponsible minority women! Theirs are the abortions we have to ban because otherwise they'll be having all kinds of immoral, recreational sex. Compared to them I've barely had any!"

## How Much Do Democrats Love Abortion?

"Ask not what your country can abort for you, ask what you can abort for your country."
### —John Kennedy

"Leave no fetus for tomorrow which can be aborted today."
### —Hillary Clinton

"It is hard to birth, but it is worse never to have tried to abort."
### —Nancy Pelosi

"The only limit to our realization of tomorrow will be all these un-aborted fetuses of today."
### —Chuck Schumer

"It's amazing how many babies you can abort if you do not care who gets the credit."
### —Barack Obama

"Every gun that is made, every warship launched, every rocket fired signifies, in the final sense, a theft of an abortion that could have been funded with taxpayer dollars."
### —Amy Klobuchar

"So, first of all, let me assert my firm belief that the only thing we have to fear is birth itself—vaginal, scheduled Caesarean, unplanned Caesarean, and water births, which paralyze needed efforts to convert procreation into forced infertility."
### —Franklin Roosevelt

# In A CNN Interview Stephen Miller Implied He Has Eaten Human Meat

February 10, 2020
New York City, NY—

Presidential adviser Stephen Miller was a total creep in a recent interview with *CNN* hosted by Jake Tapper.

Miller was booked to discuss Trump's acquittal in the Senate impeachment trial, but it quickly derailed into Miller's personal idiosyncrasies.

"The President was exonerated, and I believe that every member of Congress who voted against him ought to be put in prison, starting with Mitt Romney," Miller said. "And maybe he deserves some light torture for betraying his own party's leader. The things I'd do to Mitt... I'd start with some medical testing. You never really know a man until you discover how much bodily pain he can take before begging for its end. How would Mitt handle a little asphyxiation? I love it when victims stare at me with their bulging eyes as I squeeze harder and harder. They can't say a word, but they communicate so much with the terror in their expanding pupils as they come to the realization that I have all the power. All the control. Nothing gets me off more than seeing terror inches from my face. The anxiety and fear of death releases a peculiar, almost sweet hormonal smell. It brings back such nostalgic memories of my past experiments... Dogs, birds, rabbits, Timmy next door... Since I was a little boy, the fragile nature of life has always fascinated me. The instinctual struggle to survive captivates me. How long would it take for Mitt to squeal? I wonder if I could make him forsake his religion to make it stop. Would Mitt be willing to abandon his God and hopes for eternal salvation for a brief moment of relief from my cold fingers around his trachea? And then maybe I'd move to his extremities. Cut off finger by finger, and watch him bleed. I'd let him drip into a bowl, and I'd lap it up like a kitten sipping at a saucer of warm milk. I wonder what Mitt's blood tastes like. Abstaining from alcohol and coffee like a good Mormon boy probably gives him a unique flavor. I bet he'd be a totally new flavor for me. And then I'd bathe in his juices. If his kids and grandkids could be forced to watch the entire ordeal, it'd be even sweeter. I'd love to lick the salty tears off their cheeks as I mutilate their patriarch's flesh. Ah, I have the most curious erection right now. It's being quite impish engorging itself while I'm on live television here with Mr. Tapper! But all in good time, Mitt. Oh, yes, in good time indeed."

Tapper stared open-mouthed at Miller, who appeared to be lost in his thoughts as he licked his lips. Then Miller asked where the bathroom was, and said he needed a few minutes to himself.

# Trump Made Matt Gaetz Wear A Diaper To Become Un-Blacklisted After Voting The Wrong Way On A House Bill

February 11, 2020
Washington D.C.—

Representative Matt Gaetz recently got blacklisted by President Donald Trump for voting against his wishes on a House bill, but Gaetz has reportedly now gotten himself un-blacklisted after completing a gauntlet of humiliating pranks Trump devised.

The following are hazing activities Gaetz reportedly had to complete in order to be back on Trump's good side:

- Spend a weekend walking around Mar-a-Lago wearing nothing but a diaper, and not changing that diaper from Friday morning to Sunday evening
- Get a tattoo of Trump's face on his butt
- Contract pink eye after sleeping on a pillow that Trump, Lindsey Graham, and Jim Jordan all took turns farting on
- Submit a House bill asking Congress to adopt a resolution to formally recognize Matt Gaetz as a "b****"
- Drink an old, expired bottle of Trump vodka until he threw up
- Let Eric and Don Jr. shoot him with a BB gun
- Play two rounds of Russian roulette
- Send a dick pic to Ivanka
- Suck each of Mike Pompeo's toes for ten seconds each
- Put his hand in a mousetrap
- Get another DUI
- Write an Obamacare replacement plan that covers more people and is cheaper
- Spend a night in a Texas border concentration camp cage
- Be a dishwasher at Mar-a-Lago for a Saturday double-shift
- Drink a cup of expired milk
- Get a physical from Jim Jordan's gropey wrestling team doctor
- Leave a message on Representative Alexandria Ocasio-Cortez's office phone asking her out on a date
- Leave a message on Senator Dianne Feinstein's office phone asking her out on a date
- Egg Mitt Romney's D.C. house
- Write a 2,000-word essay on how Donald Trump has made America great again including the President's name in every paragraph
- Hang out with Stephen Miller for a night to watch his homemade horror films

# Trump Signed A $50 Million Deal To Become The Face Of CoverGirl's Makeup Line

February 15, 2020
Washington D.C.—

According to insiders at the Trump Organization, President Donald Trump just signed a major deal with the makeup powerhouse *CoverGirl* to become the face of their brand for the rest of the 2020 styling season.

"The President is actually their most loyal customer, so this is a long time coming," said Trump Organization executive Charles Prichard. "They give him a 25% 'presidential discount' because he's their highest-spending customer in the history of the company. You've noticed the way he cakes foundation on, right? How his face is just ridiculously bright orange? The bulk purchases of makeup he buys every month have to be delivered in an 18-wheeler truck. It's kind of a funny story that one time one of the trucks got knocked over in an accident on the highway and started rolling, spilling out orange foundation cases everywhere. It looked liked a giant Cheeto meteorite hit the Earth."

Regulators in various governmental oversight agencies, however, are complaining that the marketing deal goes against the Constitution's Emoluments Clause, and Democratic lawyers are looking into whether or not the deal constitutes a major campaign finance violation.

In response, Trump published the following thread on Twitter this morning:

"It's Fake News that my new *CoverGirl* advertising campaign breaks any laws. The only thing that beaks laws is my ridiculous good looks breaking the laws of physics! I always thought Ivanka was the hottest Trump, but *CoverGirl* asked me to be their spokesperson, not her (sorry, sweetie!)!"

"They want me to be on at least 3 magazine covers over the next year. I hope they want me shirtless in one. Move over, Kim Kardashian, my curves will break the Internet for real! Then everyone will see I'm not the fattest President since Taft, I'm just big-boned! And I've been told by many people that I have the best nipples in town!"

"This *CoverGirl* deal is just so crazy because I don't even use makeup. I'm 100% natural. My teeth? Totally real. My smile? Not constructed with botox at all! I'm one of those rare people whose skin gets tighter, teeth get newer, and hair gets blonder the older I get!"

# Rudy Giuliani Reveals Several Documents He Has Been Hiding Up His Rectum To Protect Trump

February 20, 2020
Washington D.C.—

The impeachment trial of President Donald Trump is over, and no one is more relieved than Trump's lawyer Rudy Giuliani, who went on Sean Hannity's *Fox News* show last night to reveal the lengths he went to in order to protect Trump.

"I am so, so glad Democrats only impeached Trump for two crimes," explained Giuliani. "Can you imagine how much longer it would have gone on if Democrats had also impeached him over the Emoluments Clause, campaign finance violations, sexual assault allegations, tax evasion, or carried on the Mueller Report's unfinished work and addressed the instances Mueller found that Trump impeded his investigation with witness intimidation and obstruction of justice? I don't think my anus could have taken it!"

"Wait, what do you mean?" asked a confused Hannity. "Is that a metaphor or something?"

"No, literally my rectum!" said Giuliani. "There were several documents I had in my possession that, well, somewhat incriminated the President, so I had no choice but to hide them in the only place I knew Adam Schiff and Nancy Pelosi would never want to look! I folded them up as small as I could, but, you know, paper only folds seven times, and, unfortunately, Trump has committed several packets' worth of crimes as regards Ukraine. But I did my duty to the President. It took a lot of stretching in the beginning, but with a lot of lube I finally got them up there safe and sound. It was a very nasty job to take them out when I had to... you know? And I walked a little funny for the first week or two, but thankfully the lining of the colon is very forgiving and elastic. Now the incriminating documents have gotten pretty fouled up, so I'm confident Schiff and Pelosi don't want to go anywhere near them. I certainly don't mind letting my rectum tighten back up for a bit. I was worried about a prolapse! And it was getting harder and harder to keep the papers up there. Sometimes they'd just fall right out. But it's probably safe now that the impeachment trial is over, and the papers are virtually unreadable anyway... I eat a lot of beans and citrusy fruits in my diet. Also I should probably get checked out because I'm fairly certain I have to be having diarrhea much more than is biologically typical or medically recommendable. It always smells like scotch, and is bright red."

Sean Hannity's face turned pale, and he called for a commercial break.

# Mike Bloomberg's Latest Ad Mocks Trump For Paying Way Too Much On Hush Money

February 23, 2020
New York City, NY—

Mayor Mike Bloomberg's upcoming national television ad for his presidential campaign will reportedly highlight the bad deals President Donald Trump has negotiated for his various nondisclosure agreements with porn stars.

The following is a leaked copy of the ad's script obtained exclusively by *The Halfway Post*:

[INTRO: WIDE SHOT on strippers dancing on a pole.]

### VOICE-OVER:
"Donald Trump paid porn star Stormy Daniels $130,000 in hush money for 90 seconds of sex."

[CLOSEUP on Donald Trump's face.]

### VOICE-OVER:
"That's $1,444 per second. America, does that sound like winning to you?"

[MEDIUM SHOT on Mike Bloomberg shaking hands with several businesswomen.]

### VOICE-OVER:
"Mayor Bloomberg pays far less for his nondisclosure agreements because he's a real business person who makes real deals. He may disrespect women, but he'd never disrespect America by overpaying on his hush money contracts. Donald Trump disrespects women, AND pays way too much to keep them quiet afterwards. We can't afford four more years of Donald Trump's bad business deals."

[WIDE SHOT of Bloomberg surrounded by piles of cash.]

### VOICE-OVER:
"Vote Mike Bloomberg, a REAL billionaire with REAL negotiating skills."

# Donald Trump Ate A Bowl Of Ice Cream In The Middle Of His COVID Press Conference

March 1, 2020
Washington D.C.—

At a press conference today President Donald Trump, while standing awkwardly behind Mike Pence during the Vice President's remarks about the seriousness of COVID-19, was handed a bowl of ice cream by his daughter Ivanka Trump.

The bowl appeared to have seven scoops in it: two chocolate, three vanilla, and two strawberry. Trump then slowly ate the ice cream, visibly savoring each spoonful. Each bite he'd close his eyes, and a few times the President audibly moaned.

Mr. Pence, meanwhile, repeatedly praised Trump's executive efforts against the pandemic's spread, and even looked behind him to give thumbs-up gestures to Trump. Pence seemed entirely unfazed by seeing the President with a bowl of ice cream, and at one point motioned to Trump that he had dripped some ice cream onto his chin.

Trump interrupted Pence a few times, once to tell White House staffers standing in the back of the conference room, "Don't give any ice cream to the evil press," a second time to tell Ivanka she forgot the whipped cream on top, and a third time to ask Dr. Anthony Fauci if he thought it'd be hot if Ivanka came back wearing nothing but a whipped cream bikini.

After finishing his scoops, he lifted the bowl to his mouth with two hands and began to vigorously lick it clean.

When it was Trump's turn to talk, he handed the bowl to Pence, who stood behind the President dutifully holding it for the remainder of the press conference as Trump ranted for half an hour about how he thought it was very suspicious no one has ever seen the coronavirus and Michigan Governor Gretchen Whitmer's period blood in the same room.

At the end of the press conference he unveiled a large banner that said "COVID: MISSION ACCOMPLISHED."

# Ted Cruz Says His Haters Are "Just Jealous" Of His "Charming Personality"

March 2, 2020
Washington D.C.—

Senator Ted Cruz is a frequent Twitter complainer, and whines often about how often he gets mocked over his political ambitions and bothersome existence.

This morning, though, Mr. Cruz told *The Halfway Post* in an unprompted phone conversation that his haters were just jealous.

"I understand why people in the media and most public places I go tend to gang up and pick on me," said Cruz. "It's obvious they're just intimidated by my rugged masculinity. I've had this intimidating effect on other boys and men since high school when the freshmen would never let me go to their parties, even though I was a senior, and I brought alcohol. They'd take the alcohol, but then lock the doors and close the curtains when I'd go around the house knocking on the windows and peering inside hoping someone would let me in. Same thing in college. I used to bring marijuana to house parties and offer to share if they'd all sign oaths swearing to vote for me for president when I ran in the future, but then it turned out that my dealer was just giving me bags of grass clippings from mowing his lawn, and weed doesn't cost $1,000 per gram. But, besides my fellow students' obvious envy of my personality, I've always been really popular. My college roommate Craig Mazin has made a lot of unfounded claims about me being unliked at Princeton, but he told all kinds of lies about me. Like when he said he walked in on me watching squirrel porn several times. I told him a million times I was doing research for a term paper in a biology class that I later dropped so the class is not listed on my transcript anywhere if you look for it, and I was only naked because I just coincidentally happened to be doing laundry all those times."

The *Halfway Post* reporter asked Mr. Cruz if he was getting off track, and Cruz apologized.

"So, what I mean to say is that the haters only mock me because they're jealous I'm the James Dean of the Senate. They're probably mad that their wives gossip about me and fantasize about being Mrs. Ted Cruz. Their wives wish they had husbands as charming, debonaire, and witty as me! Seriously, I'm really funny. When I tell the womenfolk jokes, sometimes my cleverness makes them skip laughing entirely and just throw up! I've been vomited on so many times. I think it's because my charm makes women so nervous about trying to impress me and keep up with me intellectually. I had a big problem in my twenties and thirties dating because women would always vomit all over my face when I'd lean in for a kiss. Or to hug them. Or hold their hands. Or ask them how they feel to be talking to a future president of the United States. I bet all my Democratic colleagues in the Senate never made women regularly throw up out of nervousness! I just can't control my manliness, you know? Now, I know you're probably thinking about Lindsey Graham's claim that none of my Senate colleagues like me, and that if I was murdered in the Senate and the trial was prosecuted there the murderer wouldn't be found guilty. But Lindsey Graham is a prosecutor, that's just how he flirts. And he gets awkward around me too. When I asked him if he'd be my running mate back in 2016, he was so overcome with anxiety from the idea of potentially working with the best future president in history that he just burst out laughing. Then I had to ask Carly Fiorina, who was my second choice, and she accepted immediately... right after first vomiting all over me!"

## Ted Cruz, Shall I Compare Thee To A Summer's Turd?
(Inspired by William Shakespeare)
by Donald J. Trump

Shall I compare thee to a summer's turd?
Thou art more sticky and more malodorous:
Rough winds do waft your feculence undeterred,
And your derrière hath aromatics unjustly onerous.
Sometime too hot the eye of Hell shines,
And often does his complexion look Cruz'd;
And every boner and moistness declines,
In lieu of being near him all'd rather be deuce'd.
But thy eternal miasma shall not fade,
Nor lose possession of that disgust you inspire,
Nor shall death brag he is similarly portrayed,
Or feel it fair for the damned to smell your stench in fire.
   So long as men can breathe or eyes can see,
   So long lives this, and gives warning of thee.

## Trump's Afghan Deal Gives The Taliban A 15% "Friends of Trump" Discount At All Trump Properties

March 5, 2020
Washington D.C.—

President Donald Trump unveiled his latest peace deal proposal with the Afghan Taliban, and the following details of the agreement have been criticized by Congressional Democrats and panned by media pundits:

- All Taliban members get a 15% "Friends of Trump" discount at all Trump-owned properties.
- The Taliban government will own a 33.3% stake in a proposed Trump Tower Kabul, and a 25% stake in a Trump Afghan Golf Club to host an annual Pashtun Open.
- The Taliban is committed to buying 1,000 copies of Donald Trump Jr.'s book *Triggered*, and 5,000 copies of *The Art of the Deal*.
- The Taliban will give Ivanka Trump exclusive trademarks on Ivanka-branded burqas, beheading swords, and suicide jackets.
- The Taliban will receive three years of complimentary pro bono legal assistance in rehabilitating their international image at the United Nations courtesy of Jay Sekulow and Alan Dershowitz.
- Donald Trump Jr. will host a Trump campaign rally in Jalalabad, Afghanistan, and give 50% of all "Make America Great Again" themed merchandise profits to the Taliban military for its Build-More-Missiles initiative.
- Donald Trump will give the Taliban five "Dismember-A-Journalist-Free" certificates.
- Donald Trump will lift the Taliban's "terror group" designation and instead designate the Taliban as a "state sponsor of cuddles."
- Donald Trump will move the American embassy in Afghanistan to the city of the Taliban's choice.
- The Taliban will give Russia exclusive rights to any newly discovered oil wells in northern Afghanistan through 2025, for which Russia will give Donald Trump a 20% finder's fee on all profits.
- Donald Trump will say nothing about the Taliban's human rights violations for the remainder of his time in office *a la* his silence on China and India's human rights violations.
- The national Afghan charity for children who have survived stepping on land mines will pay Eric Trump to host a fundraising gala at a Trump property, and not audit his accounting of the night's donations.
- The Taliban will publish an official declaration that says Donald Trump's hands are bigger than any other foreign leader in history who has ever meddled in Afghanistan.

# Trump Reportedly Offered Barack Obama $1 Million To Take The Blame For The Coronavirus

March 13, 2020
Washington D.C.—

According to White House insiders, President Donald Trump called Barack Obama yesterday and offered his predecessor a $1 million bribe to give a public press conference in which he would claim all responsibility for the alarming spread of coronavirus in the United States. One of Trump's White House staffers recorded Trump's end of the call on a recording app on his phone, and leaked the audio of Trump's pleas to *The Halfway Post*:

"Hey Barack, how is everything? Just thought I'd call to see how you're doing... Great. Great. Listen, as you've probably heard, we've got a bit of a COVID situation here, and I was hoping you'd be interested in a proposition I am prepared to make. I'd like you to come to the White House and help us out... You're interested? Perfect, perfect. Okay, you'd just have to do a little press conference and say it was all your fault, and that you're sorry for letting the American people down... No, why would I want your help on actually stopping the spread of coronavirus? ... No, we don't want people taking tests! ...Why? Because then our number of cases will go up! Do you know anything about dealing with pandemics? ... No tests! We want the number of confirmed cases to go down to zero. How will that happen if everyone starts taking tests? ... No tests! Do you know anything about math? Wow, I thought you were smarter than this... Look, we just need a little press conference. Just a teeny-tiny one. Okay? All you have to do is look at the camera and say it was all your fault. Say you brought it with you from a Kenya vacation on accident or something. Can you do that for us? America needs you, Barack. I need you... I'll tell you what, I'll sweeten the deal. I'll give you one million dollars to take all the blame. Okay? How about it? ... Well, how about two million then? ... Five? Ten? I'll tell you what, how about twenty million dollars? ... Okay, fine, you know what? I'll have to make some calls to Russia and Saudi Arabia, but I can probably get you thirty through a few dozen shell companies. Thirty million dollars? ... Come on. What's the matter? Don't you want to help America? This would be so great for everyone... No, no tests! Stop saying we need tests! ... Look, my polls are tanking right now, and this would turn things around for me... Screw you! Just because of that I'm going to repeal Obamacare, for real this time! ... You're so unfair! ... Come on, man. Just be cool for once. Don't you want to help America? Come on! Just say it. Say it was your fault! ... You know I hate you so, so much, right?"

Trump then slammed the phone down on his desk, crossed his arms tightly across his chest, and told his staff that Obama said he would think about it.

# Trump: "Okay, This Time I Swear I'm Telling The Truth About Coronavirus!"

March 15, 2020
Washington D.C.—

President Donald Trump hosted a press conference today about his administration's approach to preventing the spread of the coronavirus, and promised this time he was telling the truth and definitely not lying about anything or hiding any inconvenient truths like he maybe did a little bit in his other press conferences in the past.

"Okay, everyone, this time is for real," Trump said. "I promise this is the total truth on coronavirus. All the other press conferences I just had trouble remembering. This is the real one, the totally accurate one that will blow your mind how truthful it is. When I tell you, you're going to say to yourself that you can't believe how truthful it is. Everyone's talking about how this press conference I'm giving right now is one of the most truthful conferences of all time. The fake news won't give me credit for it, but I have done more about coronavirus than anyone has ever done for any disease or illness in American history. My response to coronavirus has been tremendous. Truly amazing. At Mar-a-Lago a few days ago it was all everyone was talking about. Some people at Mar-a-Lago tested positive for coronavirus since then, but it didn't get me. I have no symptoms right now, so I'm 100% sure I won't get any in a few more days. No way. And I might get tested. I might. We're working on it. I most likely will. But there's no reason to, so we'll see. In fact, I got tested already. And it already came back that I'm negative. One of the great immune systems of all time. Maybe even better than Lincoln's. And you can trust me. This is the total truth. The most truthful response to coronavirus of any president ever. No president has ever been more honest than me. Or done such great work. Extraordinary work. No one can believe the things I've done. So nothing to worry about, folks. And, whatever you do, don't take your money out of the stock market. Keep it in. We like it in. Actually, you should buy even more stocks because of how beautiful our coronavirus response has been. And if the stock market continues to go down, it's not my fault. But if it goes up, it's because of my extraordinary business brain. One of the best business brains of all time. Went to Wharton, and you know all that. Made billions and billions. But I promise there is nothing to worry about. The number of coronavirus cases has gone up a little bit in recent weeks, but everyone's doing great. That number will probably be zero in two or three days, tops. I think it might. We expect it to go very low. We've rounded the corner. But it might go up. You never know with these things. These things are very tough. The toughest things you've ever heard of. No one could have imagined how tough. And we don't want the number to go up, but who knows? We're watching it, though. Very closely. No one is watching closer than we are, I can tell you that. So everyone, keep calm. And, whatever you do, don't get tested because we want that number to stay low, low, low. So don't get tested. But anyone can get tested. We've got so many tests now. We have so many tests you wouldn't believe how many. Beautiful tests too. Tremendous tests. The best tests anyone has ever had. And everyone can get a test. But maybe in some areas there are fewer tests. A lot of people don't know this, but it's very hard to get tests everywhere. And my predecessors left me with very few. The cupboards were bare. You wouldn't believe how bare. It's criminal how bare. But we're working on it. And everywhere else you can get a test. But there's no reason to take a test. The cases are going very down. And our numbers are looking great right now. I love the numbers. No one can believe how low these numbers are. And we don't want them to go up. That would be very bad. We don't want that. Maybe some people want that, I won't say who, but you know who they are. But I don't want that. I tell everybody that we want these numbers low. So thanks, everyone. And thanks to my team. They're doing amazing things. Some of the best work of all time. But if the numbers keep going up, maybe not so great work. Maybe I'll need new people. I hope not. But we'll see. I'd give myself an A+ because of the numbers. But if they get not so good, I take no responsibility. I've done everything perfect. The fake news won't report it, but everyone is saying they can't believe how perfect. But it's very tough, okay? So let's stop pointing fingers and assigning blame, okay? Because you wouldn't believe the mess I inherited. Like I said, the cupboards were very bare. Maybe they had an explanatory booklet about catching foreign viruses early, but you can't do any testing with a booklet, can you? And no one was calling for storing more tests than me. And masks. No one. I was saying it for so long. They said I was saying it too much. They said I was obsessed with tests. They said I never shut up about the tests. Big brain. But it's going great. I'm not worried, the doctors aren't worried, and I don't think you should worry. So there's no need to take a test and raise our numbers. We want the lowest numbers of all time. And we have them. But they're going up a little. Just a little. Teeny-tiny. But we're rounding a corner. You'll see, in no time at all the number will be practically zero. Or very close. The fake news will call me a liar if I say zero and the number of cases only gets down to one or two. They're the worst of the worst. But it's going down beautifully. Almost like magic. Just wait. And the summer will wipe it out. Heat is a beautiful thing with COVID. It will be unbelievable. Unless people take too many tests. We don't like that. And the doctors are calling everything COVID. If you have a paper cut, they call it COVID. If you bruise your knee, they call it COVID. They call everything COVID. So no tests. But you can totally get a test. And there are tests for everyone. But don't take them, and definitely don't take your money out of the stock market. Alright, thank you, everybody. God bless the stock market, and God bless how perfect my COVID response has been."

## Things That President Donald Trump Has Said About His Predecessors:

"President Obama lied about his weight on his presidential physicals! He weighed way more than the low numbers he forced the doctors to write down! I bet that fatty also lied about his height to make his body mass index number lower! Unlike me, who is 100% transparent and honest with ALL of MY medical records!"

"Jimmy Carter was a peanut farmer? How did a marble-mouthed Southern hillbilly like that ever get elected president? He reminds me of Jeff Sessions, who I wake up every morning wanting to strangle for following the law and recusing himself from the Russia investigation!"

"A lot of people don't know this, but FDR was in a wheelchair. So how did he win so many elections? If I were running against him, I would have offered to roll him around for an hour, and then rolled him off a cliff or into a busy street when a bus was coming!"

"No President has ever had a daughter as hot as Ivanka! Have you seen portraits of the daughters of all the presidents before 1920? Talk about fugly! None of them are hotter than 6's, I wouldn't date any of them! Maybe that's why all the early presidents had such serious faces all the time. Their daughters were hideous. If you ask me, the women back then were so ugly they didn't deserve the right to vote. And those giant dresses were no fun at all. Way too elaborate and time-consuming to get in and out of. I'm glad my beauty pageants were in the 1990s and 2000s when clothes were much simpler and skimpier! I'd hate to have a pageant in the 1830s and walk into the locker rooms only to have to wait an hour before seeing any skin!"

"Ha! Bill Clinton and Andrew Johnson got impeached! What losers! They should have just quit life after that! How could they still show their faces in public after getting impeached? Impeached presidents should get hit with rotten tomatoes everywhere they go for being so weak and unpopular. How embarrassing!" [Trump said this before he himself was impeached... twice.]

"A lot of people don't know this, but Thomas Jefferson did the Louisiana Purchase. But he paid way too much! I would have gotten it for so much cheaper. No one does deals better than me! I would have sweet-talked the old French ladies way better than Jefferson, and even Benjamin Franklin! When I apply a little extra facial bronzer, style my hair into the perfect spray-hardened combover helmet, undo a couple shirt buttons to show off my manly, yeti chest hair, and pop in a Tic Tac, I'm irresistible! The trick is to take a broad out furniture shopping. They love it! I would have bought those French dames some nice side tables, and grabbed 'em by the *petite chats*! Then I'd buy the Trumpiana Purchase and crown myself King of Trumpland!"

"John F. Kennedy looked ridiculous with such a fake tan face! People can always tell when someone's facial skin color is way off from normal, so he was a dummy for thinking people wouldn't notice and make fun of him!"

"All of our former general presidents were idiots. I'm so much better at the military than them. I'm actually sorry the doctors wouldn't let me go to Vietnam because of the four college deferments and bone spurs. The doctors all agreed my brain was too big and brilliant to risk in war. They said that I should stay in college to be able to make great real estate deals in the future! They said they couldn't wait to stay several nights at one of the luxurious hotels they knew I'd build with my smarts! They said I had the biggest brain they had ever seen, and it would make too big of a target for the Viet Cong!"

"Nixon was a moron for accepting a pardon, which was like admitting blame for the things he did. I'd never accept a pardon, unless the Deep State prosecutes me for any of my tax evasion, wire fraud, money laundering, obstruction of justice, cyber crimes, campaign finance violations, or treason because that's all fake news! I'd take a pardon for all of that, but I'd still be 100% innocent! Sure, I had four campaign managers in a row get arrested, but that's just bad luck! It's not my fault most of the top people I picked to help me get elected were secretly criminals! Maybe Obama somehow convinced Paul Manafort, Rick Gates, Steve Bannon, Michael Cohen, George Papadopoulos, Mike Flynn, and Roger Stone to convince me to hire them in order to set me up! Their getting arrested says nothing about me!"

"John Quincy Adams, Martin Van Buren, and Dwight Eisenhower were all bald! What lame presidents! I still have the luscious, bright blonde hair of a teenager, and I don't even style it at all. How it looks right now is just how I got out of bed this morning!"

Trump only had something positive to say about one president, Lincoln:

"I respect Abraham Lincoln for the Civil War. Talk about strength! He was lucky he won his elections, though. I'm unlucky because of all the illegal voters who will make me lose reelection before I decide if I should start a civil war. I wish I could know how many fraud voters there will be ahead of time, but I won't know until they're all counted. The exact number of votes I lose to Joe Biden by is the number of illegal voters there are! I wonder if the Democrats freighted in millions of Mexican illegals by steamboat to vote against Lincoln like they're doing with the caravans to vote against me."

## Joel Osteen: "If Jesus Wanted Me To Share My Wealth, He Wouldn't Have Let Me Accumulate $40 Million!"

March 16, 2020
Houston, TX—

Televangelist Joel Osteen is facing criticism for not doing more to help the sick and needy in this COVID quarantine crisis, as critics have taken offense that Osteen is asking for donations through his website, despite the closure of his megachurch and his absurdly high net worth.

Osteen participated in an interview conducted by a local Houston television news program in which he defended his wealth as not inherently unChristian.

"Look, I view my Lakewood Church as my flock, and I look after my flock like a shepherd would his sheep," explained Osteen. "But the flock of sheep also provides the shepherd with very valuable wool that he then sells to support himself, and pay the mortgage of a mansion, and buy a fleet of sports cars. So when I ask for money donations, I am merely asking my sheep for their wool. And maybe their kids' college funds. What's wrong with that? And, besides, my church knows I'm sincere. They come to me for advice on how to be rich like me, and I help them plant their seeds for material success by taking their seeds, which are donations to my church or purchases of my books, and then burying those seeds into my personal bank account to blossom into new sports cars. But they are happy to give! They know I'm 100% authentic, and that I care about them. And though they may be my sheep, they're looking after me too. They don't want me to get coronavirus, and neither do I. Which is why, in this trying time, it is especially imperative that I continue to profit wildly. If this pandemic continues to get worse, I'm going to need to take off in my private jet, and not come back down to land for many weeks or months until the pandemic is over. Do you have any idea how expensive jet fuel is? And how much it costs to refuel in mid-air? And if all my followers die from the coronavirus I'm going to need to spend a lot of money on advertising to find tens of thousands of new dupes to buy my unimaginative, bland books. And, as the Internet accumulates exposé videos of me living a hypocritical life of immoderate luxury, and saying things that suggest I don't understand basic tenets of my own supposed religion, it's getting harder and harder to find new people willing to give me money!"

The interviewer then interrupted Osteen to ask if he remembered Jesus's line about camels and eyes of needles.

"Are you sure that's in the Bible? I'm not familiar with that. Oh, you know what, maybe it's a translation thing. You see, I've actually done my own translation and editing of the Bible. It's kind of like Thomas Jefferson's Bible, in which he edited out all the supernatural and mythological bits he didn't care for. In my Bible, I edited out all the stuff about money changers, the bits against hoarding, and all the animal-based metaphors concerning wealth and greed. Because, you know, if Jesus had been a little greedier and flashier with some conspicuous consumption, he probably would have had way more than just twelve Disciples in his lifetime. Look at me, my net worth is over $40 million, and I have hundreds of thousands of viewers of my sermons in-person and online! So clearly Jesus was a little mistaken about the value of money. Besides, why do people criticize me? Why don't they look at Kenneth Copeland? He's way richer than me! Or Jesse Duplantis? Or Benny Hinn? Or Creflo Dollar? Or Joyce Meyer? Or Pat Robertson? All these people are rich like me, and I'm not going to give up my private jets until they give up theirs! Out of all these people, my mansion is nowhere near the biggest! And if Jesus hadn't wanted all of us to live extravagant lifestyles, he wouldn't have made our followers so gullible! We're literally telling them that by giving us their money they will get more money in the future, and it never happens! And they still continue to give us money! It's incredible. That's God's fault, not mine. He wasn't such an intelligent designer with everyone, was He? So maybe God is okay with excessive televangelist wealth because otherwise He wouldn't allow us to continue doing it, right? Let's be honest, a lot of us televangelists have committed a healthy amount of tax fraud, and one God-inspired IRS audit could wreck us. But our followers still give us money for third private jets even when we already have two because we convince them Jesus will pay it forward. Isn't the prosperity gospel awesome? It's like they don't understand the basic concepts of addition and subtraction in their wallets. But where in the Bible does it specifically say not to take advantage of simple-minded people and make their lives worse by tricking them out of meaningful percentages of their paychecks? Seriously, where? I probably cut those passages out of mine."

The interviewer then asked if Osteen would donate anything to help his followers who are struggling from losing their jobs due to the economic shutdown.

"I'm not going to start being poorer just because everyone in my church is getting poorer! They should have made better money decisions, like not buying all my books! All I did was rearrange the sentences! So it's not my fault they buy every one of them. No refunds! And I recently spent all the book proceeds on a large collection of Japanese sex robots, so the money is all gone anyway. I'm a good Christian who would never cheat on my wife, but I still want some new thrills and variety in my romantic life, you know? And it's not cheating if your other woman is an inanimate, life-like pleasure doll, or ten of them from Japan! I programmed them all to call me Johann Tetzel!"

# More Religion Headlines

- Donald Trump Is Reportedly Confused Why Evangelicals Keep Telling Him To Support Israel So Jesus Can Come Back And Send All The Jews To Hell

- Jesus Christ Says He Burned His Republican Party Membership Card

- Jesus Is Embarrassed To Mention His Mere Day-Long Crucifixion Around Prometheus and Sisyphus

- Jesus Christ Return, Demands To Know Who Decided "Christians" Didn't Have To Be Jewish

- Jesus Came Back, Asked Why People Aren't Acting On The Free Pass To Sin He Gave Us

- Jesus: "What The F*** Is Christmas? I Wasn't Born On December 25th!"

- Joel Osteen Was Just Struck By Lightning For The 9th Time, Still Won't Stop Taking Poor People's Money

- Kenneth Copeland Says Jesus Told Him In A Heavenly Vision That God Thinks He Deserves A 4th Private Jet

- Jerry Falwell Jr. Says The Bible "Never Said Anything About Coveting Pool Boys And Giving Them Sweetheart Business Deals To Stay Quiet About You Watching Them Make Hot Love To Your Wife!"

- Evangelicals Admit That If The Immigrant Children Locked In Cages Were Still Fetuses They Would Probably Care Much More

- A Local Christian Group Gave Up On Praying To End Gun Deaths & Abortion, Admitted God "Is Just A Dick"

- Local Christian Woman's Claim Of What God Wants Is Suspiciously Close To What She Wants

- The Pope Revealed On Twitter He Felt A "Burning Sensation" When He Shook Donald Trump's Hand

- New Poll: 83% of Christians Wish Christianity Was As Cool As Ancient Nordic, Egyptian, Greek, And Roman Religions Were

- God Just Announced Conservative Evangelicals Have Failed Existentially, Proclaimed Liberal Atheists As His New Chosen People

- God Wants Conservatives To Know They Just Have To Pray A Little Harder And He'll Stop Shooting Up Schools

- God Admits He Really Does Get Quite A Kick Out Of Working In Incomprehensible, Mysterious Ways

- Alarmed By Evangelical Support Of Donald Trump, God Prepares A New New Testament

- God Is Reportedly Astounded How Trump Supporters Can Fail Every Single Test Of Moral Character He Gives Them

- With Coronavirus Raging Uncontrollably, God Sheepishly Admits To Praying Christians That He's Not Actually Omnipotent

- Donald Trump: "If I Was Jesus I'd Have Multiplied Gold Coins, Not Dumb Loaves Of Bread!"

- Local Evangelicals Wonder If Trump Getting Impeached Is Actually Part Of God's Master Plan, Agree God Must Have Gotten Confused

- Evangelicals Are Confident God Will Stop COVID-19 Just Like He Stopped All Mass Murders And Children's Cancer

- Evangelicals Admit They're Very Envious Of Trump's Lifestyle Of Marital Infidelity, Greed, And Being A Creepy Gross Man Around Teen Girls

- The Bible Passage Where An Old Man Makes Bears Maul Children (2 Kings 2:23-25) Voted The Bible's Best Story

- Local Christian Admits He Has Never Read The Bible, Just Really Likes Judging People

- Local Pastor Is Furious To Find Out Jesus Was A "Libtard," And All His Years Of Worship Were Wasted

- GOP Christians Don't Understand Why God Would Do A Global Pandemic When The President Is White

- Christian MAGA Fans Demand To Know Who God Thinks He Is Letting Biden Win

# A Televangelist Is Blaming COVID-19 On Captain America's Bulge In The Marvel Movies

March 17, 2020
St. Louis, MO—

Televangelist Phil Worthing of the *Straight White Christian Alliance Network* generated controversy with a Twitter thread this morning blaming the spread of the coronavirus in America on the *Avengers* superhero movies from *Marvel*, specifically Captain America:

"God is so furious right now, and it's because the Gay Agenda has rammed a fully erect heresy from Satan straight down every good Christian's throat until we gag! I'm talking, of course, about the giant bulge Captain America had in his spandex suit in all the *Marvel* movies!"

"No one wants to see Chris Evans's bulge, nor his tight butt, nor his massive pecs, nor his rock hard biceps! We're not homosexuals! In fact, I'm starting to think Chris Evans may be Satan himself! When I see his scenes in those movies, I find myself getting mysteriously aroused, and I'm as straight as can be! I suspect some kind of dark, evil magic has corrupted those films!"

"On a related note, Black Widow's suit is way too tight as well. It's revolting to see her flaunt her feminine curves like that. Is she trying to tempt good Christian women to start showing their shoulders, knees, and ankles in public? And why is she fighting crime with the other Avengers? Doesn't she have a husband or children she should be looking after? Or costume-sewing to do for the Avenger men?"

"But whatever you do, don't Google images of Chris Evans or Captain America! Satan has put tons of them online where you can see his tight, squeezable booty, and I only know because I've done some covert spying on the Devil's handiwork in the past in order to better understand his tactics!"

"Christians should immediately boycott the *Marvel* movies because watching them will lead viewers to sin, debauchery, and abominations! I caught myself just this morning Googling 'Chris Evans shirtless,' but thank God I was able to pray and stop myself just in time before Satan tricked me into doing a gay voyeurism!"

"And since this coronavirus has shut down public gatherings across America including my megachurch, I've been alarmed to find myself idling and taking naps during the day, and having dreams about cuddling Chris Evans! My fellow Christians: you must boycott Chris Evans to save your souls!"

# A New Poll Proves That 100% Of People Saying "Don't Blame Trump" Would Have Blamed Obama

March 22, 2020
St. Louis, MO—

A new poll conducted in association with several St. Louis-based universities has confirmed that supporters of President Donald Trump's coronavirus efforts would not support President Barack Obama's efforts if he were president now, even if their actions were the exact same.

*The Halfway Post* reached out to several of the poll's participants.

"Well, for starters, Obama hated America," said Pierra Donnellson, 29. "So anything he'd do would be for the downfall of America in order to weaken our country enough for ISIS to sneak in and take dictatorial control. Unlike Trump, who loves America. In fact, I bet Trump waited so long to do anything about coronavirus because the first people to get it here in America were all undercover Muslim terrorists, pedophiles, and MS-13 thugs. It's no surprise the first states to shut down were coastal, elitist blue states!"

Another Obama critic had a more interesting opinion.

"I know all about Ronald Trump," explained Jefferson Weavil, 34, "and the fact is that Ronald has never failed at anything he's ever done. He's a business genius, so I have 100% faith in him. He's had so many companies over the years, and never had to go bankrupt once for any of them! He's smarter than me even, and I had the best home-schooling anyone could have up until I dropped out in the fourth grade to help raise the livestock at my Weavil family farm. The goats get rowdy, and they're a full-time job. You have to break them in the hard way by laying with them like you would a woman. Now, I know what the Bible says, but the Bible ain't ever seen stubborn goats like my family has. I'd like to see Jesus try to break them in without any genital stimulation, and, until Jesus does, I'm going to keep doing it the way my pa, and his pa, and his pa been doing it for generations! So I'm not worried about coronavirus. If my goats don't have it, I don't have it because I never leave the farm. If Obama was still President, though, I'm sure I'd be long dead from the COVID. I hate Obama. I'll admit it, I'm racist! I wanted to join the KKK, but they said I was too racist. Can you believe that? Is there such a thing as being too factually accurate about blanket statements on a whole race of people? So they kicked me out when I made an extra hole in my Klan sheets for my pecker, and they got all concerned I was gonna seduce them. They wouldn't listen that it was for the goats! I bet Ronald understands me, though. I even made peepholes in the goat barn to be snoopy like him!"

# The Halfway Post's Top 30 Insults For Donald J. Trump

1.  Donald Trump's tough guy branding is dangerously dependent on his hair not getting wet in the rain. He skips out on WWII memorials and holding umbrellas over his wife's head to protect his nasty, fake hair combed over badly from getting moist.

2.  Donald Trump's depraved, unquenchable thirst for gauche iconification has made him the savior for an electorally declining conservative movement absorbed in an insular zeitgeist of xenophobia and ends-justify-the-means political villainy. Or, in a simpler term, fascist.

3.  Trump calls everything "the best," "the worst," and "tremendous" because he doesn't have the cognizance to describe nuance or complexity. People who can't explain things don't understand them. His basic, superlative vocabulary betrays a bad case of toddler brain. He quite literally speaks at an elementary school level.

4.  Trump's unprecedented deal making, "easily-winnable" trade wars, and ability to keep us exhausted from all his winning did not live up to the hype of his Dunning-Kruger confidence. His 2016 campaign was a spectacular Hindenburg of lies and broken promises.

5.  Donald Trump is the laziest president since Warren Harding, and at least Harding had the decency to admit he was in over his head and should not have ever been elected president. Trump has no such self-awareness.

6.  Donald Trump's Twitter was more bitchy than a teenage girl's burn book, and he got banned for being a societal danger and national security threat.

7.  The Trump family's sociopathic sense of self-importance via inherited wealth from Trump's dad and grandpa is reminiscent of why the Western world decapitated absolutist monarchs and abolished aristocracies.

8.  Donald Trump's foreign policy as president only made sense when you remember he's always in desperate need of current and future liquid cash to pay off the ludicrous loans he can't help himself from taking out from foreign banks and oligarchs because American banks have all been burned by his comically bad business sense and preposterous dishonesty. Also, his daughter and son-in-law got $2 billion from Saudi Arabia, and his golf courses are being selected for the Saudi LIV golf tour. We're just waiting on the announcement of a Trump Tower Riyadh.

9.  Donald Trump's lawyers always meet with him in pairs to counteract his lies, impulsive decisions, and circumstantial memory deficiencies.

Maybe this is why all his lawyers inevitably quit or have to get their own lawyers.

10. Donald Trump is not man enough to personally participate in firing his own underlings like Jeff Sessions, James Comey and Rex Tillerson, despite "You're fired!" literally being his former television catchphrase. But, to be fair, Trump wasn't actually the successful billionaire CEO of a successful company he pretended to be on the show.

11. Remember when Donald Trump said repeatedly he had all the best people? ...Lol. Many of those "best people" from his presidential administration, from John Bolton to John Kelly, freely admit he's a moron who has no mental capability of putting America's national interests ahead of his own personal interests.

12. Donald Trump has no idea how stupid he truly is. Malignant narcissists have that issue. He didn't even have the intellectual curiosity to read his presidential briefings after they went from daily to semi-weekly with only a couple paragraphs with his name in all of them to hold his attention for longer than ten seconds.

13. Donald Trump did not have to run for president, but because he's an egomaniac he did, and fucked up everything he touched from infrastructure weeks, to repealing Obamacare, to making deals with North Korea and China, to handling a pandemic, to running for reelection. Talk about branding failure. He could have been creeping out pornstars and paying them to sign NDAs for the rest of his miserably unloved life, but instead he felt compelled to become America's worst modern president.

14. One of the few statistics Donald Trump is first in presidential history is the number of former staffers who have said he's an idiot.

15. Donald Trump's main business accomplishment in life was to get so far into debt that his creditors had to give him an allowance in order to pretend to still be rich so they could profit off the Trump-branded properties for which he wildly overpaid and lost ownership of. Then no American banks would give him any more loans so he had to get most of his funding from Russians, as confirmed by his kids, which he lied about because the Trump family are all habitual liars about everything.

16. Donald Trump ran the government like he ran his businesses... which is why everyone in his administration leaked to the press, back-stabbed each other bad-mouthing everyone else, and wrote embarrassing tell-all memoirs when they left.

17. Trump lost by 3 million votes in 2016. Every time someone says "The American people elected Donald Trump" remember that that is not actually factually accurate. Then he lost his reelection by more than double that amount of votes. He's a consecutive election loser. He

also lost Republicans the House and Senate during his administration.

18. Donald Trump is a punching-down, sucking-up bully who acts like a little bitch when in the room with real dictators.

19. Donald Trump is so bad at deal-making that Wharton should take back his business degree.

20. Donald Trump has no depth, nuance, or complexity. He doesn't make jokes, he doesn't laugh except at the expense of others, and he speaks as if he has never opened a thesaurus. If he wasn't racist and never accused Obama of being a Kenyan citizen, he'd have no political career, and he's a baby every day about how unfair his life is when people notice that he cheats in every aspect of his life, whether it's paying contractors, being faithful to his wives, golf, or foreign election assistance.

21. Believing Donald Trump is an "alpha male" would be so much easier if he wasn't a whiny crybaby about everything, but particularly about reasonable questions from female journalists.

22. Donald Trump's critics called him too stupid, impulsive, and unprepared to make a deal with Kim Jong-un to end North Korea's nuclear program, and they were right. He now ignores the failure, and claims he and Kim are lovers… which is just too weird to guess why he'd say that.

23. The military parade Trump tried to have on July 4th was a colossal failure and perfect Donald Trump Production™: an impulsively decided, unprofessionally planned, amateurishly implemented, needlessly expensive, social-norm destroying, narcissistic effort to hijack something meant for others and make it about himself.

24. There is no word in English to describe adequately what a disgrace and joke Donald Trump's petty existence is. His hair comes closest as a sort of symbolic expression of his lunatic id.

25. If you don't count all the hush money payments to porn stars and sexual assault victims, the forced nondisclosure agreements throughout his decades in business and years as president, the ceaseless lies about even trivial and unimportant details, the omnipresent black holes of litigation to avoid consequences for his rampant fraud and insurrectioning, and all the other shady stuff his lawyers including Michael Cohen and Rudy Giuliani did for him, then, yeah… Donald Trump has barely done any cover-ups at all.

26. Donald Trump spills out word vomit so disjointed and mentally nonlinear that it's borderline impossible for editors to transcribe and punctuate in reproduction for their readers to try to interpret for themselves. It's an unmistakable sign of witlessness.

27. Trump's constant, compulsive need for personal validation betrays a crippling, omnipresent fear of personal inadequacy that is

unbecoming of a man, let alone the Office of the Presidency of the United States of America.

28. His first three kids all turned out very weird, especially the one he named after himself.

29. Someday even snorting amphetamines won't be enough to pump blood through Donald Trump's arteries clogged with decades of big mac sauce to get that rich, sweet oxygen to his brain.

30. I look forward to watching the biopic movies coming out in a few years mocking Donald Trump's spectacular business failures, cartoonish character traits, and village idiot presidency.

## Things Donald Trump Has Put Ketchup On

The following are all things on which President Donald Trump has indulged his noted passion for ketchup:

- Well-done steak
- Caesar salads
- Sunburned skin to revitalize and nourish the damaged cells
- In his nostrils to pretend he had a bloody nose to get out of gym class in middle school and high school because the pull-up bar, sit-and-reach box, and running track were all "rigged against him"
- Jared Kushner, in an elaborate and very confusing ceremony to welcome him into the Trump family
- His bald head to stimulate hair growth
- Russian hookers
- Any *New York Times* page that showed polls suggesting Biden will beat him
- He reinstalled the Taft Tub, and, once a month, requests White House staffers to fill his bathtub with 200 bottles of ketchup to take a bath in.
- The White House lawyers who took his cell phone away on January 6th so he couldn't tweet out "I demand the hanging of Mike Pence! #MAGA"
- Eric and Don Jr. on a weekly basis to show them very graphically he wishes he had aborted them
- His virginity: his first sexual partner was a bottle of ketchup in 1958. His dad caught him doing it once, and Donald shouted, "It's not what it looks like, though it is what it tastes like!"
- He has asked all his wives to wear a ketchup bikini, but none would
- The official White House portrait of Barack Obama
- In his nostrils to pretend he had a bloody nose to get out of reading presidential daily briefings

## Trump Asked Pharma Companies To Name The Coming COVID Vaccine "Trumpicil"

April 21, 2020
Washington D.C.—

According to White House insiders, President Donald Trump asked pharmaceutical company executives during a Coronavirus-themed roundtable discussion to name any COVID-19 vaccines or drugs after him.

A White House staffer requesting anonymity gave *The Halfway Post* an audio recording of Trump's request during the discussion:

"So, when we finally get a vaccine, I have some ideas I was thinking about for the name," Trump can be heard saying at the beginning of the recording. "I was maybe thinking of something like 'Trumpvax,' or 'Trumpex,' or 'Trumpicil,' or something fun and medical sounding like that. Or maybe 'Trumpazone,' with a slogan like 'Get in the zone with Trumpazone.' And what about the color for the medicine? I really like orange. I don't know why… Or maybe if it comes in pill form the pills can be gold. Who wouldn't want to take a Trump pill that's bright gold? Your stomach and immune system want a little bit of style and luxury too, you know? And I definitely want my name printed on every pill or syringe. Front and back. I want people to thank me for the COVID cure, and think of me when they get it. My poll numbers could definitely use the boost. And if the vaccines or pills are sold at Walgreens, Walmart, and places like that, I want them to be on the top shelf. It's gotta be top shelf. I definitely want it higher than the vaccines and medicine for measles, and the flu, and other low-energy viruses like those. And I want the ebola vaccine on the bottom shelf. It's gotta be the very bottom. Obama did that vaccine, so how great can it be? Did his Ebola vaccine actually start the COVID crisis? People are talking… So, yeah, very bottom shelf. Trumpicil on top. Can we make that happen? And I want the packaging for my vaccine to be black with very bold, very gold lettering saying 'Trumpicil,' or whatever name we end up with. Very big, and nothing else on the front. The disclaimers and directions or whatever can all be crammed on the back or the side in a real small font size. The front just needs to say 'Trumpicil' with 'Trump' in gold, and maybe the 'icil' part in white or a different color so that 'Trump' really stands out, you know? It has to have a real 'Wow' factor on the shelf to catch people's eyes so everyone buys it. And I should get a cut of the profit for every box of Trumpicil that gets bought since the government will be licensing my name for it. What do you think is fair, a 50-50 split? I'm good with that. I have to say, gentlemen, that I'm really surprising myself with how good I am at vaccines! Maybe I should have gone into medicine instead of real estate!"

# "Blacks 4 Trump" Group Says Having No Black Members "Isn't That Relevant"

May 1, 2020
Omaha, NE—

A local "Blacks 4 Trump" group is now only made up of white members, after an unfortunate, racially-motivated misunderstanding caused their single Black member to quit.

"It's a little ironic due to our name, I'll give the libtards that, but we're very saddened to see Darren go," explained the group's founder Thomas "Bubba" Wilkes. "It was all just a big mistake. One of our newer group members, who hadn't met Darren yet, called the cops on him while he was smoking a cigarette outside before our meeting started. This group member thought Darren looked sketchy, and was afraid Darren might try to rob us or something. Unfortunately, the cops arrested Darren for trespassing, despite doing nothing illegal, and he had to spend a few hours in jail before we could get the whole thing straightened out. Like I said, just a big misunderstanding. And the worst part is that it makes it seem like the libs are telling the truth when they say Obama's presidency didn't end all racism in America. It was just our luck to have the only police officer in America who racially profiles Black men answer the call to come investigate Darren smoking his cigarette."

Now "Blacks 4 Trump" has 49 exclusively white members, but they are adamant they won't change the group's name despite their shrinking roster.

"I don't think it's that relevant we don't actually have any Black members anymore," said Wilkes. "The idea is still the same. We're confident Trump's support in the Black community is very, very high, much higher than all the polls in the fake news suggest. Just because we can't find much proof yet ourselves doesn't mean we're going to stop trying. And we've had some promising signs. Yesterday we had a big open house event where we advertised free food, and a couple nice Black ladies actually stopped by. They said they were business owners, and were receptive to the idea of considering Trump's economic platform and proposed tax cuts. But, unfortunately, someone from our group called the cops on them, too, which made it pretty much impossible to convince them to commit to the club. But I'm sure we'll make some inroads in the Black community soon. We're learning from each of our mistakes. I'll make sure all our white members hand in their cell phones at the door for our next event so we can avoid further accidental 911 calls. Most of our members live in the rural parts of town, and it's just muscle memory for them to dial the police when they see a Black person. Repetitive, procedural motor memories can be difficult to reverse, you know?"

## Police Are Relieved Quarantine Protesters With Big Guns Don't Also Have Black Skin

May 3, 2020
Lansing, MI—

Local Lansing police officers have been busy monitoring the situation outside the Michigan state capitol building as protesters demonstrate their Second Amendment rights in response to the state-wide COVID quarantine order signed by Governor Gretchen Whitmer.

Dozens of quarantine protesters arrive every morning and parade with semi-automatic assault rifles, sniper rifles, and bulletproof vests. The police, however, say they are not threatened by such displays of potential violent carnage, and are just relieved none of the protesters waving their military-grade rifles in the air also have black skin.

"I'm very impressed with these protesters' sense of responsibility," said local Police Sergeant Paul Weims. "They've collectively brought all kinds of high-velocity weapons with probably thousands of ammo clips between them, and I even saw a few grenades, but they've left the real dangerous stuff at home. I commend these protesters' choices to not bring their Black friends, or any Black or mixed kids or step-kids they may have. If they were going to be so reckless as to bring some Black teens, things might get very dangerous around here. There's enough firepower and ammunition in the area to declare war against the entire city, so if someone had brought a Black teenager with a bag of skittles on top of all that, or an overweight Black fella selling loose cigarettes… well, I don't even want to think about that powder keg detonating!"

Other police officers echoed that sentiment.

"Sure, these protesters have all kinds of guns, but they're 100% visible," explained Officer Daniel Loopal. "These protesters are waving their rifles around, aiming them at police officers' faces, screaming and spitting on them, and threatening to kill all kinds of conspiratorial villains from space lizards disguised as their state government representatives to Governor Whitmer, who they call all kinds of horrible, sexist words. But the point is, when these protesters are walking around armed to their teeth, we know what we're dealing with. They're very transparent about their weapons. But thank God there's no Black pre-teen walking around the state capitol with an oversized hoodie on and his hands in his pockets. That'd be a huge danger to officer safety. We'd have no choice but to engage violently because we'd have no idea what could be concealed in his hands or pockets. What if he had a gun?"

# Donald Trump's MIT Uncle Thinks He's An Idiot

May 11, 2020
Cambridge, MA—

President Trump regularly speaks of his uncle who worked at MIT, and references his uncle's intelligence as an indication of his own brain power, so *The Halfway Post* reached out to Uncle John G. Trump to get his thoughts on his nephew. The following is a transcript of our conversation:

**THP: "What do you think about your nephew Donald Trump?"**
JT: "He was an even dumber President than I thought he'd be, and that's saying something because I was sure my nephew would be absolutely terrible, inept, incompetent, and emotionally unfit for the job. I've known him his whole life, and, unfortunately, all those paint chips he used to eat as a kid clearly had negative effects on his brain development. His parents were always catching him licking the walls, and eating the flakes he could pick off when they weren't looking. Every time I'd come over to visit they'd be yelling at him for it. And, don't forget, in those days the paint was loaded up with lead. You're not supposed to have lead in your system when you're growing up, and Donald J. Trump is a perfect case study of why."
**THP: "The President points to you for why he's smart."**
JT: "Donnie is such a moron. I'm not his father, so it's not like he directly inherited all my genes. Me and his dad were quite a bit different, you know? I spent my life studying medical applications of high voltage machinery to clean up city wastewater and doing cancer research, whereas Fred became a slumlord. Maybe my brains were a family fluke. And, of course, Donnie's mother had a whole different set of genes that she passed on to him. And no one can know what all that lead did to his DNA methylation."
**THP: "Do you feel Donald has sullied your family's name?"**
JT: "Absolutely. He's not even a good business man. My brother left him $400 million. Donnie is always saying how his dad gave him a small loan of $1 million, as if that was a small loan everyone gets from their parents anyway, but it's a total lie. And he lost it all wildly overpaying for those massively stupid Potemkin casinos because he's an idiot who shouldn't be running a neighborhood lemonade stand, let alone a sprawling real estate empire. I mean it! I can't stress this enough for your readers that my nephew's neurons are probably jam-packed with lead particles blocking all his axons from efficiently transmitting electrical signals. That's why the guy is the poster boy of Dunning-Kruger idiocy, and he is incapable of empathy, and he always has been. I saw his childhood bedroom when he was growing up. It had teeth marks up and down the walls, on all the wood moldings and door frames, and all the furniture. It may have looked like the gnawings of a rat, but it wasn't no rats! It was Donald J. Trump!"

# Nowhere In The Constitution Does It Say We Can't Turn RBG Into An Immortal Cyborg

May 12, 2020
Washington D.C.—

This is just a reminder that the Constitution is very vague on turning old, frail, liberal-leaning Supreme Court justices into cyborgs by replacing their failing organs with indestructible robotic machinery so they become physiologically immortal.

Ruth Bader Ginsburg has again visited the hospital due to a gall bladder-related health issue, and there is no doubt in anyone's mind that, if she would retire suddenly due to health reasons, Senate Majority Leader Mitch McConnell would ram a Trump-appointed replacement through a Senate confirmation if there were but ten seconds left in Trump's presidency, despite his preposterous rationale to block Barack Obama's last Supreme Court appointment, Merrick Garland, in the last year of his presidency.

So why not give Ms. Ginsburg a new gall bladder made of titanium that will never fail, and is even bulletproof? In fact, let's replace all her organs with complex robotics that will keep her on the Court deep into at least the 23rd Century.

The Constitution only stipulates that Supreme Court justices have lifetime appointments, but has no regulations on how long those lifespans can be artificially and technologically extended. With no limit on Ginsburg's potential judicial service, why not upload her national treasure legal mind into a weapons-grade cyborg soldier capable of defending the rule of law militarily as well as intellectually?

She could have a missile launcher attached behind each shoulder blade, a flamethrower arm, a twin turbine jetpack for flying, retractible knife blades for fingernails, dual machine gun muzzled eyeballs, and we could even design a hydraulic exoskeleton cooling vent system featuring her elegant and iconic fashion flair for lace jabots. With supreme firepower Justice Ginsburg would take the "extra" out of "extrajudicial punishment."

We have to start somewhere with the fusion of humanity and technology, why not start with the Notorious RBG, and ensure liberals don't lose another Supreme Court seat when America has popularly voted for Democratic court nominations in every election since 1992 except only 2004?

# Trump Offers To Sacrifice His Son Eric To Open Up The Economy

May 15, 2020
Washington D.C.—

President Donald Trump today offered up his son Eric as a sacrifice to the coronavirus in order to get the economy bustling again.

Trump made the following remarks during a press conference:

"We need to open up the economy, okay? It's time. We can't wait any longer. We need to open up. It's totally safe. The only reason the number of COVID cases and deaths in America is so high is because Democrats demanded all this dumb testing. If we never did a single test, we wouldn't have any cases of the coronavirus. Zero. We'd be so healthy! It's simple. But we need to open up. Some people are going to get sick and die, but that's life. Look, no one is more pro-life than me, okay? Nobody. I'm the most pro-life president, maybe of all time. Maybe Washington was more pro-life. Who knows? But it's time, okay? Grandma and grandpa lived nice, long, beautiful lives, but we need the economy back open. Grandma and grandpa want big, tremendous stock market profits. They want America to be great. And I'm willing to sacrifice as well. I offer up Eric. Eric will take one for the team, and get COVID so we can open up the economy. Eric is a great son, and I hate to see him go, but we need to open up. Stocks need to go back up, okay? And they can't go up if people are hiding in their homes, and taking their money out of stocks. So we're going to open up. There will be some deaths, but I think everyone who dies will be happy they're dying as a hero for the economy. And I'm also going to be effected. Eric is a great son. But it's what he would want for the stock market to rally. A lot of people don't know this, but I'm really going to miss Eric—hahahahahaahaha! Sorry, I couldn't say that with a straight face. Ivanka, now she would be a sacrifice I'm unwilling to make for stock gains. If she got COVID, I'd shut everything down, and arrest everyone who broke the quarantine. Everyone would get $1,000 a week to stay home and not risk getting a single extra COVID droplet anywhere near my sweet angel during her recovery. I'd test everyone hourly, and trace their every footstep to make sure they don't come within a mile of Ivanka. Things don't have to slow down so much for Eric. We'll keep chugging along…. I'd miss him— that's hilarious. Why do people say I'm not funny? But I'll tell you what, Eric will watch over everyone's grandparents up in Heaven, okay? He'll make sure they have a great time. They'll wish they would have died from COVID way sooner. I promise. So, everyone, call up grandma and grandpa, say goodbye, and thank them for saving the economy. And stocks are going to come roaring back like never before, I guarantee it!"

# A Newly Discovered STD That Turns Penises Orange Was Named After Donald Trump

May 19, 2020
St. Louis, MO—

A recent discovery of a new sexually transmitted disease has just given President Donald Trump his life's latest honor.

The disease, scientifically classified as *Trumporrhea trachomatis*, is a mushroom-shaped bacterium that infects primarily male urethras, and turns the surrounding skin surface area orange in a manner that its medical discoverers thought bore a striking resemblance to Trump's orange foundation makeup.

"The orange kind of flares out from the urethra's opening, but in circumcised men it rarely extends to the edge of the penile head," explained Dr. Harold Weinerman, who thought up the name for the new disease, and said his surname did indeed inspire his chosen field of medical study. "The orange discoloring is a trademark indicator of Trumporrhea's infection, and it almost perfectly imitates the President's classic, minstrel-esque makeup look where he paints himself real orange but doesn't quite blend it all the way into his hairline or jaw so there's always a distinctive border where his neck is just a completely different color from his face. I myself thought it also amusingly familiar that another common symptom of Trumporrhea is a burning sensation while urinating just like America's democracy gets a burning sensation every time Trump opens his mouth to whine about how mean and unfair everyone in the world is to him."

Dr. Weinerman said he wanted to assure everyone that Trumporrhea is not a disease to worry much about, as it is easily treated with antibiotics.

"Trumporrhea's cell walls are so quickly burst through by penicillin during treatment that I like to think Trumporrhea bacteriums yell out just before dying that biology is 'rigged against it.' And it probably hates me for accurately diagnosing it as an STD, so it probably calls any diagnosis of it a 'hoax,' and yells out in its little microscopic voice that I and the rest of my medical team are 'enemies of the people.' And when we diagnose patients with Trumporrhea, it probably holds a little STD press conference saying, 'Chlamydia, if you're listening, hack Dr. Weinerman's emails!' And it tells infected patients' most gullible, nearby penile skin cells that its orange inflammation is going to 'Make the Penis Great Again.' I've thought of like a hundred of these, and could keep going all day. Nothing has given me more pleasure and satisfaction in my career than naming an STD after Trump, who is, without a doubt, the most STD-like president we've ever had."

# Trump's Physician Reportedly Has To Hide His Blood Pressure Pills In Hotdogs

May 20, 2020
Washington D.C.—

According to several White House staffers, President Donald Trump does not like taking medicine to keep his high blood pressure under control. As a result, White House Chief Physician Mark Loredo must hide the pills by stuffing them into the hotdogs Mr. Trump requests for lunch while golfing.

"The President really likes the hotdogs that are served at his golf courses," explained a Trump staffer requesting anonymity to describe the President's healthcare regimen, "and he always makes a big, loud stink about taking his medicine, so Dr. Loredo eventually figured out Trump doesn't notice the pills if they're inserted into hotdogs cooked well-done and smothered with ketchup. Trump's alarmingly high blood pressure is essentially a matter of national security for continuity of governance, so the lengths we have to go to in order to trick him into taking these pills is totally called for."

Another staffer confirmed these details with *The Halfway Post*.

"It was a pretty big learning curve for us at first to figure out how to get Trump to take these pills," confirmed the second staffer. "We had to use a lot of trial and error. Initially, we tried stuffing the pills into his ice cream, but he'd melt the ice cream in his mouth, spit out the pill, and start fussing for a new bowl of ice cream that hadn't been 'tainted.' Then we tried sneaking the pills in his Big Macs, burrito bowls and fried chicken, but he always found them. We even tried dissolving the pills in his Diet Coke cans, but he could always tell that the flavor of the Diet Coke was off. He'd knock the can off his desk and start screaming for Jared to bring him a new one. We'd pretend the Diet Coke was normal, but then he'd remind everyone he has been drinking twelve cans of it every day for 35 years, and that he can tell when something is amiss. Finally, we found that hotdogs worked. His golf resort buys regular-sized hotdogs, but they cut each individual one in half like Trump likes, and we think he's just so pleased with how big his hands look holding the mini hotdogs that he doesn't notice the pills. When a platter of them are brought out, he squeals with delight and claps his hands, and can't wait to grab one and start talking with very animated gestures as he makes remarks about how delicious the 'totally normal-sized' hotdogs are. His golf buddies treat it like an emperor's-new-clothes type of thing, and they take turns remarking at how big the hotdogs are, and how they're so full after just one. It's really odd, but if anyone doesn't go along with it Trump gets very upset and suggests Steve Mnuchin ought to investigate their tax records."

## Local Police Officer Really Regrets The Advent Of Cameras On Smart Phones That Everyone Has

June 1, 2020
Splinterville, MN—

*The Halfway Post* reached out to the Splinterville police department today, and asked for their opinion on the murder of George Floyd and the subsequent race riots that followed it.

One police officer was rather introspective.

"Policing has really changed over my career," explained Ralph Strippy, a 30-year veteran. "When I started, back in the early 90s, our rules were very relaxed. People didn't have cameras on them all the time like they have now, so you could put your foot over the line of sadistic brutality a bit and get away with it. You could be out at night on a rural highway, find a car of a couple Black kids, and, uh, no one would ever find out what you did, you know what I'm saying? Nowadays, both those kids would be live-streaming the whole interaction onto Facebook from before you even walked up. And when the camera is on, you actually gotta go by the book. The police lawyers can't help you out with he-said-she-said defenses if there's publicly broadcast evidence. So if they're taping, and you still have to do a brutality or two, you have to do it fast. And the less talking the better, because if you get sued it looks bad when the jury can see you were the one running your mouth and escalating things. Yep, things have changed quite a bit over the years. Assaulting an officer and resisting arrest used to be magical citations like a one-size-fits-all free pass to arrest anyone. You could brush someone with your shoulder and use that as a pretext to get to do whatever you wanted to a guy or gal being temporarily detained for whatever reason you made up afterwards. We used to have some real creative writers on the force who could come up with the perfect retroactive excuses or conduct rationales for your reports if you got carried away and maybe trampled on a few civil rights. But the body cameras we wear now rat us out. And there's more paperwork than ever because you have to be accurate. It obviously looks pretty bad if your report doesn't resemble anything like what got taped. But, all in all, I'd have to say cops are substantially less violent and wild than they used to be because of the increased accountability. I suppose that's a good thing. You should have seen some of the crazy stuff I saw back when I started 30 years ago. You think the brutality in 2020 is bad, yowza! Back then you could practically get away with it all. I actually feel a little guilty for these young cops today. They think they're above the law now, but they'll never know how unsupervised policing used to be before everyone could film you at a moment's notice. Yep, I'm sad to say it, but the golden age of policing is long gone."

# Steve Bannon Is Selling A Face Cream Made Of White People's Semen

June 6, 2020
New York City, NY—

Godfather to America's Alt-Right Steve Bannon has officially registered his latest invention with the US Patents Office: a facial moisturizing cream in which the main active ingredient is white people's sperm.

Mr. Bannon is selling the moisturizer he calls "Patriot Cream" on his website for $19.99 a jar.

The venture is a partnership with neo-Nazi Richard Spencer, whose own foray into the white semen industry began with an Alaskan White Sperm Doomsday Vault project that collected and is currently preserving 10,000 mason jars of white sperm in the event that white people ever become an "endangered race." Spencer sells Bannon surplus sperm donations.

"I'm very excited for this cream product," explained Bannon in a phone conversation with *The Halfway Post*. "I use it every day, and it has really cleared up my splotchy face. Who knew white DNA had other benefits beyond making pure, Aryan babies. And this is just the first product, but I have so many other ideas. I thought up a white sperm-based toothpaste I'm thinking about calling 'Mein Cumpf Paste,' and a white sperm derived mouthwash called 'Kristallnacht Fresh,' and a white sperm botanical-infused shampoo I was thinking about calling 'Ges-STOP-o Dandruff.' I've been truly delighted with all the cosmetic and pun possibilities!"

Bannon's semen business marks a dramatic reversal from his previous political efforts canvassing across Europe to gin up support for various ethno-nationalist movements in conservative, Eastern European countries.

"I got a little burned out on all that," said Bannon. "It's just such an uphill battle to convince people that destitute Muslim refugees are somehow going to plot the overthrow of governments, and put all the Christian whites into slavery. I realized I was being too divisive, and I decided I wanted to shift my focus. Instead of focusing on so much negativity, I found I could have a bigger impact, and make more money, focusing on some of the more positive aspects of white pride. I thought to myself, what Klansman, neo-Nazi, or involuntary celibate doesn't want smoother, clearer skin? And what better way to get that clearer skin than by liberally applying God's purest substance on Earth all over their faces? White sperm is a miracle remedy for acne and dozens of other common ailments we've only cracked the surface on!"

## Several Televangelists Hope Jesus Is Fake Because Otherwise He'd Be Furious At Their Bank Accounts

June 24, 2020
Dallas, TX—

A convention of Evangelical televangelists got together this weekend in Dallas, Texas, hosted jointly by Joel Osteen, Jim Bakker, and Kenneth Copeland.

The purpose of the convention was to figure out new ways to take their congregants' money during this time of economic uncertainty, and, of course, the COVID-19 pandemic.

"My congregants are being real stingy," said Kenneth Copeland, "They're barely giving me any money at all! I used to get 10% of their income every week, a real Godly tithe I deserved. But now I'm lucky if those selfish jerks give me a measly 2%! If they keep stiffing me, I'm going to have to fire one of my breakfast waiters at my mansion. I can't eat breakfast with only four waiters, I need all five! What if my toast cools to room temperature? And I don't want to start dipping into my net worth savings just because my congregants are worried about themselves. Give me liquid cash!"

Other televangelists agreed that times were rough.

"I've tried everything," said a visibly exhausted Joel Osteen. "I threatened God's wrath and several extra plagues if they didn't continue to pay, I threatened to tell God to dig up all the seeds they've already planted with previous monetary gifts to my church, and I even tried to convince a young, pregnant woman that babies were expensive and she should just abort so she can save her money for my church, but nothing will convince these self-absorbed peasants to give me more of their money!"

Jim Bakker's presentation got uncharacteristically honest.

"You know something?" asked Bakker rhetorically. "I've gotten a little reflective due to all my lawsuits, and I want to say that I for one am glad that Christianity is largely fictional. The other day, I actually opened up my Bible. I don't know what came over me, but I had to blow off the dust because it has probably been 25 years since the last time I looked in there. I found this amazing passage where Jesus gets upset with the money changers in the Temple, and starts overturning tables and causing a ruckus. I didn't know Jesus had that kind of masculine rage in him. I had never heard this story before, and it really got me hot imagining Jesus all sweaty with his muscles glistening from throwing tables around. Maybe he also had a whip, and started whipping the naughty money changers for being bad boys. I got so aroused spiritually. Well, long story short, after a trip to the bathroom to plant a seed of my own in the sink, it dawned on me that maybe we televangelists are just like those money changers. I don't think Jesus would be happy with how rich we all are, and I just want to say that I'm glad most of the Bible is probably just a bunch of fluff written down by goat herders who had to be reminded not to sex up animals or eat unsalted, unrefrigerated pork and seafood, and isn't literal. Can you imagine any of us seriously spending our lives passively praying to a silent, invisible, seemingly indifferent God to make things magically better for us, and expecting good things to happen without actually doing any of the required work ourselves? Like really praying, and not just a theatrical show for our dupes? You know? Cause God didn't just drop our multi-million dollar mansions, and private jets, and our small armies of life-like, Japanese sex dolls into our laps. We worked hard to get where we are! You know how many hours of my life I toiled to convince fools they'd soon be rich if they gave me part of their paychecks? It was not easy or quick! I earned my half billion by myself, with no Heavenly assistance! Prosperity preaching may not be honest work, but it certainly is hard work! So, anyway, I thought that since I've been in the Bible business for 50 years, I might as well try to finally read it, and, let me tell you, this book is wild! Truly wild. I lost count of how many instances of incest there were in the first 40 pages alone! I can't believe I've told so many people they could solve their problems just opening up to any page in the Bible and reading from there for an hour! What if they opened up to the part where Lot's daughters get him drunk, sleep with him, and get pregnant? Whose problems would that story solve? I was astounded to learn what crazy stuff I've been subjecting these poor people to all this time! The Bible should probably be banned since it's way more gross and corrupting than *Harry Potter*, or any other books we tell good Christian children to burn. It's literally filled with violence, murder, and genocide! And can you imagine any one of us being satisfied with the answer 'God works in mysterious ways' when bad things continually happen to good people? It would piss me off if someone told me that if I crashed one of my Porsches! I guess I'm feeling a little guilty about all the circular, logical fallacies we have to repeat to our congregants when they ask why Christian theology doesn't make very much sense when you stop and think about all the convoluted stuff about the Trinity, transubstantiation, theodicy, the ethical problem of Hell, predestination, free will, the Old Testament's dystheism, and all the other scriptural incongruities and theological paradoxes. But I digress. I guess my advice for all you other televangelists hurting from dwindling church donations is to get into the survivalist market. I'm having great success selling a bunch of COVID-related products like buckets of beans and fake vitamin cures. The FDA's lawsuits have dipped into my profits a bit, but I always recover. It's always easy to recover in our business!'"

# Eric Trump Just Launched A 2024 Presidential Campaign Ahead Of Ivanka And Don Jr.

August 3, 2020
New York City, NY—

The sibling rivalry between President Donald Trump's oldest children is heating up as Eric Trump just announced his 2024 presidential candidacy.

Eric is the first Trump kid to officially launch a presidential campaign, though both Donald Jr. and Ivanka are rumored to be planning runs as well.

"I was first," explained Eric in a brief phone conversation with *The Halfway Post* this morning. "Don and Ivanka can suck it! I have dibs so they better back off. Ivanka thinks she should be the next president because she's a girl and she's our dad's favorite, but she's just a stuck-up, bossy phony. I don't know why people think she's hot. She's gross. I totally disagree with my dad on that one. And don't even get me started on Don Jr.! Did you know he eats his scabs? He goes hunting a lot and gets a bunch of mosquito bites, and then he always picks them until they bleed. When they scab over, he picks those, too, and eats them! He says it's what Green Berets do for protein and iron when they're stranded in the wilderness behind enemy lines, but I don't believe him. I also think he might be racist because he gets chegros a lot while hiking and camping, but he calls them 'chiggers.' I try to tell him that 'chiggers' is a derogatory slur, but he never listens. Unpresidential, if you ask me! The 'Woke' people are not going to like finding out about that!"

Asked what kind of campaign platform he would be running on, Eric said he would be quite a different president than his Dad.

"You'd be surprised how much of my own man I am," continued Eric. "To be honest, I don't think my father's presidency has been as effective as it could have been. He doesn't really like to read, or listen to the advice of experts, or respect women. That last one is big difference between my father and me. I've just always thought my dad would have been more successful in life if he hadn't disrespected and harassed women so much. It always seemed to me like such a big distraction having to spend so much time worrying about lawsuits, and paying off victims, and planning with lawyers, and financing catch-and-kill stories. I learned from watching him that life is just easier and cheaper when you don't regularly sexually assault women. Also, my father only hires young, attractive, mostly blonde women for his advisers and staff members. He says he hates hiring uglies, but I always thought that was a big waste of potential. I've found that some of the smartest, hardest working, most capable women are at least a little ugly and out of shape."

# Eric Trump's Top 10 Deepest Secrets

1.  Eric stole Pokémon cards from kids with cancer while visiting them in the hospital. It's how he got his holographic Charizard.

2.  Eric hosted several charity events at his father's properties to try and earn an "I love you, son" from his dad, but his dad still called him a "regret" when Eric gave a leukemia charity a 1% discount on a purchase of a bottle of Trump Wine.

3.  He lost $1.3 million in June of 2014 in a cryptocurrency scam called "Billionaire Bucks" for which he thought he'd get fabulously rich being the first investor. Unfortunately, he was the only investor.

4.  He used to practice French-kissing with Donald Jr. until age 16 so they'd be good at it when they got girlfriends.

5.  He loves to crochet, but has to hide his passion for textiles from the rest of his mean-spirited family. He has made them all beanie hats, but can't gift them because he knows they'd just laugh and mock him.

6.  He hates ketchup because of several traumatizing memories of his father abusing him and his brother with a ketchup bottle when their mom would undercook steak to a medium temperature instead of well-done, and he'd explode with rage.

7.  He wanted to study botany in college, but his dad wouldn't let him.

8.  His favorite band is *Nickelback*, his favorite movie is *Showgirls*, and his favorite television show is *The Jerry Springer Show*. He cherishes seeing glimpses of families more screwed up than his own. His favorite episodes are ones where men take paternity tests and find out they're not the father because he likes to imagine Donald Trump is not his real dad, and he has a different father somewhere out in the world who will accept him, love him unconditionally, and not call him a "loser" every day in front of his wife and kids.

9.  His most proud moment was when he punched Jared Kushner in the jaw for telling a joke that implied the Trump family wasn't actually rich, but he later apologized when he found out it was true.

10. He gets very upset when his dad mocks him for not having cheated on his wife yet because it's not like he hasn't tried.

# Jim Jordan, Lindsey Graham And Matt Gaetz Started A Congressional "Dictator Club"

August 5, 2020
Washington D.C.—

A group of Republican lawmakers in Congress founded a new caucus last week they're calling the "Dictator Club" to promote President Donald Trump's authoritarian interests in Congress.

The Dictator Club will have two chapters, one for the Senate and one for the House of Representatives. In the House chapter, the founding members are Jim Jordan (OH), Matt Gaetz (FL), and Louie Gohmert (TX). In the Senate chapter, the founding members are Lindsey Graham (SC), Ron Johnson (WI), and John Kennedy (LA).

Senator Ted Cruz (TX) really wants to join as well, but the other members have yet to invite him for fear that Cruz's membership will scare away other prospective Dictator Club members.

"We're trying to attract some female members, and Ted Cruz's existence is the biggest c***-block in history," explained Matt Gaetz. "There's something about him that makes women feel uncomfortable and unsafe. Several women have told me that when Ted Cruz makes direct eye contact with them they all of a sudden get their periods. It's like their bodies are subconsciously so disgusted by Ted Cruz that their uteruses just start flushing everything to ensure there's no chance in Hell that even a single strand of Ted Cruz DNA gets anywhere near their eggs. Susan Collins told me that when Ted Cruz introduced himself to her on his first day in the Senate and shook her hand, she got her first menopausal hot flash. Her very first impression of Ted literally made her body just give up on ever reproducing."

The Dictator Club is planning to meet every Wednesday afternoon for an hour. Members will participate in a number of activities, including perusing magazines for pictures in which President Trump's hands look big so they can tear them out and show him, recording informal polls amongst themselves so that Trump can finally get some poll results where he's not losing his reelection, and taking turns doing each other's makeup so they can all have an orange facial appearance like Trump.

The Dictator Club is also conducting a weekly contest to see who can convince foreign governments to fabricate the most dirt on Joe Biden's family, and the weekly winner gets the honor of putting on an Obama mask and letting Trump lock them in a dog kennel and then kick it off the White House roof."

Jim Jordan won the honor last week, and Trump was so delighted he invited Jordan to come over to the White House residency last Thursday evening.

The other Dictator Club members were very curious about what Trump and Jordan did in the late-night visit, but Mr. Jordan said he'd never tell.

## More Media Headlines

- America Suspects Jon Stewart Could Have Saved America From Donald Trump By Not Retiring

- Pope Francis: "I Would Rather American Catholics Watch Hardcore Gay Porn Than *Fox News*!"

- *Breitbart* Just Hired A Suspiciously Pro-Trump Writer Named John Barron

- Obama's New *Netflix* Project Will Investigate Trump's Orangutan Ancestry

- North Korean State Media Claims Kim Jong Un Won Every Season Of Trump's gameshow *The Apprentice*

- *Fox News* Claims Donald Trump Does Not Poop, Invented Burgers

- *Fox News*: "COVID-19 Wouldn't Have Happened If Liberals Would Just Pray To White Jesus Once In A While!"

- New Study Shows *Fox News* Is A Worse Cultural Influence Than Violent Video Games, Death Metal Goth Music, And Pornography Combined

- Tomi Lahren Admits On *Fox News* That She Receives Money From 16 Separate Welfare Programs, But Says She Still Distrusts The Government

- The Most Popular TV Show In Russia Is A Cartoon Titled, In Translation, *Doofy Donnie & The Downfall Of America*

- Sean Hannity Demands To Know Where In The Constitution It Says We Can't Have A Dictator, Constitutional Experts Say "Page 1"

# Bombshell: Donald Trump's Russian Sex Tape Has No Women, Just Big Macs

August 7, 2020
Washington D.C.—

A shocking development in the Russian collusion scandal has thrust President Donald Trump's suspected kompromat videotape back into the spotlight.

*The Halfway Post* conducted an exclusive interview with Russian fracking oligarch Dimitri Kuznetsov, who confirmed the Steele Dossier's authenticity.

"Your President wasn't hard to lure into a classic sex tape espionage sting, let me tell you," Kuznetsov explained. "The Steele Dossier was spot on. But it wasn't a golden shower. That was a mistranslation from Russian of 'golden arches,' meaning McDonalds. We were partying after the Miss Universe contest and he wanted fast food, so we drove him to a McDonalds as he requested, and I have never seen a more disgusting order. I've quite literally seen a full-sized Siberian brown bear fill up on less garbage than your President. He ordered four Big Macs, two large fries, two Filets-O-Fish, and three large chocolate shakes, which he explained were for him to drink one on the way back to the hotel, one while he ate the sandwiches, and the third for dessert afterwards. We had planted a camera in the room, so we asked him if he wanted us to send any of the best prostitutes Moscow had to offer up to his room, and the guy, to his credit, said no. He was munching on the first Filet-O-Fish, and he told us he was going to go to bed early. So we went into the office in the basement to monitor the camera feed of Mr. Trump's room, and what we witnessed I will never forget. The sexual acts with which your President violated those McDonalds products made our AV technician vomit several times into a wastebasket. Trump quickly undressed and lathered himself up to his neck with the other two chocolate milkshakes. I could not in good conscience explain to your readers where Mr. Trump stuffed his french fries, and I have never found the right words in English to adequately describe the fate of that poor, unfortunate, second Filet-O-Fish. The next morning when your President checked out to fly back to America, we found the bed littered with mutilated Big Mac buns. The ones he hadn't eaten during his night of ravenous lust probably wished they had been eaten. The horrors would have been over much quicker for them."

Kuznetsov sighed. Then he continued.

"There's a reason your president has entirely forsaken his oath to protect your country's national security and domestic interests from foreign meddling, and it's because this tape he knows we have is magnificently embarrassing."

# Rudy Giuliani: "Trump Is 100% Innocent... But If He Ever Turns On Me I'll Rat!"

August 8, 2020
Washington D.C.—

Trump lawyer Rudy Giuliani just published a Twitter thread responding to claims that President Donald Trump might throw him under the bus by accusing him of going rogue and doing all the quid pro quo extortion of Ukraine's President Zelensky without the knowledge of the White House.

The following are Mr. Giuliani's tweets:

"President Trump is 100% innocent! He's the cleanest president I've ever seen. And he'd never turn on me like some in the Fake News are suggesting, I promise you that... Because I have so much dirt on him and so many receipts that it would make his head spin. But, again, Trump is not guilty whatsoever, so nothing to worry about."

"All this Ukraine stuff is entirely a hoax. We're just a couple of straight shooter guys who have never broken a law in our lives, and we're incredibly close. He's not a rat, and I'm not a rat, but we have a bit of a mutually assured destruction kind of thing. You hear that Donald? But again, all this is hypothetical, cause there was no collusion, no extortion, and definitely no quid pro quo."

"I can't get into too many details because of client-attorney privilege and executive privilege, but take my word for it that President Trump has never lied about anything in the world. And he's a very smart guy, so I know for a fact that the President knows better than to ever throw me under any buses to protect himself from impeachment. Cause the second he tries, he knows I'll hit him with ten buses of my own!"

"However, I cannot emphasize enough that there has never been any criminal wrongdoing from either of us. Though if I ever have to go to jail, let me tell you that the President will spend much, much longer in prison. But it will never have to come to that because we're both 1,000% innocent... but the President better never forget that I'm a little more innocent!"

# Televangelist Says Women Should Be Imprisoned For Stealing Men's Virginities

August 9, 2020
Boise, ID—

Local televangelist Herbert Brock made controversial statements this weekend about women being responsible for every lost virginity in America.

"No man has ever, in the 6,000-year history of humanity, wanted to lose his virginity," claimed Brock in his Sunday church service. "That kind of idea could only be generated in the deluded, easily manipulatable mind of a girl or woman gullibly succumbing to the corruption of Satan. It pains me to think of all the pure, innocent boys and men who have been lured into sexual slavery by succubus women with their overseer vaginas cracking their whips of promiscuity. It's like women have two brains, and can't help themselves but only think with the brain in their labia. It's particularly tough for young men in high school and college these days. Taking your studies seriously is hard enough, but add to that the constant threat of girls asking them to send sexts! Girls these days must be watching too much pornography because they have become addicted to seeing pictures of penises. Women need to show more respect for consent. There is a terrible trend in society thanks to 'hookup culture' where women text men on a nightly basis asking for dick pics. Men don't want this, and they certainly don't enjoy sending them. I can't tell you how many men I talk to who say they're grossed out and disgusted by how often women, who are total strangers, beg them for dick pics. So let's take a moment now to pray for America's men, and ask God to help them stay strong while avoiding women's omnipresent demands for sex..... thank you."

Brock then described legal remedies for this societal problem.

"I think we really have to get the law involved," Brock continued. "The problem is that serious. Girls and women just need to learn that men's virginities are precious, and they have no right to tempt males for sex before they're married. I think any time parents find out their son has had premarital sex, they should call the police right away to drive to the girl's house and arrest her. I think 3-5 years of prison would teach America's harlots to keep their vaginas closed, out of sight, and quiet whenever a boy is nearby. And the girl's parents would surely agree that a brief prison sentence is for the benefit of all of society. Sexual desire is a female plague, and they need to learn to control their urges. Incarceration is the only way for women to learn to 'keep it in their pants' as the kids say these days. Alright, everyone, take out your Bibles now, and let's all read together the part where God kicks Adam and Eve out of Eden, and it's 100% Eve's fault."

# 86% Of The Republican Men In Congress Believe Female Orgasms Are A Myth

August 10, 2020
Washington D.C.—

An illuminating new poll of Congressional sentiment conducted by a consortium of St. Louis-based universities has unearthed some wild findings.

The most surprising discovery is that the vast majority of Republican men in Congress believe female orgasms do not exist.

"I know for a fact my wife has never had an orgasm," said Senator Ted Cruz. "Sometimes we'll go at it practically for forever, as long as I can humanly last, and even after a full, agonizing thirty seconds of my holding off as long as I possibly can by thinking about unsexy things like a future in which I am not elected President, she still doesn't feel anything. Riddle me that one, science!"

"One time I heard several of my female colleagues talking about female orgasms," explained Representative Louie Gohmert, "but they must have all gotten on the same menstrual cycle and been hysterical from being on the rag because they kept mentioning something called a clitoris. Talk about being delusional! I'd love for some coastal elitist scientist to point on my body where my clitoris is!"

The poll also found wild COVID beliefs held by Congressional Republicans.

"I'm so sick of these idiot leftists always trying to get government involved in our personal lives!" said Representative Patrick Broff of Idaho. "It's just not the government's job to tell citizens what to do. The government has no business telling us not to go out into public without masks, or not to open restaurants for inside dining, and so on. Liberals are always telling us what we can and can't do, and what's a public danger and what's not, and I'm sick of it! Everything liberals say makes freedom-loving patriots like myself want to do the opposite. We're individualist capitalists, not glasses-wearing, *NPR*-listening Marxists! We don't mindlessly believe like sheep everything published in medical journals by brainwashed doctors from socialist medical schools. We think for ourselves! Hell, if I want to lick the ground around the base of toilets in airport bathrooms, or pull out the garbage bags in trash cans along the street so I can cut a whole in the bottom and drink all the mystery liquids that come out, I will! And, as a real American, I'm going to continue going out in crowded places with no mask on until either the Democrats admit COVID is a hoax, or this real bad cough, fever, and loss of taste I'm getting from seasonal allergies gets any worse!"

## Trump: "Joe Biden Will Turn All Suburban Marriages Into Biracial Marriages!"

August 11, 2020
Washington D.C.—

President Donald Trump today made unusual claims about Joe Biden's presidential platform.

"Joe Biden hates same-race marriages even more than he hates God!" exclaimed Mr. Trump in a press briefing that quickly went off the rails. "All the suburban white women out there who are thinking about flipping to the Democrats better understand that Joe Biden does not respect you or your husband like I do. He will make you divorce your husband, and force you to marry someone else. Someone way different. A jihadi, an African immigrant, or a Chinese. Biden will make you spin a wheel to find out whether your new husband is Black, brown, yellow or red. Normal colors will no longer be allowed. If you don't want to have to marry a member of al-Qaeda, I'd suggest you reelect me. Democrats are going to abort your marriage, and Nancy Pelosi will personally convert your kids into multiracial mulattos, the ones she doesn't eat. If you want your kids' skin to stay white, you better vote Trump, that's all I'm saying. You wouldn't believe what Joe Biden wants to do. If I told you, it would blow your mind. Biden wants to mandate your husband grow a beard, wear a turban, memorize the Koran, force you into a burqa, take away your driver's license, and marry ten other women besides you, each one more biracial than the last! I know I said this about Obama and Hillary, but my election stopped them from doing this just in time. And Biden will finish the job! Trust me. You'll have to choose for your kids to convert to Mexican or Arab. There will be taco stands or hummus bowls in every room of your house! If you're a suburban white woman, it'll be game over for you if Biden wins! You're not going to be suburban anymore. Maybe not even a woman. Who knows? The way things are going... Joe Biden will ruin your life. I guarantee it. Biden will sign an executive order that your house gets torn down, and he'll replace your comfortable home and pretty little yard with a low-income housing unit, and cram in dozens of immigrants, thugs, MS-13 gang lords, abortion doctors, and Antifa. He's going to turn your suburban life into an urban one, and he'll convert all your kids into little urbans. You won't even recognize them anymore. Trust me. Your little Timmy is going to turn into big Tyrone, or Osama the Terrorist. The suburbs will be totally over. You'll never see a suburb again. America will be nothing but urban. So suburban white women better stop flipping over to the Democrats! I love you, and Joe Biden hates you. Seriously. He will feed your children to Nancy Pelosi. It will be their new tax. A children tax!"

# Ivanka Trump Won The White House Talent Show Judged By Her Dad For The 4th Consecutive Year

August 12, 2020
Washington D.C.—

The Trump White House just held its 4th Annual talent show, and the winner was, for the 4th time, Ivanka Trump.

President Donald Trump was the judge for the 4th consecutive time, and the other contestants complained about his blatant lack of impartiality.

"My dad always does this!" said Eric Trump, who came in last place out of all 19 contestants. "He always picks Ivanka for everything! It's not fair! Her routine was just acting like a little kid sitting on Santa's lap and pretending our dad was Santa! How original for her! And how did I get last place? I pulled a freaking rabbit out of a hat, and spent a lot of money on my cape and wand for my costume! My dad can go to heck!"

The following were some of the other, more notable talent performances:

- **Betsy DeVos**—she performed a short one-act play she wrote about being a plantation master reprimanding slave children for trying to learn to read.
- **Mark Meadows**—he sang karaoke of Celine Dion's "My Heart Will Go On," and then cried.
- **Stephen Miller**—he did that creepy thing where he turned his eyelids inside out and showed off how many Madagascar hissing cockroaches he can keep in his mouth while making pig squeal noises with the lights turned off, a strobe light flashing, and death metal music playing. He ultimately fit seven cockroaches.
- **Mike Pence**—he recited several passages of the Bible from memory (Pence was awarded second-to-last place just in front of Eric).
- **Kayleigh McEnany**—she performed an improv game where she let Trump pick a random object and she let him direct her flipping back and forth between hyping it as the greatest invention ever and the worst invention ever depending on whether his thumb was up or down.
- **Wilbur Ross**—he sat in a chair and slept. No one was sure if that was his talent, or if he just fell asleep.
- **Ben Carson**—he flipped through a catalogue of office furniture, and commented on which new dining set he'd love to get if taxpayers weren't so stingy.
- **Rudy Giuliani**—he stop-and-frisked himself for six minutes.

# Pastor Who Claimed "Only 100% Hell-Bound Pedo Gays Get COVID" Just Got COVID

August 13, 2020
Tulsa, OK—

Christian Pastor Thomas Philbertson of Tulsa just announced he will be taking a two-week break from pastoral duties due to infection from the coronavirus.

While this would usually be a sad story to report, the irony of Mr. Philbertson's positive COVID-19 test is, frankly, hilarious.

Philbertson has spent the last three months promising his congregation that it was physically impossible for heterosexual Christians like himself to catch the coronavirus, and has frequently used church services to show off his certainty by walking up and down the aisles and licking his church members' palms.

Philbertson went viral a month ago after posting a now-ironic video of one of his sermons on YouTube. The following is a transcript of that video's most controversial excerpt:

"Folks, I'm not worried about the coronavirus one bit. I trust in Jesus Christ. And Jesus only lets queer, homo gays get the COVID. They should have named it the QUEERVID. And pedophiles can get it, and criminals, and Democrats, and Catholics, and Unitarians, and Lutherans, and atheists, and agnostics, and Muslims, and girls who show too much cleavage, and squirrels, and the Chinese. I will never get it. Because I am none of those. You see, Jesus comes to me in my dreams, and He tells me who is getting COVID and who will be safe. Then He tells me who is getting into Heaven and who isn't. And I am definitely going. Jesus said I don't even have to wait in line at the Pearly Gates. And Jesus said He'll let me tell some of the gays they're not allowed in, and pull the lever that opens the trapdoor in the clouds that makes them fall down to Hell. What an honor. Jesus told me He'll let me do it because I'm the straightest person to ever live. I'm a heterosexual VIP. Jesus said that. I'm 100% straight. Maybe even 110% straight. Y'all here in this church need to study my example of godly straightness. Look at these skinny denim jeans I'm wearing, and these colorful boots with the red, white and blue of the American flag. Gay people don't dress so American as I dress. And all these sequins on my denim jacket are because it blinds Satan. They're very shiny, aren't they? When I'm walking around, it's like I'm blinding Satan's eyes, so he can't touch me with his slender, well-manicured gay fingers of flaming homosexuality he just wishes he could slip into my anus and make me climax by rubbing my male G-spot. And then use cucumbers and other phallic-shaped, satanic vegetables. But that would never happen. I'm too Godly, too pure of faith. I never even eat a phallic-shaped vegetable. No pickles, zucchini, carrots, or eggplants have ever gone into my mouth. That's how not gay I am. My heart burns for only one man, and no others. Jesus of Nazareth. You see, because I'm so straight, my heart will never burn for plumbers who come over to fix my kitchen sink, and lean over so that their tool belt makes their pants slip down and their butt cracks show a couple quarter-inches. And my heart will never burn for shirtless cowboys throwing giant stacks of hay into the backs of trucks single-handedly with washboard abs. My heart will never burn for manly firefighters rescuing me from a burning building and holding me in their massive arms to safety where they'll set me down inside an ambulance, throw one of those ripped arms over my shoulder, rub my back up and down to warm me up, and then give me their phone number and ask me to call them for coffee sometime next week. Not in a million years, Satan! My heart only burns for Jesus Christ. And because I'm not gay, Jesus will never let me get COVID. And he won't let any of you get COVID either, unless you're secretly homo. In which case, as I mention every Sunday, my house is always open at night after 8pm to come over and talk to me about it. It will be just the two of us, so you don't have to worry about a thing. No one will ever know what kind of secrets you want to disclose to me, or role-play out so I can get a visual understanding of your sexual anxieties and guilts. We will pray very, very passionately, and figure things out about our sexuality together. Just gay men, though. No lesbians. Lesbians are too disgusting and satanic for my Christian powers to put back on the straight and narrow path of Godliness and heterosexual purity. I can't do anything for lesbians. Talk about unmanageable the way their four cumbersome breasts must get in their way all the time. I don't know how lesbian couples ever get anything done! And the idea of two moist vaginas rubbing together makes me want to vomit. Ew, I'm gagging right now. I can't even look at one vag. They give me nightmares! I swear, nature never created anything so horrifying and aesthetically useless as a naked woman. So sorry, lesbians, I can't do anything to keep you out of Hell. If there are any lesbians out there, don't come to my house! I don't want to hear a word about your problems. But closeted gay men, y'all just ring my doorbell. Tonight if you want. We'll light some candles, pour some wine, and see where the night of prayer takes us. If you're worried about coronavirus because of your gay-ness, I'm here for you. Because I'm 110% straight. Alright, everyone, it's licking time, so get out your Bibles, turn to Leviticus 18:22, and read aloud from there with your neighbors until I get to you and lick all the way up to your elbows, at which point you can head out to the lobby and enjoy our refreshments. We have donuts with brown frosting, sausage links, and country-style gravy, and I actually recommend eating them together. Dip the sausage tips into the gravy, then rub 'em on the frosting and get 'em good and lathered up, and stick 'em in the donut hole for a delicious mix of sweet and salty. It's my favorite!"

# Mike Pence Demands Kamala Harris Not Show Her Ankles At The VP Debate

August 15, 2020
Washington D.C.—

*The Halfway Post* obtained a leaked list of Vice President Mike Pence's demands for the upcoming vice presidential debate between him and Senator Kamala Harris:

1. Harris, and any female moderators, must not wear any clothing that reveals their knees, ankles, shoulders, clavicle, lower back, or more than a half-inch of mammary gland cleavage (rulers will be brought and utilized!).
2. Harris must not make eye contact and hold it for longer than three consecutive seconds (stopwatches will be brought and utilized!).
3. Handshakes only! No hugs. Harris's mammary glands must not get within six inches of the Vice President's chest.
4. Harris must wear a bra, though preferably two, to make sure no devilish nipples distract the VP from his godly focus on America.
5. The following words are strictly prohibited: vagina, uterus, labia, vulva, clitoris, cervix, G-spot, breasts, taint, or perineum. Only "pussy" is allowed, per the precedent of presidential acceptability wisely endorsed by God through President Trump's immaculate electoral college victory over Hillary Clinton. Also, no other words even remotely related to female sexuality or female-specific anatomy will be permitted (a thesaurus will be brought and utilized!).
6. Under no circumstances will Harris be allowed to familiarly refer to the VP on a first-name basis. She must refer to him only as "Mr. Vice President" or "my male superior."
7. Harris must not use any words from Ebonics, Hindi, Bengali, Marathi, Jamaican Creole, or any other languages Harris's diverse family might speak at home. The VP only speaks standard American English.
8. No references to rap music, R&B, jazz, basketball, the Harlem Renaissance, the Harlem Globetrotters, kente cloth, soul food, Kwanzaa, or Beyoncé can be made. References to any of these will make the VP uncomfortable, create a hostile atmosphere, and give the VP permission to terminate the debate immediately.
9. No uses of the Bible or Jesus's memory will be allowed to come out of her sinner Californian mouth. The right to discuss Christianity in any political context is granted exclusively to the VP.
10. Under no circumstances will Harris be permitted to utilize her jezebel power to turn the VP to stone, and if her hair spontaneously turns into snakes she must not let any of them bite him.

# Trump Just Reignited His Twitter Feud With Paul McCartney

August 16, 2020
Washington D.C.—

President Donald Trump just launched a series of tweets reigniting a Twitter feud he started with Paul McCartney back in 2018 after the Beatles singer called him a "mad captain."

The following are tweets Trump posted insulting McCartney:

"The Beatles are the most overrated band in history! Their music isn't catchy at all, and Paul McCartney is less talented than even Ringo! Their songs are all trash except the one that goes 'She was just 17, you know what I mean?' I totally know what they meant on that one!"

"'Can't Buy Me Love?' Are you kidding me? I buy love all the time! And then I pay extra to keep the girls quiet! I thought Paul McCartney was rich... I guess not! Maybe that's why he wrote the song 'Penny Lane!' If I had written it, I'd have called it 'Hundred Dollar Lane!'"

"'Taxman?' Paul McCartney pays taxes?? What an idiot! He's even dumber than I thought! 'Fixing A Hole?' I hope Paul didn't pay that contractor after fixing his hole! Paul will never get rich like me paying his taxes and his contractors!"

"'Paperback Writer?' Not me! *The Art of the Deal* is a hardcover masterpiece! You make more money with hardcovers, everyone knows that! Except Paul McFARTney I guess! And only a loser writes a song like 'Yesterday!' I'm using my unpresidented IQ to Make America Great Again TODAY and TOMORROW!"

"'Hey, Jude?' Is that a song for Jews only? I think there are fine songs on BOTH sides! 'I Wanna Hold Your Hand?' Talk about a real beta move! Not like me, who is a total ALPHA! I grab women full on by the pussy! And I don't announce it ahead of time. They swat your hand away if you do that!"

"Even worse is the song 'Blackbird,' which only encourages ANTIFA thugs. I'd like to hear a song about law-abiding WHITEbirds! And I have some obvious ideas on how to improve the theme and lyrics of 'Golden Slumbers!'"

# COVID Czar Mike Pence Just Released 10 Tips On How To Avoid Catching The Coronavirus

August 18, 2020
Washington D.C.—

Vice President Mike Pence, the acting COVID Czar, just publicly released a brochure on the White House website he says is full of the best, up-to-date medical advice on dealing with the coronavirus.

However, health professionals across America immediately described the pamphlet as "absurd," "wildly unsanitary," and "spectacularly ill-advised."

The following is the brochure's list of top ten coronavirus-related recommendations Pence authored:

1. Don't wash your hands! Germs spread much more easily when your hands have been recently washed because your skin acts like a Slip 'N Slide on which the germs can slide right off your fingers into vulnerable entry points of your body like your eyes, nose, and mouth.

2. Sneeze into your palms so you can keep any COVID germs locked away in your closed fists until you can throw them away the next time you pass a trash can.

3. Pray every night and morning. God will never let a good Christian patriot in America get a godless, communist illness from China!

4. Cough in people's faces to help clean each other. The wind force power generated by your lungs will blow off any germs lurking on your friends' and family members' faces they don't even know are hiding there. Your lungs clean the air in your body, so any air coughed out on others' faces is likely much cleaner than the air all around us.

5. Stand very close to strangers in public places. When a bunch of human bodies are clumped together, you have better odds that the coronavirus will choose to infect someone other than you.

6. Stop drinking water. When your body is hydrated you urinate more, and when you're urinating your body is exposed for coronavirus to sneak in through your urethra.

7. Poop in the street. The coronavirus can hide in old, antiquated city pipes and wait to get you when you least suspect it by sneaking right

into your colon. Keep your toilet lid closed, and seal it with tape until at least the month of May to keep coronavirus out of your home.

8. If you're a good Christian, help keep your community safe by licking door handles, subway and bus handrails, and all other often-touched public surfaces. God will protect you and kill any coronavirus germs you get in your mouth or stomach, and this will help clean public places so even the non-Christians are better protected against coronavirus. They don't deserve it, but if all the non-Christians die from this pandemic we will have no one left to judge and feel intrinsically superior to, and that's just not fun!

9. Drink your urine. Your pee is actually sterile, and you just can't trust coronavirus to stay out of our water supply. Even water bottles! The more times you recycle your urine back into your body, the cleaner it gets, so you can stay alive for months at a time if you're just careful to preserve all your pee.

10. Act like COVID isn't happening. President Donald Trump's reelection depends on a healthy stock market, so it's imperative that stocks don't continue to decline like they have been. No matter how bad things get, always do your duty to Trump and act like everything is fine, because the positive perception of the stock market's health is much more important than real humans' health in order to MAGA!

Later in the day, though, a defeated-looking Pence held a press conference.

"I give up," Pence said. "After hours of praying ceaselessly, my efforts have yielded no results. I gave it my all, but COVID is just too strong and won't go away. Why is God forsaking me? I've tried speaking in tongues, baptizing myself again, handling snakes, self-flagellation, self-mutilation, stoning a neighbor I found working on the Sabbath, forcing my wife to sleep on the roof when she got her period, sacrificing animals, going to Walmart and opening all the condom boxes and poking holes in them with a thumbtack, protesting Planned Parenthood, tearing out all the pages on the reproductive system and evolution in the local high school's science books, launching a lawsuit against Hollywood for all its gratuitous female nudity in movies, and I even circumcised myself a second time! What else can I do? I've never seen God so tempestuous and angry before! What did the gays do to provoke His wrath? Is it the new Lady Gaga song? Was it Pete Buttigieg winning the Iowa caucus? Did RuPaul crown too flamboyant a drag contestant? Tell me, Lord! Tell me so I can make everything right!"

Pence then collapsed to the ground and sobbed on the floor.

# Jim Jordan Claims Donald Trump Ran A Mile In Under 6 Minutes Last Weekend

August 21, 2020
Washington D.C.—

Representative Jim Jordan claimed today that President Donald Trump is a big fan of jogging.

"A lot of people don't know this, but President Trump rarely uses a golf cart when he goes golfing," Jordan said in response to a question from a constituent asking him to reveal something voters don't know about Trump. "He loves to jog from hole to hole, and I thought I was in good shape, but I can barely keep up! People think that he's not in good shape because of his diet of almost exclusively fast food, and the fact that he starts to breathe heavily when he talks for more than twenty seconds, but I can assure you that the President has more endurance than anyone I've ever seen. He really loves running. In fact, I raced him last weekend in a mile, and he beat me! I couldn't believe it. By the end of the four laps of the track he was about to lap me! His final time was under six minutes. The guy who timed us said Trump's time was 30 seconds faster than Barack Obama's personal record. There's just nothing Donald Trump can't do better than Obama, is there? And you totally don't expect Trump to be a good runner, you know? You'd think that the way he stands with his pelvis curved and his hips bent awkwardly with his upper body leaning forward about 45 degrees and his arms dangling down as if he were a knuckle-dragging Cro-Magnon would impact his running form, but nope. I guess it makes him more aerodynamic or something! You know, Donald Jr. and Eric both stand like that, too, so I wonder if they're great runners as well. Maybe agility is just in the Trump genes, like their great dealmaking. I'd guess that Trump is probably the fastest president we've ever had. He's obsessed with physical exercise. He's always jogging when I see him going in and out of meetings at the White House. He goes up and down stairs skipping every other step, and often turns them into lunge exercises. He's got pull-up bars on most of the doorways in the West Wing so anytime he leaves or enters a room he'll do a quick set of 30 pull-ups real fast. The generals can't believe it. He's like a superhero. I've never seen anyone be able to keep up with his energy. The President told me he used to go jogging with Dr. Fauci, who is another big fan of running, but Fauci got upset and quit their jogging club because Trump was in such better shape. That's why Fauci is lying about the coronavirus hoax. He's just jealous that the President's mile time is so much faster than his! And, let me tell you, Donald Trump looks great in his tight, little running shorts. His varicose veins just won't quit until America is made great again!"

## The RNC Will Show A Montage Of Melania Swatting Trump's Hand To Showcase Their "Christian Love"

August 23, 2020
Washington D.C.—

According to GOP insiders, the Republican National Convention will showcase a montage video of all the times First Lady Melania Trump has swatted away her husband's attempts to hold her hand in order to showcase examples of their "unprecedentedly Christian marriage."

"President Trump's union with Melania is probably the most Christian marriage America has ever seen," said RNC producer Stephen Thompson, who edited together the video. "You'll never see them showing disgusting displays of affection, familiarity, or even any warmth at all. The Obamas were always throwing their love and marital satisfaction in our faces. Maybe it's a Muslim or Kenyan thing, but it's very unAmerican and unGodly. Thankfully, the Trumps could not offer a more profound and desperately needed contrast with the eight satanic years of the Obamas' horrifying spousal socialist propaganda. Watching Donald and Melania together is like a master class in Christian love and devotion. There have been just so many teachable moments in their time at the White House, but you have to watch closely because they're humble and hide their love well. But you absolutely cannot deny it's there. If you don't have a good eye, you'd probably think Melania absolutely detests Donald, and is physically repulsed by the thought of letting him touch her, but that could not be further from the truth!"

Our *Halfway Post* reporter asked Mr. Thompson if he was serious.

"I've never been more serious about anything in my life!" Thompson continued. "You're just not used to it because you let the Obamas brainwash you about what a healthy marriage should be like, and you don't understand Christian marriage when it's right in front of your face! Whereas Michelle would playfully make fun of Barack, and he'd laugh and make self-deprecating jokes forever soiling the honor and dignity of the Office of the Presidency, Melania instinctively knows only to smile in public when her husband turns his head to her during speeches. Then, the second Donald turns his head back, you can see her obediently resume her facial expression of dour seriousness so focused on Christ you'd swear she was unhappy, depressed, and trapped in the position as First Lady as if against her will! What a magnificent Christian wife! And you can tell by the way that she's always swatting away Donald's hand to remind him about staying chaste, and to save room for Jesus. Donald Trump does not give into base impulses and desires of sexual gratification, I guarantee it!"

# Eric Trump Is Crushed To Learn His Dad Didn't Watch His RNC Speech

August 26, 2020
Washington D.C.—

Eric Trump delivered a fiery speech for his dad at the Republican National Convention, but was reportedly crushed to find out his father hadn't watched.

"Eric was so excited that he stayed up late for weeks editing his speech, rehearsing it over and over in front of a mirror, and asking around for advice," explained a Trump Organization executive, who requested anonymity to discuss Eric's private feelings. "Eric kept telling us that this speech would finally get his father to say that he loves him, and that he respects him. Naturally, everyone at the Trump Organization was really pulling for him, you know? Eric is kind of the runt of the family, and you want to see him kind of step out of the shadow of his dad and older siblings and succeed on his own. He tries so hard to impress his stone cold father, and anyone would cheer for an unloved underdog, right? So Eric invited a bunch of us Trump Organization executives to come to the convention and see him deliver it in person, and as soon as Eric got off stage he called up his dad to see what he thought. He put it on speaker phone as the call was ringing, and started fist pumping excitedly for that long overdue 'I love you, son!'"

But things turned awkward fast.

"Donald answered the call, and asked 'Who is this?' Eric kind of laughed, and said, 'It's me, Dad, Eric.' And then Donald Trump said 'Oh,' and mentioned that he had just gotten a new phone a few months ago, and some of the contacts hadn't transferred correctly. Eric laughed lightly, and then said, 'So, Dad, what did you think?' There was a long pause on the phone before the President asked 'About what?' Eric's eyes got real wide, and then the President said 'Oh, shoot! Did I miss another one of your ball games, sport? I just get so busy here at the office, you know?' I saw Eric's soul drain from his face. Then Eric reminded him of the speech, and Trump said it totally slipped his mind. Everyone around Eric kind of started shuffling their feet. We all felt so bad for him, you know? We could see the tears start welling up in his eyes, but Eric put on a brave face. He said, 'I worked really hard on my speech for you, Dad.' There was another pause, but then the President asked Eric if he had seen Tiffany's speech. Trump said that Tiffany really surprised him with her delivery, and that he was so proud of her. At this point the dam broke for Eric, and tears started streaming down his face. Then his dad said, 'And who knew Tiffany had filled out so well! Maybe I shouldn't have ignored her for her whole life!'"

## "Why A Woman AND Black?!" Screamed Mike Pence At God After His First Debate Prep Session

August 26, 2020
Washington D.C.—

Vice President Mike Pence is apparently unhappy about having to face off against Kamala Harris in the upcoming vice presidential debate.

A White House staffer, who requested anonymity, leaked to *The Halfway Post* an audio recording of Pence yelling at God in his office following his first debate prep session. The following is a transcript of the recording:

"Are You kidding me, God? Kamala Harris?! After all I've done for You? How many Sundays in a row have I woken up and gone to church? I haven't missed a service in 55 years! So why are You doing this to me? After all those times I've punched myself in the nuts to distract myself when the Devil got into my ears and whispered that I should masturbate! Why, God? I've been nothing but pure! It's bad enough I was going to have to be in a room with a woman debating her as if she were my equal, but a Black woman too? Why are You torturing me, God? Why couldn't I have gotten a white man again like Tim Kaine? You've really hurt Mother's feelings by forcing me to be onstage with a woman! She thinks I secretly wanted and prayed for Kamala to be the VP pick! You've got to make this right, God! Why are You threatening my marriage, and forcing me to be uncomfortable on live television? What if Kamala speaks in urban slang? Or references Cedric the Entertainer? I won't know what to do! What if she challenges me to a dance-off? You know I have no rhythm, God! I'd stand no chance dancing against someone Black! So why are You ruining me?! Is it to punish me for accepting the VP role from Donald Trump? I know he's a disgusting sinner, but I did it for You, God! I thought You were telling me he would be impeached or have a heart attack, and You wanted me to be able to take over. But neither of those things happened, did they, God? So You're actually the one who owes me an explanation! I've debased myself for four years while You taunted me dangling the presidency so close yet so far away from my grasp! Do You have any idea how many horrifying stories I've had to listen to Trump tell me about his adultery? Of course You do because You're omniscient! So why are You forcing me to debate Kamala? Is this some kind of Abraham-Isaac thing where You're testing my faith by ruining my life? Well I've had enough, God! Just kill me! Kill me now! Killlllll meeeeeee!"

The recording then goes on for nine minutes of Pence apologizing profusely for losing his temper with God, and offering to flagellate himself if God gives him a sign in the next five minutes that that is what God requires for penance.

# Melania Trump Reportedly Left A Dozen Rats Inside Ivanka's White House Office

August 27, 2020
Washington D.C.—

According to White House insiders, the feud between Melania Trump and her step-daughter Ivanka has intensified in recent weeks.

Melania has reportedly been upset about Ivanka always getting more attention from her husband than her, and has recently begun making her feelings about Ivanka known.

"It has gotten way out of hand," explained a White House staffer, who requested anonymity to discuss the chaos. "Melania snuck into Ivanka's office a few nights ago and left a dozen rats she had purchased from a local pet store. Then she took a can of red spray paint and wrote 'Eat up, you snake!' several times on the walls. This was Melania's revenge from an incident a week ago when Ivanka took some of the cockroaches from the terrarium in Stephen Miller's office and left them in Melania's bed in the White House residence, which, of course, is separate from the bedroom where the President sleeps. Ivanka also left several printed, glossy photos of herself with her father when she was a teenager where she was sitting on his lap in a very creepy, inappropriate way. I have never seen the First Lady more furious. And the President refuses to get involved. He says it turns him on that the two of them are fighting over him. He said he didn't think Melania had it in her, and is interested to see how far they'll take it. But it's becoming a substantial waste of taxpayer money to fix the damage they're doing. This morning Ivanka ran through the freshly planted flowers in the Rose Garden that Melania had just finished renovating, and destroyed lots of the flowers kicking them and cutting them with a pair of scissors. Then at lunch, while Ivanka was eating, Melania came up behind her and spit gum into Ivanka's hair and sprayed ketchup all over Ivanka's dress. Melania yelled that Donald would really be attracted to Ivanka now, which made Ivanka stand up and slap Melania in the face so hard it left a handprint on her cheek. But then Melania started laughing maniacally, and revealed that she had periodically snuck into Ivanka's purse and replaced her birth control pills so that they were all placebo pills and Ivanka would have more children than she wanted. Ivanka screamed that she had only wanted one kid, but now had three, and that Melania had ruined her life. The smile on Melania's face as she said 'The kids will keep you too busy for Donald' literally gave me chills. The Trump family is really f***ed up. I'm going public with this because their fighting has got to stop. I'm terrified of how much further this feud will escalate! It's approaching *Godfather*-calibur stuff."

# Jerry Falwell Jr. Says He Prayed Long And Hard, And God Has "Totally Forgiven Him" For His Sex Scandal

August 28, 2020
Lynchburg, VA—

Disgraced Evangelical leader Jerry Falwell Jr. has taken to Twitter to announce that God has forgiven him for his transgressions against Christian values in his recent pool boy scandal.

The following are Mr. Falwell's tweets:

"Listen, everyone, I know I've not lived up to the strict code of conduct I wrote for Liberty University students, but I have spent the last several days praying to Jesus and asking God for forgiveness. I can now report to all of you that God said me and Him are cool."

"He said it wasn't my fault, but that my wife Becki shoulders all the blame. Then Jesus chimed in and said that, just like Adam, my Eve had tempted me into the Devil's arms with the evil fruit of voyeurism and sexual socialism. God told me that I was still a VIP for Heaven, but Becki maybe not so much."

"God informed me that, because I've lived my entire life so devoutly while spreading His message, I get a free pass for a couple dozen or so fraudulent business deals misspending university money to pay off a few sex-related extortion schemes here and there."

"Then Jesus told me it was 'no biggie,' and that Satan had tried the pool boy trick with Him plenty of times, but luckily He didn't have a wife like Becki to betray Him like I did. So, as you can clearly see, I'm all good and forgiven!"

"Now, I know there are a bunch of liberal atheists out there who will say I'm making all this up, but they don't understand the glory of faith so they could never possibly appreciate God's grace. In fact, Jesus showed me a vision of all my atheist critics burning in Hell! But guess who wasn't there? Me!"

"Then Jesus showed me a vision of me and all my supporters partying it up in Heaven on a yacht. We were all having the best time, and everyone had their pants unzipped and our arms around young women who weren't our Judas wives! Jesus said that's what Heaven is all about!"

"Then Jesus snapped His fingers and brought me back to Earth. But, before He left my prayer session, He told me not to worry about all the Liberty students who I expelled for breaking the same university rules I did because they weren't forgiven, only I was."

"All the Liberty students who got in trouble for not abiding by the strict code of conduct knew they were sinning, unlike me, whose only sin was trusting my wife to behave like a Christian when she was serving Satan instead!"

"So all the slutty, gay and misbehaving Liberty students who got expelled: don't bother trying to get back in… unless you send me some sexy photos on Instagram, then we can talk. I know a couple pool boys who'd love to see those!"

## More MAGA Fan Headlines

- "Liberals Are Snowflakes!" Say Conservatives Currently Boycotting The NFL, Hollywood, Books, Nike, Starbucks, Netflix, Mainstream Media, All Music But Country, NASCAR, France, Healthy Foods, Public Politeness, Cultural Tolerance, And Anything Created Or Sold By A Person Of Color

- A Florida Man Stood At The Edge Of The Ocean And Screamed For Several Hours At Hurricane Irma That It's A Liberal Hoax

- "All Lives Matter" Pedantics Remind Hurricane-Flooded Houston That "All Cities Matter"

- White Supremacists Hate Being Called Nazis So Much That They're Threatening To Literally Become Nazis

- "Milo Yiannopoulos Shouldn't Be Kicked Out Of Bars!" Scream Neo-Nazis Who Want To Deport A Minimum Of 30 Million Americans

- White Nationalist Poster Boy Peter Cvjetanovic Is Stunned To Learn His Family Immigrated To America

- Gun Rally Man Wearing Three AR-15s Says He Feels Threatened By Biracial Couples

- Armed MAGA Protester With Trump Flags On His Truck And A Bible In His Hand Is Having Trouble Explaining How He's Different Than ISIS

- GOP Voter Realizes Sharia Law Sounds An Awful Lot Like The GOP's National Party Platform

- Local Conservative Finally Reads The Second Amendment, Is Astonished To Learn It Calls For "Well Regulated" Militias

- Trump Voter Realizes His Crappy Life Will Never Be Improved By The GOP's Tax Cuts For The Super Rich

- Local Evangelical Trump Voter Admits Bob Mueller's Jawline Has Made Him Question His Heterosexuality

- Alt-Right Neo-Nazis Insist Feminists Are "The Real Nazis" Because They Can't Get Laid

- Alt-Right Neo-Nazi Takes Back Avocado-Picking Job From Deported Mexican, Quits After 20 Minutes

- Local Good Guys With Guns Got Shot By Other Good Guys With Guns Mistaking Them For Bad Guys With Guns

- Local Trump Voters Admit Trump Is A Terrible President, But Still Support Him Because Blatant Corruption And Obvious Governmental Incompetence Makes Liberals So Upset

- Local Nazis Are Concerned That, If Jews Supposedly Control Everything, Maybe Jews Are Actually The Real Master Race

- The KKK Wants You To Know They're Wearing Hoods Because They're Racist, Not Because Of COVID

- MAGA Fans Claim Leaked Audio Of Donald Trump Calling His Supporters "Stupid Idiots Who Are Dumber Than Rocks For Donating Money To My Campaign" Somehow "Owned The Libs"

- Trump Killing His Own Voters By Downplaying The Seriousness Of The Medical Risks Of Getting Infected With COVID And By Suggesting Fake Cures To Them Is Quite Some Impressive 4-Dimensional Chess

- MAGA Fans Are Pointing Out That The Constitution Does Not Specifically Say Democrats Can Vote

- "Jimmy Kimmel Should Stick To Comedy" Says Every Republican Who Tells Scientists That Evolution, Climate Change, And Vaccines Are Hoaxes

## Local Police Are Relieved Black Man They Killed Had An Overdue Library Book So His Murder Is Justified

August 29, 2020
Mobile, AL—

Police in an Alabama town shot and killed a Black man this afternoon who was quietly reading a book in a public park.

A Black Lives Matter protest has been organized for tomorrow in front of the town's police department, which the entire town accuses of recurring racism and brutality.

"The thug was reading his book in the park very menacingly," explained Police Chief Ralph Meegan in a press conference a few hours after the incident. "And his book happened to be a biography of Colin Kaepernick so we can obviously infer that the thug hated our brave troops fighting abroad, and loathed America and all of our freedoms. The thug also had a substantial afro hairstyle so it is my opinion that the officer was warranted in thinking the victim probably belonged to a gang, and was therefore an immediate threat. We don't have any gangs in our fair city, and we police officers try to keep it that way! Therefore the officer was also perfectly warranted according to our protocol guidelines in sneaking up behind the thug on the park bench and firing his weapon several times with no warning into the thug's back. The officer promised me that he truly felt his life was in imminent danger, and I believe him. Upon inspection of the thug's body we noticed a comb in his pocket, which, of course, besides being a simple tool to comb his afro hair, can also be used as a weapon with many potentially sharp prongs. So I am thankful our brave, totally not racist officer was not harmed today, and was able to protect his own life in the face of such terrifying book reading. We also ran through the police database, and we found a case from a couple counties over with a description that vaguely matches the guy, so it turns out actually that our officer was totally retroactively warranted to suspect this thug of being a criminal in the first place. So this incident of deadly force happens to be just an unfortunate misunderstanding. Besides, let's be honest, a Black male between the ages of 18 and 65 ought to know not to hang around outside in public places. That demographic matches literally thousands of police profiles around the country! I would also like to report that we did an extensive background check on the thug, and we found that the book the thug was reading was, in fact, overdue by a day, which means that criminal owed the public library an entire nickel. It frightens me still to think about that criminal stalking around our peaceful town all day with an overdue library book. Ooh, I just got the chills again! Who knows what other books that thug might have checked out and not returned in a timely fashion had our officer not intervened. And let's not forget that the thug was reading a book about that Kaepernick America-hater, so who knows what acts of civil disobedience he was no doubt getting inspired to commit in the future. He was radicalizing against America right there on that bench! What a terror! This thug was probably going to go from book reading straight to kneeling during our beautiful anthem, and who knows what horrible displays of America hatred next! It was no doubt only a matter of time before that thug pulled his comb out on some innocent citizen, or kept his overdue library book even longer! I would like to commend the officer in today's incident for bravery, and I hope that the whole community continues to pray for the police officers, who every day risk their lives keeping our park safe from criminals like the one neutralized today."

Another cop in the police department, however, had a different perspective, and said the incident today gave him an epiphany that cops killing unarmed citizens seems to make a lot of members of the community get upset.

"I was eating my lunch sandwich when all of a sudden I had this idea," explained Officer Rutgers to *The Halfway Post.* "I started thinking about how it looks when citizens somehow die in police custody, or ironically get arrested for the logically dubious charge of resisting arrest, or get shot by cops while unarmed. I put myself in the shoes of an average, law-abiding citizen, and I realized that if I weren't a cop, I'd probably be upset about those instances happening myself. I started looking up videos on YouTube of police brutality, and I was very surprised how many hundreds of videos there are of cops killing family dogs needlessly, of resource officers beating up kids in schools, of cops starting fights with calm people on the street, of cops pulling guns out on people seemingly indiscriminately, and of police officers getting caught planting drugs on people while their cameras were still on. Then I saw some of the videos of these social justice protests where dozens of police at a time are shooting people in the head with rubber bullets, pushing down the elderly, clubbing people on the ground, attacking journalists, and so on. There are public videos of literally hundreds of cops around the country straight up brutalizing Black Lives Matter protesters, and who deserve to be arrested, charged, and jailed for assault and other violations of civil rights ASAP, but they still have their badges and are working today. Assault gets other people arrested, so why shouldn't all these violent, psycho cops be arrested? It made me realize that maybe our Blue Wall of Silence is like a cult that illegally stifles accountability. So I started thinking about the way I do my job, and I realized that maybe aspects of my training to escalate situations I get into so I can provoke resistance from citizens and then respond with overwhelming force leading to unnecessary bodily injury or death is maybe not the best way to do my job in a manner that earns the respect, trust and faith of my community. Maybe American policing could use some reform!"

# Trump Is Suing His Grandchildren For Violating NDA's He Made Them Sign As Infants

August 30, 2020
Palm Springs, FL—

Donald Trump has just filed lawsuits against each of his grandchildren for leaking details of his personal life to teachers, classmates, and sports coaches.

As soon as they started making babbling sounds as infants, Trump reportedly put a pen in their tiny hands and forced them to sign. He also reportedly gave them each fifty cents in hush money.

The following are details of Trump's private life that his grandchildren have let slip in various public situations:

- "Grandpa is scary without his hair and makeup done."
- "I technically have three grandmas, and Grandpa says bad things about all of them!"
- "Grandpa is mean to Daddy" (Eric).
- "What is a 'f***ing idiot,' and why does Grandpa call Daddy that every day?" (Don Jr.).
- "Grandpa must really like sugar because he's always snorting it. His favorite is blue sugar."
- "One time, Grandpa's teeth fell out, and I hid them, and he got very angry and hit Daddy a lot" (Eric).
- "Grandpa calls himself a 'babe magnet,' but I always see women running away from him, not toward him!"
- "I'm not going to fetch Grandpa any more Diet Cokes until he pays me. He says he'll give me a dollar for each can I deliver, but he never pays!"
- "Grandpa said his next girlfriend will be my age" (13).
- "Why do Grandpa's friends all look like scary, vampires?" (Rudy Giuliani and Stephen Miller).
- "Grandpa doesn't let Daddy eat until Grandpa's already full, and all the food is cold" (Don Jr.).
- "Grandpa calls Daddy a 'globalist' a lot" (Jared Kushner).
- "Grandpa always borrows my middle school yearbooks, and never gives them back."
- "I've caught Grandpa stealing money from my piggy bank two times."
- "Grandpa only remembers Aunt Ivanka's kids' names, and says he wishes he could have been in her womb too."

# Stephen Miller Unveiled A Human Centipede He Made Out Of Three Immigrant Children

September 1, 2020
Washington D.C.—

Stephen Miller, executive adviser to President Donald Trump, just unveiled a human centipede he created, and defended his work claiming that the only effective deterrent to keep migrants and refugees from crossing America's border and requesting asylum is to separate families and turn all the children into human centipedes three at a time.

Pundits on *Fox News* unanimously commended the Trump Administration's new immigration policy, and said it was comfortably within the purview of long-standing American values. Sean Hannity said the human centipede policy was a stroke of political brilliance designed to solve all the immigration problems President Barack Obama never could, and Brian Kilmeade said if he was in a human centipede he'd like to try being at the back end.

Trump-supporting Evangelical groups across the country affirmed that Jesus would approve of the new human centipede policy as a "perfectly Christian" method to keep America safe and secure from Muslim terrorists sneaking across the border disguised as refugee children. Jerry Falwell Jr. said sewing an immigrant child's butt cheeks to another immigrant child's face cheeks seemed vaguely enough like what Jesus meant when the Savior told His followers to "turn the other cheek."

Senator Mitch McConnell said he had no comment.

Representative Louie Gohmert said the centipedes were more morally acceptable than Democrats having power and turning America communist.

Senator Susan Collins said the centipedes "concerned" her, but did not go so far as to actually commit to using her Senate authority to hold the Trump Administration accountable in any way.

Executives from the National Rifle Association said they were interested in partnering with the Trump Administration to buy and transport some human centipedes to nature reserves to let Second Amendment fans hunt them.

First Lady Melania Trump incorporated the human centipede project into her anti-bullying "Be Best" campaign, and claimed it proved that her husband's administration does not mistreat migrant children, but instead turns them into beautiful new creatures like a metamorphosis.

## The Top 10 Medical Cures For COVID-19 Donald Trump Has Endorsed

The following are medical cures President Donald Trump has endorsed in his coronavirus press conferences:

1. Lysol: "Lysol is a beautiful product, tremendous product. There are many ways you can kill COVID with Lysol. There's injection into your veins, you can huff it for several hours, you can mix it into any liquor during happy hour, or you can pour some into your palms and rinse your eyes with it. Great disinfectant!"

2. Adderall: "I snort Adderall every day, and I haven't gotten coronavirus. Dr. Fauci says my Adderall cure is only correlation at best, not causation, but it's worth a shot, right?"

3. Drano: "People have been seeing some great results from taking a kitchen funnel, lying on the ground on their backs with their legs lifted up to angle their buttholes straight toward the ceiling, putting the funnel into their exposed anuses, and then pouring Drano inside. They say you have to keep pouring till it comes out your mouth."

4. Fake tanning: "Another thing I do every day. Maybe it works, maybe not. But if you look great and have a healthy glow like I do, you'll start feeling better. People say my tan is even sexier than Jack Kennedy's tan."

5. Autoerotic asphyxiation: "My executive aide Stephen Miller was telling me about this one. He says he was feeling some of the COVID symptoms, but that choking himself out cured him. He said he used to get himself off by choking other people, but, since social distancing has started, he's had to get creative by himself."

6. No exercise: "Why exercise and waste your energy? You have a finite supply of it in your life, and you need all the energy you can get to fight off COVID. That's why I spend most of my day in bed watching *Fox News* and tweeting congratulatory tweets to *Fox* show hosts for recognizing how much of a genius I am. It's also why I golf every three days. I don't want to play a real sport and unnecessarily sacrifice my valuable energy!"

7. Lindsey Graham massaging your back: "I don't know if this has anything to do with my immune system, but every day Lindsey

Graham massages my back for 45 minutes. I like to make him grovel at my feet for 15 minutes first, and apologize for all the nasty things he said about me before I got the Republican nomination. And before Russia hacked everyone in the Republican Party's private emails. All while I whip him on the back with my belt. It might just be a placebo effect, but it makes me feel younger than ever."

8. An exclusive diet of fast food: "If you eat a lot of fast food, the grease coats your internal tubes, and your veins and arteries are too slippery for the coronavirus to sneak up and latch on anywhere. It's like trying to run on a freshly waxed floor with socks on."

9. Trump campaign donations: "If you donate $100 or more to my 2020 campaign, I guarantee that God will never let you get infected with coronavirus!"

10. Don't test: "Whatever you do, don't take a COVID test! If you never take a test, you'll never test positive for COVID!"

President Trump has also claimed that, if he gets reelected, he has a 30-day plan to defeat the coronavirus once and for all.

"If I win reelection, COVID-19 will just give up when it hears the news about my next tremendous landslide Electoral College victory," Trump told reporters. "COVID knows I have a big, beautiful plan to destroy it, and there's no chance it will survive my second first 100 days. But I'm not going to tell how I'll do it because we have to start being unpredictable. The scientists and the doctors are all way too predictable. They say everything we're going to do out loud! They say we're going to shut this down, or we're going to limit that activity, or we're going to use this quarantine approach, and the coronavirus hears it all and adapts its schemes! We have to start being unpredictable, folks. I won't be letting the fake news spill out all our secrets in my second term. COVID particularly loves Don Lemon from *CNN*. Listens to him every night, and takes notes. So I'm not going to say my plan out loud. It's going to be a surprise, but you're going to love it. Trust me. COVID's days are numbered, I guarantee it. I'm going to give the doctors total authorization to do whatever it takes. There will be no rules. No limits on drone strikes. Maybe even nukes. Who knows? You'll have to wait and see. So just 30 days after I get reelected the coronavirus will be gone. Like magic. We're already rounding the corner, but we'll round all the other corners too! You're going to love it. You're going to say, 'Wow, President Trump, I can't believe how fast you did it!' It'll be a beautiful thing. And it will be the last thing COVID expects. COVID will never expect this plan in 100 years. Even if it watches Don Lemon every night. So vote for Trump!"

# Steve Bannon's White Sperm Vault Lost Power, Ruined His Collection Of 20,000 Jars

September 2, 2020
Anchorage, AK—

A few months ago Steve Bannon bought Richard Spencer's Alaskan White Sperm Doomsday Vault project, and has invested heavily since to ramp up production of its collection of white people's sperm.

The vault's first goal was to maintain a large enough supply of sperm with DNA coded for white skin in order to repopulate the Earth with white people if immigrants and interracial marriage ever lead to a future where white skin is genetically endangered, but Bannon expanded the goal to save enough white sperm to populate whole other planets with white people as well.

Just last week Mr. Bannon finally capped his 20,000th mason jar of white sperm, and he celebrated with a giant party for his financial backers and sperm donor friends. An attendee told *The Halfway Post* that it was themed like a giant bachelorette party, with guests all bringing penis-shaped candies, balloons, masks, and other phallic decorations.

However, tragedy reportedly struck last night when a power outage occurred and the emergency back-up generators failed to activate, thawing and expiring all 20,000 jars of sperm.

"It was literally the worst day of my life when I woke up and discovered that the power had been out all night," explained Bannon in a brief telephone call with *The Halfway Post*. "I was in Hungary at the time for a European conference on adapting Nazism for the 21st Century, so it took me a whole day just to get back to North America. When I finally got there, I must have opened up and smelled 500 of the mason jars to try and find even one that was still fresh. But, sadly, they were all rancid. I even dumped a few out on the ground and tried to give them CPR compressions and mouth-to-mouth, but it was just too late. Each little sperm was like a child to me. A beautiful, white potential child. I guess Heaven got a trillion new angels this week."

However, Mr. Bannon is not quitting the project.

"I got very depressed for a few days," continued Bannon. "But then I thought about the oath I swore to preserve the future for white children when I was elected Grand Dragon of the Alt-Right, and I realized I couldn't just give up. So I called up Richard Spencer, Stephen Miller, Sebastian Gorka, and Tucker Carlson and we met up, each brought a mason jar, and got right back at it."

# Mitch McConnell Just Sold His Soul To Satan Live On C-SPAN To Keep His Senate Majority

September 5, 2020
Washington D.C.—

Senate Majority Leader Mitch McConnell just gave a speech on the floor of the Senate in which he appeared to offer Satan his everlasting soul in exchange for letting him keep his Republican majority in the Senate.

The following is a transcript of the related excerpt of Mr. McConnell's speech:

"If my colleagues in the Democratic Party want to pass their socialism into law, consider me the Grim Reaper of the Senate. As long as I am Senate Majority Leader, socialism will never come to America. But things are not looking good in the polls for us, to be frank. We're going to lose senators, that's for sure. But the question is how many? So I am prepared right now to offer my soul to the Dark Lord Satan in order for Republicans to win at least five of the upcoming toss-up Senate elections. Preferably more, but I will leave that up to Satan to decide in His infinite evil wisdom how big the GOP's majority should be. It just has to be a majority. Satan, are You listening? I, Addison Mitchell McConnell Jr., renounce my faith in Jesus Christ, and put it instead in You, the august Dark Lord! I will gleefully spend all of eternity in the flames of Hell for just two more years of GOP Senate majority power! I must have two more years to install enough Republican federal judges and Supreme Court Justices to fully turn America into a theocratic, fascist state, and I will trade my everlasting soul to make sure the government is corrupted enough for Democrats to never have control of a branch of government ever again, no matter how many more millions of votes they get than Republicans! Satan, I offer myself as collateral for a GOP victory! Yahweh, I firmly and with full, willing, conscious intention put Satan before You against Your specific commandment! I renounce the Holy Spirit, Jesus Christ, and Christianity in their entirety, and am henceforth a loyal adherent to and servant for the Church of Lucifer! Satan, if You let me stay on as Senate Majority Leader, my soul will be Yours to do with as You please! I will gladly praise Hell's stench of burning flesh, worship the cacophony of piercing shrieks and screams, and cherish the ceaseless sights of torment and suffering! I will eagerly drink from Your great underworld fountains of blood, and feast upon Your maggoty corpses! I consent to immortal affliction and all unimaginable cruelties in Your name, Lucifer, I pray! Thank you, Mr. Speaker, and I yield the remainder of my time. Alright, that concludes today's session, the Senate will adjourn until tomorrow at 9am for the vote on renaming the post office in New Mexico's 2nd District after Pete Domenici."

## Ted Cruz, To Prove His Loyalty To Donald Trump, Admits His Wife Is Ugly

September 8, 2020
Washington D.C.—

Senator Ted Cruz was widely mocked this morning for sucking up to President Donald Trump in the most opportunistic way imaginable: admitting Trump was right when he called Heidi Cruz, his wife, ugly.

Cruz displayed his loyalty to the President in the following Twitter thread:

"I am fully endorsing President Donald Trump to defeat Joe Biden and the socialist Democrats. I know I've said some mean things about him in the past, but that was when we were caught up in the heat of the campaign. I lost, and President Trump is clearly a better, more virile man."

"And I'm glad I lost because President Trump is the best president ever. He's so honest. He never lies. In fact, he was telling the truth when he called my wife ugly. My wife is ugly! She's way uglier than Melania Trump! I know I attacked Trump for saying it, but I was just upset about how right he was!"

"President Trump was also right about everything else he said about me and my family. My dad DID help assassinate Kennedy! The underside of my office's desk IS covered with bloody boogers. My wife DOES scream out Donald's name during intimacy, though Donald would of course never be with her—she's way too ugly for him!"

"So I'd like to thank President Donald Trump for always telling the truth! I hope his MAGA supporters are hearing me say this! I hope they'll remember my humiliating loyalty to the President in 2024! I'll do anything for their votes!"

"I'll pay porn stars for sex, I'll say some locker room talk about my daughters, I'll steal money from kids' cancer charities, or anything else voters who love Donald Trump want to see me do! I'll divorce Heidi right now on Twitter if that's what it takes! Heidi: we're over! Pack your things and get out!"

"If I come home and find you're still there, I'll throw you out. Hey @RealDonaldTrump, not only can you call my wife ugly, from now on you can call her homeless!"

# Trump Agrees To Allow Mail-In Voting If Everyone Writes Either "Dem" or "Rep" On The Back Of Their Envelope

September 13, 2020
Washington D.C.—

President Donald Trump has finally consented to Congress allocating federal money to bolster mail-in voting initiatives to help people worried about COVID-19 get their votes submitted.

He specified one condition, though, in a Twitter thread this morning:

"Okay, I'll let Democrats do their mail-in voting! But on one condition: voters have to write whether they're voting for me or Biden by writing DEM or REP on the back of their envelopes! This is so Postmaster General DeJoy can make sure USPS does a great job getting these mail-in ballots processed promptly and efficiently!"

"We are devising a state of the art sorting system in which the mail-in ballots will be separated accorded to party, but I promise on a Bible or any other book you want to give me that all the ballots will be counted fairly! No one loves free, fair, and accurate elections more than me!"

"The Democrats will claim this is an attempt by me to collect all the Democratic ballots separately and then destroy them, or slow them down enough that they don't get counted in time, but that is total fake news! I love Democratic votes! Believe me that no one would hate more than me for Biden votes not to get counted!"

"Because there's no way Biden gets even 10% of the REAL vote when everyone can tell Biden hates Jesus! Unlike me, who is a total Jesus lover! He did so many amazing things. Like when Jesus was going to sacrifice His son to prove His devotion to God. Taught me so many lessons. Eric, watch out! Ha, just kidding, but maybe someday…"

"And when Jesus cut the baby in half to make a point for the arguing parents, wow! What wisdom! You know, Jesus was even tougher on kids than I am on Don Jr.! But I bet Biden doesn't know any of these stories. He should read the one about the Goliath again because he's just like the Goliath, and I'm Jesus with a slingshot!"

"So, if you like Jesus, you have no choice but to vote Trump and let me part the Blue Sea of coastal socialist elites again, just like Jesus parted the Red Sea and led the Jews to Sodomy and Gonorrhea!"

# Mike Pence Is Concerned About Kamala Harris's Lack Of Chaperones On The Campaign Trail

September 24, 2020
Washington D.C.—

Mike Pence raised a lot of eyebrows with the following Twitter thread he tweeted this morning about Senator Kamala Harris:

"I cannot remain silent anymore about the fact that I am very concerned about Kamala Harris's conspicuous lack of male chaperones on the campaign trail. I'm worried about the terrible message her promiscuous galavanting about town sends impressionable young girls across these United States!"

"The way she gets up onstage without explicitly showing the audience she has her husband's permission to speak publicly really offends good Christian women everywhere, and embarrasses the good Christian men who have to listen to her! It's just not a woman's place to speak about what direction the country should take, especially without her husband standing behind her telling her what to say!"

"Now, if she got up onstage at campaign events to talk about baking pies, or to warn young men about devilish liberal girls trying to steal their sacred virginities with their satanic, atheist vulvas, or apologize on behalf of Eve for eating Eden's fruit and damning our Earthly existences to chronic suffering, I'd be all for her wanton, unchaperoned traveling!"

"But the fact is that she is mostly traveling alone in a large company of unrelated men without any male family members there to officially represent the Harris family and ensure she doesn't dishonor her husband, marriage, or father! God is very much not happy about her campaign arrangements. Couldn't she at least bring along a nephew or something?"

"I'm almost thinking about canceling the VP debate! The liberal media has refused all of my preconditions about Ms. Harris making sure she covers her knees, ankles, and elbows with thick, wool clothing (no polyester, per the Bible), and promising not to speak in any sultry tones or use any sensual double entendres!"

"And the DNC won't make her promise not to lick her lips, wink at me, or blow a kiss in my direction! The Democrats clearly don't respect the fact that I only make room in my life for one mother: my wife! I want a dignified, Godly debate, not some floozy California debate!"

## Rudy Giuliani Mysteriously Tweeted "The Aliens Have Anal Probed Me FOR THE LAST TIME!"

September 27, 2020
New York City, NY—

Rudy Giuliani this morning published several mysterious tweets alleging past alien abductions and anal probings.

The following are Mr. Giuliani's tweets:

"The aliens came back last night, but they were not gentle like they promised they would be! They got right up in there with no decency or foreplay to loosen me up or stretch me out a bit! I told them last time I wasn't just a piece of meat for them to poke, prod, probe and monitor internally, and now I'm serious! No more! I'm cutting them off!"

"If the aliens come back again I'll be ready for them! Starting tonight, I'm sleeping with a loaded shotgun under my pillow! From now on, Rudolph William Louis Giuliani's sphincter is only an exit, not an entrance for their spindly little green fingers and metal machinery! They don't even warm up the cold, metal boxes first before jamming them up there! They have no bedside manner!"

"And I'm sick of the beeping! If they have inter-galactic technology, why can't they build an anal probe that's quiet instead of beeping audibly every 3 minutes! It's driving me crazy! So mark my words, my anus will no longer be their biology experiment! They can go anal probe some other schmuck! I've been extra-terrestrially sodomized for the LAST TIME!"

The tweets were displayed on Mr. Giuliani's Twitter account this morning from 3:51am to 7:21am before they were apparently deleted.

## Paul Ryan Endorsed Joe Biden, Apologized For His Emasculated Spinelessness

September 29, 2020
Washington D.C.—

Former Speaker of the House Paul Ryan today published a shocking Twitter thread endorsing Democrat Joe Biden for President over Republican incumbent Donald Trump.

The following are Ryan's immediately viral tweets announcing his 2020 endorsement:

"Hey, everyone, it has been a long time since I've last tweeted, but I have to clear my conscience for myself, my family, and my beloved nation: Donald Trump CANNOT be reelected. He cannot be given four more years as president of our great nation."

"Donald Trump has been cruel and horrible in a million ways, and having a Republican in the White House is just not worth dealing with the sociopathic and fascist apocalypse of democracy he has conjured upon America. Democrats simply have to win, and return our country to a psychological sanity that Republicans, at the moment, are incapable of giving us."

"The Faustian bargain I made to leverage Trump's demagogic appeal and MAGA voting base for a full Republican government in order to pass extreme tax cuts has backfired, and now the endurance of America's democratic experiment is at stake. Like all Faustian bargains, I was hoisted by my own petard…"

"…As my Frankenstein-ish monstrosity of a House Republican caucus commandeered by Trump's childish, unleashed id bested my political abilities to wrangle the contemporary GOP's factional insanities, ended my political enthusiasm for public service, and ultimately left me soulless."

"Though dealing on a daily basis with Trump's 5th grade intelligence, utter inability to think of anything or anyone other than himself, and his early signs of dementia were punishments I could barely withstand…"

"I cannot help but lie awake at night thinking how much worse existential vengeance I have earned. I deserve to have to try to explain to his toddler brain how complicated healthcare is every day for a torturous eternity."

"Like all conservative coalitions expecting to control a racist demagogue before me throughout history, I too lost control of my electorally useful sociopathic fool, and was entirely emasculated trying to maintain the illusion of normalcy while that wannabe dictator mangled and dismantled every safeguard of nonpartisan governmental professionalism standing in his way of corrupt intentions."

"All those times I said I hadn't heard his base appeals to Americans' worst instincts, or I said I hadn't read his offensive tweets, I was lying. I knew all too well the damage he was doing to our society and culture. Yet I was a coward, and I put my desire of letting already mega rich people and corporations pay even less money in taxes ahead of the institutional stability of the country."

"I was silent when I could have, and should have, said something or done something. And I wasted several reclusive years after leaving Congress avoiding my responsibility to reign in the political monster I helped set free to quietly profit personally in the lucrative private sector world of lobbying and executive boardroom membership thanks to those tax cuts I passed."

"But no more. I now fully own up to my abject spinelessness; my moral, masculine, and historical cowardice; and my personification of everything that is wrong in contemporary politics. I accept fully the blame for enabling Donald Trump's worst impulses, his Constitutional subterfuge, and our current governmental psychopathy. I admit that I am the worst."

"It is much too late to prevent Trump from getting elected, but I hope to help prevent his reelection. So I fully endorse Joe Biden with my whole heart. I may never recover my soul from my Faustian bargain, but I hope to reclaim a sliver of my heart, which quivers with despair every time I look into my children's eyes and see the democratic and free society they will inherit burning in the reflection."

"So please vote for Joe Biden. America cannot handle another four years of President Donald Trump. There will be no America left. He will degrade it, destroy it, and abandon it like he has degraded, destroyed, and abandoned everything else in his life, from his marriages, to his casinos, to all his personal relationships."

"So I repeat one last time that Joe Biden is our only hope. Donald Trump cannot be trusted with any quantity of authority or responsibility, no matter how small and insignificant. He is unequivocally the very worst president this nation has ever suffered through. Sorry again for helping push us this close to the precipice of fascism!"

# Thirteen Ways Of Looking At A President

(Inspired by Wallace Stevens)
by Donald J. Trump


## I

Among copious elitist billionaires,
The only tremendous thing
Was the big brain of the President.

## II

I was of three minds
Like my three wives,
I'm past due for a fourth.

## III

My hair whirled under the ceiling fan.
Time for some more hairspray.

## IV

A man and a country
Are one.
A man and a country and an Electoral College
I won.

## V

I do not know which to prefer,
The beauty of impeachment acquittal
Or the beauty of revenge,
The Democrats losing
Or just after.

## VI

Her revulsion filled the doorway
With barbaric disgust.
The shadow of the younger wife
Crossed it, to and fro.
The mood
Traced in the shadow:
Sex tonight is a lost cause.

## VII

O, liberal women of cities
Why do you imagine female presidents?

Do you not see how the male Commander-in-Chief
Walks around the locker rooms
Of the women about you?

## VIII

I know tax evasions
And lucid, legal loopholes;
But I know, too,
That the oligarchs are involved
In what I know.

## IX

When another chief of staff resigned,
It marked the edge
Of one of many ovals.

## X

At the sight of buxom daughter
Walking down the hallway,
Even my rod of euphoria
Would cry out sharply.

## XI

He flew over flyover country
In his airborne coach.
Once, a fear pierced him,
In that he mistook
The fault of someone else
For his own.

## XII

The retweets are adding.
The President must be winning.

## XIII

It was executive time all afternoon.
*Fox News* was playing
And it was going to play.
The President sat
In his bed with his phone.

## "Blacks 4 Trump" Group Caught Using Blackface To Pretend They Have Black Members

October 14, 2020
St. Louis, MO—

President Donald Trump has been desperate to attract Black voters to his reelection campaign in order to turn around the polls that show him losing to Joe Biden by a significant margin, and a local "Blacks 4 Trump" group has been trying to help.

Unfortunately for the President, they have been unsuccessful signing up a single Black voter onto their club roster in the last five years of canvassing.

"I don't understand it!" exclaimed Ralph Hartman, the group's frustrated president. "We've done everything we can think of to get some Black members! We've advertised in local papers and on Facebook about our open-house events, but we've gotten absolutely no traction in the Black community! I don't understand why no Blacks are interested. And it's not like we need a lot of them. We just need a few for some photos to upload to our social media accounts to finally make it look like our group is authentic. Or if we could at least get one Black person I guess I could copy and paste the face on several other bodies in our group photos to make our group look more diverse. But it's costing our club a ton of money to buy all the makeup every weekend. We want potential Black members to feel comfortable joining, so for each of our events some of our members use dark brown makeup on their faces to look like they're African-American. We actually had a Black guy attend one of our chili cook-offs a little while back, but he got upset and left when he realized our 'Black' members were actually caucasians wearing disguises. Apparently Black people don't appreciate blackface. Who knew? And we really went to a lot of trouble to make our 'Black' members seem indistinguishable from real Black people! We got them du-rags, pants that don't fit, fake wigs with dreadlocks, and we had them walk around carrying in their hands biographies of Malcolm X and DVDs of *Bad Boys II*. It looked pretty authentic to my untrained eyes! I guess I'll just have to resort to photographing them for our site photos, and hope any prospective Black people checking out our social media pages don't look too closely or zoom in and see the bits of white skin sticking out around their eyes."

## GOP Senators Are Excited For Trump To Lose To Finally Say What They Think About Him

October 19, 2020
Washington D.C.—

According to reports on Capitol Hill, Republican senators are increasingly eager to get the election over with so they can finally say what they really think about President Donald Trump after he loses to Joe Biden.

"November 4th can't come soon enough!" said Senator Ben Sasse. "I know Trump is a sociopathic idiot lunatic like everyone else, but obviously I can't say that out loud in public! My voters loyal to Trump would all turn against me! So I stifle those thoughts of reality deep down in the bottom of my soul along with all the other thoughts of reality I keep hidden from my voters, like how climate change is real and average conservatives have no educational or professional authority to claim otherwise. And how the US healthcare system is an amoral, inefficient, needlessly expensive mess that obviously needs more democratic socialism. And how the Second Amendment unambiguously calls for gun regulations in its first three words. And how gays getting married doesn't affect me or my marriage in any way. And how evolution is the undeniable bedrock of all biological sciences, and is provable in a million ways independent of the fossil record. And how tax cuts have never once led to federal budget surpluses, and never will!"

"Donald Trump might be just a little bit wrong about..." began Senator Chuck Grassley. "Donald Trump is slightly misguided to think that... He should reconsider his position on... Gah! I just can't definitively say anything bad about him until he officially loses to Joe Biden! But I could end those sentences so many different ways. So many ways! Check my Twitter the morning of November 4th because I'm going to be tweeting for hours all the things I really think about Trump!"

"Once Trump loses reelection, I'll finally stand up for my wife and dad!" claimed Senator Ted Cruz. "No one will ever emasculate me and mock my family once they no longer have an electorally impressive number of voters I am trying to woo for my future presidential campaigns!"

One Senator was not excited for the prospect of Trump losing the election:

"First I lost John McCain," said Senator Lindsey Graham, "and if I lose Donald Trump I have no idea who I'll fanboy over next. If Ted Cruz becomes the new standard-bearer for the Republican Party, I will resign and move to the most rural place in South Carolina I can find."

# Susan Collins Vows To Use Harsher Words Than "Concerned" And "Troubled" To Describe Donald Trump If He Loses

October 28, 2020
Washington D.C.—

Maine Senator Susan Collins today vowed to take her gloves off rhetorically if either she or President Donald Trump loses reelection.

"If the President or I lose, and his MAGA supporters' continued approval is no longer relevant to my career," said Collins to *The Halfway Post*, "I will really unload on what I believe are the President's moral shortcomings, administrative failures, and unpatriotic threats to our democracy. I will use words much more profane and colorful than 'troubled' and 'concerned,' I guarantee that. If Trump loses, you can expect me to really speak my mind, and use words such as 'horrified,' 'disgusted' and 'repulsed!' In fact, I may even be so saucy as to say that President Donald Trump is a toddler-brained f**kwit c*** with a d***ably omnipresent sociopathy that turns even the most mundane and ceremonially easy parts of his job as POTUS into clusterf***s of b****y a**holery disgracing forever the historical prestige and honor of America... Wow, that felt good. That felt so lovely finally coming out of my mouth. President Trump is the taint of US presidents! The frothy taint littered with diarrhea dingleberries! He is the biggest pussy president we've ever had! He's such a pussy when it comes to standing up for American values around the world I wouldn't be surprised if he spends his six scheduled 'Executive Hours' every day grabbing himself by his boy pussy just to practice his form and technique! F*** Donald Trump. Donald Trump is the biggest piece of s*** human being who ever lived! He's disgusting, disturbed, and worst of all just incredibly, wildly stupid! He's the biggest dumbf*** I have ever encountered in my life. He's the biggest team-killing dumbf*** in American history! He's the most idiotic dumbf*** in human history! I hope the Southern District of New York f***s him so hard he spends the rest of his miserable dumbf*** life in prison with his dumbf*** fake hair falling out, his dumbf*** fake teeth falling out, his dumbf*** kids going to prison, too, and his dumbf*** name in the history books forever being followed with an asterisk leading to a footnote spelling out to every elementary schooler in history class, from now until the universe expands so far that gravity ceases completely and all the atoms spread out light-years apart from their closest neighbors and freeze and their electrons reach absolute zero degrees on the Kelvin scale, that Donald J. Trump is the biggest dumbf*** organism to ever metabolically exist! ...Wow, I really got carried away there, didn't I? If you liked that sample of my outrage just wait until Trump loses!"

# Trump Is Reportedly Wondering If It's Too Late To Replace Mike Pence

November 2, 2020
Washington D.C.—

According to White House insiders, President Donald Trump is second-guessing his decision to keep Mike Pence as his Vice President.

"The President asked several of us top advisers this morning if voters would mind if he replaced Mike Pence with Nikki Haley or Ivanka," explained an executive staffer, who requested anonymity. "We told him that his voters likely wouldn't have minded if he had done it several months ago, but that, since the election is literally tomorrow, it would look pretty bad and raise lots of questions. And that's to say nothing about the fact that it's way too late to change the ballots, which all have Pence's name printed on them. Trump is nervous about the polls showing he's losing in the swing states he desperately needs. He thinks suburban women are only shifting to Biden because he has a female running mate, so he tried to convince Pence to transition into a woman to win some of the suburban women back. Pence didn't like that one bit, and told the President that transgender identities go against the teachings of Jesus, at which point Trump asked 'which one was he again?'"

However, Pence has concerns about the election as well, and is conflicted about various Trump decisions and strategies. He reportedly regrets that the administration did not fight harder against the territorial gains in the culture wars the sinister Gay Agenda has made in order to excite and mobilize Evangelical voters, who make up a core bloc of Trump's political coalition.

While congratulatory to Trump on the President's decisions to bring troops home from Afghanistan and other countries in the Middle East and Africa, Pence is frustrated that Trump has ignored his calls for redeploying those soldiers in liberal cities to combat the proliferation of "gayborhoods," or LGBTQ+ friendly neighborhoods.

In recent months, Mr. Pence has been particularly upset that Trump's military assassination priorities have been against Iranian generals and scientists, without even going after one general from the Gay Agenda.

Pence has vigorously argued with other national security officials in recent months that generals from the Gay Agenda are much easier and cheaper to find and assassinate with drone surveillance than Iranian generals because of how colorfully they dress, and how flamboyantly they do their plotting and scheming.

## MAGA Christians Can't Believe God Would Make Such A Big Mistake

November 4, 2020
Tulsa, OK—

The apparent election loss of President Donald Trump has been a shock to devoutly Christian MAGA fans convinced Trump's narrow Electoral College victory over Hillary Clinton in 2016 represented Heavenly endorsement of Trump, and suggested he would get two terms.

"Don't get me wrong, I have total faith in God's eternal master plan," said Benny Daniels, 47, "but I believe God got this one way wrong! Is God asleep? Can the angels wake Him up and let Him know *Fox News* has called Arizona for Biden? It's just not like God to make such historic mistakes like this!"

Other MAGA Christians agreed.

"I've been a 100% committed Christian my whole life," explained Sarah Malcolm, 35, "but, with God screwing this election up and letting the socialist, communist, baby-eater Democrats win, I may have to start shopping around for a new monodeity! I'm not about to start praying every day to a libtard!"

"Honestly, my whole world has turned upside down," said Samantha Havers, 28. "How can I have faith in God's omniscience and omnipotence if He would let a Democrat win? And he's letting Biden get the same number of electoral votes as Trump got in 2016. That's just offensive! It's bad enough God keeps letting Democrats beat Trump in the popular vote, but now they're winning in the Electoral College as well? God has gotten so obnoxious and insufferable!"

"God has been my one and only all these years," explained Dan Lipp, 41, "but I've started doing a little window shopping on some other religions. I've started looking into Hinduism a bit, and I have to say I like what I see. One of their gods is Shiva, whose role is to destroy the entire universe, and that's a very attractive deity to worship now that the political party I don't like is going to be in power in the executive branch for four years! I hope when the universe gets rebuilt anew Shiva won't let there be any liberals in it! So, starting today, I'm only praying to Shiva. Come on, Shiva, destroy the universe as quickly as You can! I'd prefer that all existence in this universe be ended rather than have the government expand Obamacare or Medicare, raise the minimum wage for the first time in over a decade, or slightly raise estate taxes on billionaire children's inheritances."

## Questions Trump Should Have Been Asked In The Election, But Wasn't

The following are questions *The Halfway Post* would have loved to hear Donald Trump be asked to answer in his classic, nonlinear word-vomit:

1. "Without saying you'll reveal it 'in two weeks,' what is your Obamacare replacement you said would be cheaper and cover more people?"

2. "Which specific book of the Bible is your favorite, and why?"

3. "Why do you always defend Vladimir Putin? Why did you want to leave NATO? Why weren't you interested in defensively supplying Ukraine?"

4. "Michael Cohen is currently serving a prison sentence for crimes you participated in and directed. How will you plead to those crimes when you're no longer president, and are suddenly indictable again?"

5. "If the Saudis chopped up your son Eric, would you still make excuses for them? Lol, jk, we mean Ivanka."

6. "How much money would you estimate you have spent on taking women who aren't your wives out furniture shopping?"

7. "Which bankrupt company of yours do you most regret running into the ground?"

8. "Why, specifically, did you betray the Kurds, and break America's promises to them?"

9. "Rex Tillerson said he stopped you from repeatedly breaking the law, what were some of those things he stopped you from doing?"

10. "Would you like to publicly apologize for mocking Obama for golfing now that you've golfed way more?"

11. "Why did Eric and Don Jr. both say on television that your family company gets all its funding from Russia if you claim you have no deals with Russia?"

12. "Are you currently blackmailing Lindsey Graham?"

13. "Don't you think you should get a get cut of all that windfall money Jared Kushner made while serving in your administration?"

# Mitch McConnell Says As A Token Of Bipartisanship He'll Let Biden Confirm One Federal Judge

November 6, 2020
Washington D.C.—

Georgia is currently planning for two runoff elections, and control of the Senate hangs in the balance. If Democrats win both seats, the Senate would be divided 50-50 with a tie-breaker vote wielded by Vice President-Elect Kamala Harris, otherwise Republicans will keep a narrow majority.

However, current Senate Majority Leader Mitch McConnell says if Republicans keep majority power in the Senate he hopes he can work together with Joe Biden despite a divided government.

"I believe Joe Biden and I will be able to work together," McConnell told reporters this morning. "Critics of my tenure as Majority Leader have mocked me for my perceived utter lack of policy idealism, my pyrrhic approach to acquiring political power, and my alleged dearth of red-blooded circulatory warmth, but I want Americans to see that I am capable of good faith political brokering. So, as a token of my congratulations for his victory, as well as a Republican peace offering in the name of bipartisanship, I will allow Joe Biden the opportunity to appoint one federal judge in his term as President. No Supreme Court justices, though. There will be no new Supreme Court justices in Biden's term if I am majority leader. I have paid dearly for the conservative majority on the Supreme Court selling my soul and pledging eternal allegiance to the Dark Lord Satan, and I do not intend to give it up. I don't care if a meteorite strikes Earth and obliterates all nine Supreme Court justices, we will just have to settle with having zero Supreme Court judges until either a Republican president wins, or Democrats manage to pry the Senate's majority from my cold, purple hands in the upcoming runoff elections in Georgia… Or if Joe Biden can somehow procure a Galápagos tortoise from the government of Ecuador for me. I am only willing to trade a Supreme Court seat for a pet Galápagos tortoise. They're virtually impossible to obtain, and, if I get one, my turtle collection will be complete. Someday, when me and Elaine are ready to retire and downsize our living situation, I'm going to convert our D.C. mansion into a turtle petting zoo. I have turtles from every continent they live on, and it would be very educational for kids. If you ask me, turtles are the unsung heroes of nature. They play a vital role in Earth's great food web, and help maintain healthy beds of sea grass and coral reefs, which provide happy and safe habitats for more sea creatures than I could count! Oh, look at me, going off on a turtle tangent again! But let me repeat that a Supreme Court deal is not entirely off the table. The shell is in President Biden's court, as they say."

# A Brand New 2021 "Platinum Club Memberships" At Mar-A-Lago Now Come With A Free Pardon

November 16, 2020
Washington D.C.—

Recent document leaks from President Donald Trump's finances and tax returns have revealed deep debts and money-losing real estate properties, and Mr. Trump is reportedly desperate to think up creative ways to pay off his various loans.

Trump's latest scheme is a new "Platinum" level of club membership at his Mar-a-Lago resort advertising complimentary pardons as a sign-up bonus.

The following is a copy of a marketing offer that was recently mailed to current and prospective Mar-a-Lago members:

## NOW OFFERING:
### A BRAND NEW MAR-A-LAGO MEMBERSHIP OPTION!!!

Time is running out, but if you sign up for the all new 2021 **PLATINUM**-level membership before noon on January 20th, you'll receive a Presidential Pardon from Donald J. Trump himself **FREE**!

A few criminal exclusions apply, but Platinum members' previous run-ins with the law will be pardoned away for the low, low price of **$250,000** to become a Platinum Mar-a-Lago **PATRIOT**!

So sign up now! Before you know it, the Trump presidency will be over, and you **DO NOT** want to miss this opportunity of a lifetime to have your past criminal misdeeds expunged!

Pardons are transferrable as well, so if you happen to be squeaky clean you can transfer your complimentary Platinum-level pardon to a more delinquent family member or friend! And there's **NO LIMIT** to how many you can buy! This Christmas you can get pardons (and Mar-a-Lago memberships) for everyone on your shopping list!

And if you're interested in bulk purchases, our deal gets even sweeter! If you buy **TWO** Platinum memberships, we'll throw in a **THIRD** pardon for **ABSOLUTELY FREE**! Christmas just got a whole lot more innocent!

So buy today because **TIME IS RUNNING OUT**!

# Ivanka Trump Wants Her Father To Fire Mike Pence, Appoint Her As VP For 2 Months To Boost Her Resumé

November 19, 2020
Washington D.C.—

According to White House insiders, Ivanka Trump is trying to convince her father, President Donald Trump, to fire Vice President Mike Pence for the last two months of his presidency so that she can replace him.

"The President says he likes the idea of injecting some last-minute sex appeal into his lame duck administration," explained a White House staffer, who requested anonymity to discuss the ongoing internal deliberations, "but Pence is furious about the idea after four years of unquestionable loyalty to even the most morally and intellectually deranged aspects of Trump's decision-making and leadership. In retaliation, Pence called Ivanka a 'hussy' the other day, and tried to appeal to the President's ego by arguing that keeping him on as VP for the remainder of the term proves to everyone that he is, in fact, a stable genius. Ivanka, meanwhile, wants to be able to put 'Vice President' on her resumé to promote her future political and commercial ambitions, and has been stoking Trump's incestual jealousies by telling him that she thought Pence was kind of a cute dad to his daughters hoping that Trump would fire him to keep all of Ivanka's paternal attention to himself."

Mr. Pence was reportedly already upset with the President before this incident when he noticed earlier in the week that the Bible he gave to Trump as an inauguration gift had a thick coat of dust on it.

"Mike got real upset when he noticed that," explained a VP aide anonymously to candidly discuss the emotions Pence would never reveal publicly. "Mike has tried so hard to turn Trump into a religious man, but the President just doesn't have a humble bone in his body. Mike even took the time to pick out Biblical verses he thought related to the monumental task of being president, and put color-coded sticky notes on the pages for easy searching, but those little color tabs sticking out from the pages are coated in dust as well. Trump obviously hasn't touched the book in four years. Pence was distraught because he considers himself a Bible foster parent, and he spends much of his free time collecting Bibles from local thrift stores so he can take them for 'walks' where he gets them out one at a time to recite a passage from each of them so every Bible gets a chance to be read from daily. He simultaneously hopes to find a new anti-gay reference no one has ever found before. But he got very upset thinking how that poor, lonely Bible had been miserably abandoned and neglected in Trump's solely decorative library all these years next to Trump's copy of *Mein Kampf*."

## Rudy Giuliani Tucked In His Shirt For 25 Minutes During Today's Election Fraud Testimony

November 20, 2020
Detroit, MI—

During courtroom testimony in which President Donald Trump's lawyers were suspiciously alleging voter fraud only in counties with large minority populations, Rudy Giuliani reportedly had his hand in his pants for a full 25 minutes.

Several courtroom sketch artists drew Mr. Giuliani leaning back in his chair with his eyes closed, and the court stenographer recorded several moans coming from the former mayor on the official testimony transcript. Several beads of sweat formed at Mr. Giuliani's temples, and rolled down his cheeks leaving distinctive dark trails of apparent hair dye spray.

After about twenty-five minutes, Mr. Giuliani removed his hand from his pants, sniffed it, and asked the judge if the testimony could be sped up because he had a lead on another potential Hunter Biden laptop he wanted to go check out before business hours were over.

Giuliani was later reportedly seen in the men's bathroom standing in front of a hand dryer with his pelvis thrust up so his crotch was under the heater.

After the courtroom sketches went viral later in the day, Giuliani defended himself claiming he was only "tucking in his shirt."


## Ode To Ted Cruz
by Donald J. Trump


Ted Cruz is a monster unleashed accidentally,
He deserves an electric chair kind of death penalty.
His birth was not vaginal or even Caesarian,
He was found in a pile of cemetery carrion.

Ted Cruz, you're mushy with no solid core,
You'd still suck up if I called your wife "whore."
When you lose reelection and scream and complain,
A bipartisan Congress will pop some champagne!

# Donald Trump Blames The Military's Respect Of Human Rights For Why He Lost Reelection

November 22, 2020
Washington D.C.—

According to White House leakers, President Donald Trump is blaming the military for why he lost reelection in phone conversations with foreign leaders.

The following is a transcript of Trump's end of a phone call with Russian President Vladimir Putin that was secretly recorded and leaked to *The Halfway Post*. Its verbatim accuracy has been confirmed by three Trump Administration sources:

"Sorry, Vlad, I know… I know, it's f***ing bulls***… I knew I should have taken your advice and started pushing journalists and Democrats off roofs… I was waiting for the second term for stuff like that… I know, but I had to get reelected first… Yeah, presidents can't be indicted, but it's way harder to campaign if everyone is blaming you for murder… Well, I can't cook the books and invent votes like you can because our elections are decentralized… I could have made some public examples of my enemies in other ways, you're right… Tell me about it. … Trust me, I tried that, but my military has so many dumb rules. They're such rule-followers. Be glad your military does what you want. My generals are so lazy. I can't even get them to pepper spray protesters. I had to get Bill Barr to do that with Department of Justice goons… Hey, it's not all my fault, you know, I remember a certain someone telling me their hackers and Twitter trolls would keep Pennsylvania red! You said that, didn't you? … Yeah, yeah, yeah… Of course I'm still going to pull America out of all the arms and peace agreements so you can do whatever you want and blame America later… Obviously I'm going to try to get rid of the sanctions again, but that's an uphill battle. … Well, you didn't give me the emails of enough GOP Congress people, and I can only low-key blackmail so many myself… And what about your end of the bargain?… No, we agreed Trump Tower Moscow would be 45 stories tall, not 44! What the f***?! That's Obama's number! … So what if I didn't get reelected? A deal is a deal! … Come on, Vlad… What if I make Eric be your slave for a year? … Five years? … I can't pull all our troops out of Germany, believe me, I tried… We can't make it too obvious, Vlad! … Well, what about you? Your shell company superPAC didn't spend quite as many rubles on TV ads in Georgia and Arizona as you claimed it would, did it? … Fine, 44 stories. But count the basement as the first floor so we can say in the marketing brochures that it's 45 stories. And don't forget to make sure on all the tax filings that it's listed as only 35 stories. I'm not f***ing paying taxes on all 44!"

## Donald Trump Claims He's Looking Forward To Having More Time For Melania, Charity, And Church

November 23, 2020
Washington D.C.—

President Donald Trump appears to finally be accepting the reality that Joe Biden won the election, and will be taking his job on January 20th.

He tweeted about his post-presidency plans this morning:

"Maybe it'll be nice to have some free time if I LET Joe Biden be President, even though he TOTALLY cheated and had 50 million illegal immigrant votes in the most rigged election in US history! He's so desperate to take credit for the accomplishments of his predecessor, which I'd NEVER do!"

"I suppose it'll give me time for things that really matter. My biggest regret these last four years has been not having more time to turn my head behind me to see Melania's beautiful smile full of unconditional love for me, or hold her hand. When I leave D.C. we might just hold hands for days at a time to catch up on all the lost time!"

"And I miss doing charity work as well. Since starting my new Florida foundation I have learned so much about non-profit laws. I promise this time I won't accidentally spend millions of dollars on personal and frivolous expenses! My problem was I kept the old foundation's debit card right next to my credit cards in my wallet, and by mistake I kept grabbing the wrong one!"

"And, most of all, I can't wait to start getting to church more often. Being President kept me so busy, and every Sunday morning when I got all dressed up for church, someone would come in with my daily briefing. I told them to keep it to one page because Jesus was waiting, but sometimes they'd never put in pictures and it'd take all morning to get through! And they'd insist that I had to read it at golf courses for national security reasons!"

"So maybe taking a break before my next presidential term isn't such a bad idea. I never wanted the Presidency to change me, and as a private citizen again I can return to my trademark interests: faithfulness to Melania, selfless and altruistic generosity for others, and humble devotion to a power higher than myself!"

Trump then took a two-hour break from Twitter before adding one last tweet:

"Oh, and also Barron!"

## Donald Trump Is In Talks With Joel Osteen To Set Up A Televangelist "Church Of Trump"

November 25, 2020
Washington D.C.—

It looks like President Donald Trump has finally decided what he wants to do post-presidency: become a televangelist.

According to White House insiders, Mr. Trump spent most of last week's "Executive Hours" in the Oval Office calling several rich televangelists for advice on how to set up his own mega church. A Trump staffer requesting anonymity secretly recorded Trump's end of the call for a portion of a talk with Joel Osteen. The following is a transcript of the recording:

"…So you're telling me there's no taxes on churches? Wow… So I can tell the state of New York and federal prosecutors to go f*** themselves because all my money is for Jesus or whoever? That's incredible! … I should have started a church decades ago! How much money do you make from your congregation in donations? … Oh, so you write a lot of books and stuff, and make money that way? … Right, of course, you have to pretend the actual church crap is not about the money… Okay, very smart, Joel. So the compassionate sounding fluff is the hook to bring them in, and you're basically just hawking a lot of merch? … Ha! Not taking a salary, that's clever! But you get your followers to peer-pressure each other into buying your products, and compete to see who has them all, and judge the ones not buying the latest books… Interesting business model… Yeah, guilt is a great motivator… And it works, look at your mansion! You are one rich son of a b****! … Exactly. You know, that's what I do here at the White House. I say I don't take a salary, but I make soooo much more money from taking the Secret Service along with me to my golf courses and hotels, and charging the government for everything but the air I breathe… Ha! You put your hand in the hats and take some of the church cash when no one is looking? I'm so going to do that at the Church of Trump! I'll have a high net worth like you in no time! For real this time! … Wow, you bought a private plane in cash with all ones and fives? I can't imagine how many suitcases that took to carry it all! … I'll tell you a little secret of my own, I don't actually donate my presidential salary. I do the photo-ops with the paychecks and everything, but I just cash them anyway! … So, what kind of design should I have for my church? What do gullible Christians like? …Hmm. Well, I like a lot of gold. I want gold accents everywhere. If I had to critique Jesus on anything, I'd say his homeless look was a real branding mistake. They say you should dress for the job you want, not the job you have, and I don't even want to know what job Jesus was dressing for! Can you imagine if Jesus came into my church? I'd have to kick him out for getting poor all everything! Poverty can be contagious, you know? It's like Jesus never paid attention to the prosperity gospel. Kind of lazy considering He's the one who wrote the Bible! ... You don't let the homeless in your church either? ... Ha! That's hilarious! 'No shirt, no shoes, no salvation!' You're a clever guy, Joel! Unless the shirtless person is a hot model, and then I have a locker room she should totally change into before the service starts! Actually, there's an idea! I want big locker rooms in my church, with peeping holes I can use. Sneaking inside is fun and all, but the girls always cover themselves up when they see me. And I've found that they're way more likely to yell and scream, and say 'no' immediately when I solicit them for sex while they're in the middle of changing... From Japan, you say? ... Yeah, give me that guy's number later... And the sex dolls are totally life-like? Wow! ... You have a new one for every day of the week? ... You're a cultured guy, Joel, but I'll take just blonde and white! ... Okay, so far I have written down big locker rooms I can peep in, and gold accents everywhere. I really want the prosperity aesthetic to shine through, you know? But in good taste. I want my church to kind of suggest the theme of monastic devotion to the Bible, but still scream subliminally 'Give me that sweet, sweet, seed-planting money, you idiot suckers!' You know what I mean? ... Ha, of course you do! You perfected it! ... So for the stage I was thinking I want my name real big up above of where I'll be delivering my tremendous, amazing sermons. I guess I can have Jesus's name somewhere nearby, but mine definitely higher and bigger, you know? It's my church... Oh, that's an interesting idea. So you almost never include Jesus's name anywhere in your book titles and merch and stuff? ... Oh, you're right, Jesus's sermons about not being rich do kind of cramp our style, don't they? ... Yeah, I agree, I definitely want when my church followers are thinking about salvation to be thinking 'Trump' and not 'Jesus.' I don't want them to buy any of Jesus's books, they need to buy my books! I want them to buy my future *Art of the Prayer*... Exactly. So the Church of Trump will be like a traditional church with all the praying and 'Yay God' stuff, and whatever else the Christians do, but, you're right, I have to build my personal Christian brand for the real money... Logo? You know, I had this interesting idea the other day. I was thinking that all those cross necklaces that the Christians wear are basically the letter T already, so what if I had all my congregants cut off the little bits at the top to turn the crosses into capital T's? Would that be offensive? ... Maybe you're right. Maybe I'll just sell my own cross necklaces, but have the 'T' part of it gold and the little bit at the top silver. That way you can be worshipping Jesus and Trump at the same time with just one necklace. It could be my first piece of merchandise to hawk... Wow, selling them in a bunch of collectible colors is a great idea, Joel! You're so clever about economizing Christianity! You've made such an impressive fortune off of the charity of Jesus! ... Ha! You're right! Why should we have to do all the legwork raising money for God? God's got enough money, I want mine!"

## Steve Bannon Is Collecting Donations To Build A Fake Trump Presidential Library

November 29, 2020
Washington D.C.—

The following advertisement from Steve Bannon's latest money-making venture was forwarded to *The Halfway Post*:

Donate\* **NOW** to help build\*\* the

# <u>Donald J. Trump</u>\*\*\*

## Presidential Library\*\*\*\*!

(The **evil Libs** don't want you to do it, so you **totally should!**\*\*\*\*\*)

\* We're a for-profit organization, so technically your money is not a donation, and you can't write it off for tax purposes.
\*\* Proceeds won't actually be going toward the construction of a physical library.
\*\*\* President Trump is unaffiliated with our organization other than a 25% kickback we'll send him for licensing his name.
\*\*\*\* There won't be any books.
\*\*\*\*\* Steve Bannon will use all proceeds for hanging out shirtless and drunk on a Chinese billionaire's yacht.

# Trump Secrets Leaked By White House Staffers

- He has several framed Rubik's Cubes around the Oval Office he claims he finished by himself, but no one believes he has anywhere near enough patience to figure out the algorithms.

- He has accidentally texted his Chiefs of Staff Reince Priebus, John Kelly, and Mark Meadows "Ivanka, u up?" several times.

- He has White House staffers search the Rose Garden lawn for dropped coins after every press event and ceremony held there.

- He once did a photo-op with the women's national college championship softball team after accidentally using green foundation makeup instead of his usual orange.

- He uses a finger-lengthening contraption each morning for a half hour.

- He once asked Secretary of State Mike Pompeo during a briefing on North Korea's nuclear missile program which porn stars he had paid for sex. When Pompeo said he hadn't ever done that, Trump was silent for a moment, and then said he hadn't either.

- He once told a White House janitor that paint used to taste better before "socialism ruined it" by banning lead.

- One time he texted Rudy Giuliani "Ivanka, u up?" and when Giuliani self-identified himself Trump texted back, "If you cross-dress again with big fake jugs I'm still down."

- Kim Jong Un catfished him pretending to be a sexy, teenaged aspiring model from North Korea, and got him to text the North Korean government a picture of his genitals.

- Putin writes him personal letters addressed to "Collusion Boy."

- He didn't know South America existed until 2017, and always thought it referred to Mexico.

- His father used to lock him in the family dog's kennel until he was 14, and that's why he's the first president in a century not to have a dog.

- He has a tattoo of his own signature on his mons pubis.

## A Televangelist Turf War Is Brewing As Donald Trump Looks Into Starting A "Church of Trump"

December 27, 2020
Washington D.C.—

There is tension brewing in the televangelist community as President Donald Trump is reportedly looking into launching a televangelist ministry to raise money to pay off his substantial personal debts.

Yesterday, a meeting of the Five Families in The Commission, headed by Joel Osteen, Kenneth Copeland, Creflo Dollar, Jim Bakker, and Pat Robertson met to discuss how to respond to Trump's potential entrance into the televangelist racket.

"Kenneth Copeland immediately wanted to kneecap Trump to send him a message," explained an insider informant, who would only discuss the meeting under anonymity for fear of his life, "but Joel Osteen cautioned patience. He pointed out that Trump has failed at pretty much everything he has ever done, from Trump Steaks, to Trump Airlines, to being a one-term president, and said their fears that Trump's competition would ever cut into their own ministry profits were overblown. Creflo Dollar then suggested The Commission invite Trump to their next meeting to let him know they were willing to accommodate him as long as he stayed out of their regional turfs."

Pat Robertson and Jim Bakker were not so open to that idea.

"Bakker got a little upset, and accused the other family heads of capitulating to an even bigger fraud than all of them," said the insider. "He complained that Trump knew the least about Christianity than everyone there at the table, and would make their televangelism look bad by association. He pointed out that Trump doesn't even try to pretend he cares about Jesus. Then Pat Robertson finally spoke up, and agreed with Bakker that Trump would inevitably discredit their very profitable prosperity gospel churches with his bad business sense, gaudy personal vanity, and utter disregard for moderation of any kind. Copeland pointed out that Trump would betray them all if he thought it would earn him $5, and that The Commission ought to be unanimous against him for its own existential sake. He warned that a Church of Trump could implode so spectacularly it might even threaten their holy grail of profits: televangelists' tax-free status. Hearing that, Creflo Dollar vomited, and Joel Osteen broke down into tears. The matter was settled as The Commission agreed to unanimously oppose any effort by Trump to cut into their racket. Then Copeland said that one day soon Trump was going to wake up with some of his beloved Diet Coke cans decapitated in his bed."

## Donald Trump Declares Candidacy For Pope So He Can Become Joe Biden's Boss

December 29, 2020
Washington D.C.—

President Donald Trump just announced some truly surprising post-presidency plans on Twitter:

"Since Joe Biden cheated so much to take my job, I've decided I'm going to run for Pope instead of continuing my election legal challenges (even though I could totally win them all easily because the fraud was so obvious)! Let's see how Biden likes being President when I become his Catholic boss and can tell him what to do! MAGA!"

"And it will be so easy! Pope Francis is even sleepier and more brain-dead than Biden! People are saying Pope Francis is the most lying, crooked, corrupt, and low-energy Pope we've ever had! And I've already got Rudy Giuliani snooping around the Vatican as we speak, so we'll be finding out very soon if there are any old, forgotten Papal laptops lying around!"

"So, effective immediately, I'm changing my name to a more Italian-sounding name to better fit into the Roman Catholic scene. You can now call me either Donaldino Trumpini, or Father Trumpini when I'm in a holy place. And I will win with 90% of all the Pope votes (unless that election is rigged against me like all the other elections)!"

"I will be a tremendous Pope. Trust me, I'm going to make being Catholic great again! The other Popes will be calling me up and telling me they can't believe what a great job I'm doing for the Catholics. Because I never sin. Nobody sins less than me! And just wait to see how I take that Pope hat and make it 100 times better!"

Meanwhile, the White House is busy planning for President-Elect Joe Biden's transition, and insiders have told *The Halfway Post* that staffers were pleasantly surprised to learn that Mr. Biden would not be forcing them to sign loyalty pledges, nondisclosure agreements, or affidavits swearing Biden's hands and inauguration crowd size are the biggest they've ever seen like Trump did.

National security officials have similarly been impressed to learn that Biden actually reads the presidential daily briefing he has begun receiving, and has not once complained about there not being enough pictures or printings of his name with compliments in every paragraph.

# Betsy DeVos Announced A Plan To Give Coronavirus Vaccines Only To Rich Students

January 2, 2021
Washington D.C.—

Education Secretary Betsy DeVos released a revised budget proposal today for her department, and one of its most controversial details concerns how she plans to allocate funds approved by Congress to combat the spread of the global coronavirus pandemic in schools throughout the nation.

"I cannot stress enough to parents across America that I'm taking serious my responsibility to protect our students from the coronavirus," DeVos explained in a press conference this morning. "I asked Congress to give the Education Department more funding for vaccines, and I think with the resources I've received I can save a substantial number of students. Unfortunately, there just aren't enough vaccines to go around for every student, and I've been grappling with how to distribute the limited supply fairly. There's just too many white students in America for me to divvy up the vaccines according to the obvious choice of race, so that's not practical. Then I wondered if I could give out the vaccines according to religious belief, but, again, there's just too many Christian children who would be left out by that process. But then it hit me to go by wealth, and I can't believe I didn't think of it first because it's so pertinent! I think we can all agree there's no reason to vaccinate a bunch of disadvantaged students whose parents are too poor to afford professional writers to author their kids' college application essays in order to get them into Ivy League schools. We should give the vaccines to students whose parents have enough money for the necessary bribing of college administrators and sports coaches to ensure admittance into schools that aren't just gross community colleges or trade schools. So disgusting! I just threw up in my mouth at the thought of my own kids ever getting a blue-collar job! And this decision works economically as well because rich parents have the best connections for their kids to get high-paying corporate jobs right out of college. That's the kind of winning our economy needs! So, effective next week, my department will be giving the COVID vaccines to students whose parents make over $300k a year. These students have the kind of life opportunities ahead of them we need to safeguard. But I promise that this isn't about hating financially doomed children born into poor families. It's just a rational metric to most effectively maximize the outcome of distributing our very limited supply of vaccines. And, who knows, maybe because poor kids don't bathe very often the dirt on their skin will protect them from COVID. Rich kids are cleaner, so they're more at risk. They don't have a protective layer of filth between COVID and their beautiful, smooth white skin moisturized with expensive name brand lotions and creams!"

# QAnon's Top Tips For Patriots Preparing Themselves For "The Storm"

January 5, 2021
St. Louis, MO—

The conspiracy ringleader Q of QAnon just posted a QDrop with a list of the following tips for Patriot believers to prepare themselves for Donald Trump's upcoming arrest of Joe Biden and return to the presidency:

- Douse your children with your urine as an olfactory disguise every morning so Democrats can't smell their rich, youthful blood. It has been rumored that Nancy Pelosi can detect the scent of a toddler from up to 25 miles away.
- Smear your own feces across your forehead as a sign to other Patriot believers that you have their back, and will join them when the Storm arrives and things get messy.
- Stop bathing. You need to be ready to head into the hills and start a guerilla-style war outside the nearest liberal-run city to form a blockade and cut off their supply lines, and the sooner you get used to the stench and grossness you'll experience in the field will only make you a more valuable guerrilla teammate. The effort to violently reinstall Emperor Trump could take years or even decades. Prepare yourself to keep on fighting long after Trump is even alive.
- Keep in a butt plug at all times. You never know when the civil war will erupt, and the top secret Deep-Deep-State Trump loyalists in the FBI and CIA have special acoustic weapons that will make only Antifa, BLM, and socialist terrorists defecate on themselves in public, as long as you keep in your special, Q-approved butt plug. Remember, it's not gay if you're doing it for Trump, even if he is a man.
- Get a swastika tattoo on a conveniently revealed location on your body, but one that is easily covered up when in public for your protection, like a forearm, calf, or your chest. When the Storm arrives, this will be our mark to prove loyalty. It also nicely gets back at all the libtards who called us Nazis for so many years. They were so wrong about that, weren't they? And now the joke is on them because we're actually going to BECOME Nazis to get back at them! Ha! Take that, libs!
- Eat a lot. Most of you are overweight anyway, and the more obese you can get before the Storm means the longer you can last in the wilderness with your body converting your fat into valuable energy.
- Single men only: if women want nothing to do with you, keep trying to impress them in all the impotent, loser ways you typically flirt. We need all the pent-up, involuntary celibate rage your unf***able personalities can generate for the Q cause.

## Trump's Staffers Built Him A Fake Twitter App To Distract Him From Inciting More Violence

January 8, 2021
Washington D.C.—

Following President Trump's ban from Twitter, several White House staffers reportedly raised $30,000 to quickly develop a convincing fake Twitter app to load onto his phone that lets him post tweets to nowhere.

"The app looks just like Twitter, and has most of the same functions," explained a staffer, "though, because of the quick turnaround that the riot situation demanded, we took some shortcuts. The app doesn't keep his tweets longer than a day, but he hasn't seemed to notice. He just seems happy to be able to type out angry and offensive tweets again, and the app sends him nonstop notifications of supposed likes and retweets. He claps his little hands together and squeals with delight, and he loves showing us how many millions of retweets he thinks he's getting. I have to admit I'm very relieved Twitter banned Trump, because these fake tweets he's writing are truly appalling."

The following are tweets Trump has written out on his fake app:

"My protesters should violently rebel! I hate America and all the Americans who voted against me! Punish them! Start up new concentration camps! If I can't have the presidency, no one can! Who knew US elections could be even more rigged than the Emmys, who never gave me one for *The Apprentice?*"

"I've got hidden cameras in all my hotels' rooms! That's why Congressional Republicans do everything I say!"

"I sell all my daily briefing reports to Vladimir Putin for $5 each!"

"Eric's father really is Gary Busey. And I have six illegitimate kids running around somewhere in the world, whose mothers I paid off to stay quiet! I'm going to swap one of them for Don Jr. so I have a 'Jr.' son who isn't a loser!"

"My saucer nipples are no one's business but my own!"

"Rudy Giuliani and I made out one time, big deal! He had cross-dressed with giant fake jugs, and let me get to 2nd base! He was a high-class broad! I'm not ashamed, so say what you want. But his BJ wasn't good, so I didn't pay him at the end. He was all teeth, and have you seen his bottom row? Yuck!"

## Mar-A-Lago Just Ordered 45 Pounds Of Kool-Aid Mix To Be Delivered On January 19th

January 16, 2021
Palm Springs, FL—

According to a national distributor of Kool-Aid mix, President Donald Trump's Florida resort Mar-a-Lago just ordered 45 pounds of red Kool-Aid powder to be delivered on January 19th, which happens to be the last full day of Trump's presidency.

A spokeswoman for the White House, however, denied rumors that Trump was planning a Jim Jones-style mass suicide event.

"I believe the President will only be preparing this giant supply of Kool-Aid for refreshments during his 'Thanks, President Trump!' themed gala at Mar-a-Lago on the night of January 19th," the spokeswoman said. "The President may have said some offhand remarks here and there over the last few weeks about directing his most loyal followers to drink poison in order to leave their material existences behind and enter into a new metaphysical dimension in which he will be President for eternity so America will be made great for real, and Ivanka will be his girlfriend, but no concrete details have been confirmed, as far as I know, to actually go through with poisoning the punch and demanding his guests die alongside him."

The event is sold out with approximately 300 guests RSVP'ed for the various festivities, including a golf tournament during the day, a McDonalds-catered lunch, and a father-daughter dance in the evening.

Ted Cruz announced on Twitter this morning he would definitely be tasting the Kool-Aid, unless everyone at the party talks about not voting anyone for president who drinks the Kool-Aid, in which case he definitely would not drink the Kool-Aid, except if they later say they're just joking, and would, in fact, vote someone who drank the Kool-Aid for president, in which case he'd drink more Kool-Aid than anyone else at the party.

# Mike Pompeo And Steven Mnuchin Are Both Now Using Orange Foundation Makeup Like Donald Trump

January 18, 2021
Washington D.C.—

In an act of solidarity with President Trump, Secretary of State Mike Pompeo and Treasury Secretary Steven Mnuchin have both begun using the orange foundation that Trump favors.

"With a healthy tan glow like the three of us have, we made America respected around the world again," said Pompeo in a joint press conference this morning. "Our totally natural faces reflect the youthful vitality and vigor of America, and no one laughs at us like they used to under Obama!"

A *CNN* reporter then pointed out they were obviously wearing makeup.

"What makeup are you referring to?" Mnuchin asked. "See, this is why we call *CNN* 'fake news.' We went golfing with the President yesterday, and it was sunny outside so we tanned a bit. I take offense that you would insinuate the President wears makeup. The color of the President's face is not different than the rest of his body. In fact, when we were done golfing, we hit the showers and, while discussing totally harmless locker room talk, I could see that the President's facial skin color matched the rest of his nude body. No makeup. Also, I saw the President's peepee, and I can 100% confirm that it's definitely not mushroom-shaped. It is a majestic penis, and I only wish mine was half as beautiful as the President's penis because then it would still be more beautiful than any other man's penis I've seen. And I've seen many."

Pompeo then took a notecard from his pocket, and read aloud from it.

"Also, for the record and for posterity, the President's hands are very big, much bigger than mine. And he does not slur any of his words, ever, because his teeth are totally real, and he's never once had a problem with them slipping out while giving speeches. The President only weights 165 pounds, and it's only that high because muscle weighs so much more than fat. He does not try to catch Republican officials in sex stings for blackmail material. That's a complete fabrication from the sub-human reporters who work at *The New York Times*. The dozen anonymous sources who they claim have confirmed it are all liars who should be put in jail for being rats. Also, that information is highly classified, so the leaks were illegal. It's totally fake news, but if we find out who leaked, they will be prosecuted for breaching the terms of their very specific nondisclosure agreements. Now go f*** yourselves."

# The Halfway Post's Dispatches From The Capitol Riot Insurrection, the Second Donald Trump Impeachment, And The Biden Inauguration

January 6-20, 2021
Washington D.C.—

Eric Trump sent Georgia's Secretary of State Brad Raffensperger 11,800 faked votes for his dad, but signed his own name on all of them.

Donald Trump promised Mike Pence he'll never force a mistress to get an abortion again if he overturns the Electoral College vote for him.

Ted Cruz reportedly told Josh Hawley to "back off," says being the most hated senator is HIS thing.

"MAGA" has been distilled at last to its purest essence: a riot mob occupying Congress with a noose outside chanting "Hang Mike Pence" as his four years of mindless loyalty is negated in their eyes forever by a single, unforgivable, purely administrative recognition of already-certified state votes.

Ted Cruz is currently calling friends and advisers frantically asking if they think he'd be more likely to become president if he renounces the insurrectionist mob or joins them.

Cops are relieved none of the insurrectionists are Black Lives Matter activists, or they'd finally have to start violently suppressing the Capitol siege.

There's nothing funny about these insurrectionist Capitol riots, except that the likelihood Stephen Miller accidentally kills himself with autoerotic asphyxiation masturbating to all the fascism on TV has gone way up.

Americans agree to repeal the 25th Amendment's part about removing an unfit president because, if Republicans won't use it after Trump incited a literal riot to attack the entire legislative branch of government, it will never be used and is just cluttering our Constitution.

Josh Hawley, sobbing, tells CNN he wasn't intending to incite violence with his election lies, and was only trying to get ahead in Iowa's next presidential caucus.

Donald Trump casually reminded staffers horrified at the Capitol insurrection playing on every television that "all press is good press."

After being banned from Twitter, Trump is now frantically attaching messages to pigeons' feet and telling them to fly to anyone wearing a red MAGA hat.

Trump is reportedly suffering severe withdrawal symptoms just ten minutes after being locked out of his Twitter account, and is chugging multiple cases of Diet Coke every hour.

Past Trump behavior suggests he's going to regret releasing his conciliatory, taped video clearly dictated by lawyers asking his followers not to kill more people in about two hours when he decides it makes him look weak. Then he'll get furious at the advisers who told him he had to call for peace, and double down on his and his followers' sense of victimhood until his lawyers explain again that he can be put in prison for incitement.

Conservatives are currently debating how storming Congress to overturn a democratic election and ending American democracy compares to kneeling during the National Anthem on the scale of "hating the troops."

Matt Gaetz: "How do we know Hillary Clinton didn't clone herself a thousand times, and all those insurrectionists weren't just the clones dressed up like Trump supporters?"

Elaine Chao, wife of Senator Mitch McConnell, resigned from the worst, most corrupt administration ever at the full turtle speed of 3.99 years.

Betsy DeVos just resigned, said she can't focus on resegregation efforts based on the proliferation of charter schools in such a toxic administration.

Wilbur Ross just woke up from a two-day nap, is asking where everyone else in the cabinet went.

Josh Hawley was forced to eat lunch today at the Senate misfits table with Ted Cruz.

Asked about a second impeachment following the insurrection riot, Susan Collins said she's "super duper sure" Trump has learned his lesson this time.

Trump claims he inherited the insurrectionist mob from Obama.

With riot coverage everywhere in the media, Ben Carson is asking if this is a good time to ask for some new dining room furniture for his office.

Eric Trump just asked his father, "Daddy, are we bad people?"

Ted Cruz is relieved that everyone already hates him so Josh Hawley is getting more blame for the riot than him.

Donald Trump, burying his head in Ivanka's chest as she consoles him, is muttering to himself, "Most admired man! Biggest inauguration crowd! Big hands!"

Kim Jong Un just distanced himself from Trump, says they were never "lovers" like Trump has claimed in the past. Kim said he only "used Trump" for his body in a "regrettable moment of corpulent lust."

Republican members of Congress are complaining that Trump was kicked off Twitter despite always saying they never read any of his tweets.

President Trump is currently roaming D.C. alleyways asking passersby if they can spare just one tweet.

Donald Trump is preparing to give several 15-second press conferences 280 characters at a time.

Eric Trump on his new Parler account is asking his followers if they know any good children's cancer charities he should follow.

Ted Cruz reportedly can't hear the choruses calling for him to resign over the sound of his roaring presidential ambitions.

Trump hopes inciting the violent insurrection riot doesn't take him out of the running for the Nobel Peace Prize.

Jeb Bush is somewhere watching news coverage of the riot with a tear falling down his cheek while he softly claps for himself.

Kevin McCarthy: "We Republicans MAY have gotten a little carried away with all the lying and fake moral outrage turning every political battle into an all-encompassing, culturally existential crisis for our mob-like voters who have now turned violent against democracy and even us... oops."

Mike Pence told Trump that his mother won't let them be friends anymore.

Donald Trump's Tumblr account, which he uses to post "tasteful, body-positive" self-portrait nudes, has not yet been removed like all his other social media accounts.

Jared Kushner reportedly thinks he may have married into the wrong family.

Republicans say that, in the interest of unity, Democrats should let Mitch McConnell stay Senate Majority Leader for two more years.

Bigots will soon be adding Trump flags above their Confederate and Nazi flags in their basement, and tell people "It's not offensive, it's my heritage!"

Donald Trump just started a hunger strike in the Oval Office to protest being banned from Twitter.
UPDATE: Seven minutes later he asked for a Big Mac.

Trump is reportedly claiming he was "so close" to finishing out his presidency scandal-free.

Ivanka Trump says that every time her father did something illegal, immoral, racist or fascist, she was in the other room working on women's empowerment issues.

Trump is desperately asking aides what distraction he should create to distract from the coup that distracts from his COVID failures and election loss.

Kellyanne Conway claims Trump's insurrection wasn't a coup, it was just an "alternative concession."

Mike Pence wants to blame the Gay Agenda for the rioters chanting "Hang Mike Pence," but is frustrated he can't find traces of glitter anywhere in the Capitol hallways to prove it was them.

Republicans say if Democrats are going to admit D.C. and Puerto Rico as states, they should be able to admit the "State of Denial" into the Union and get two extra senators who claim Trump really won.

Republicans say a new tax cut for the rich will trickle down and unify the country of all our political divisions.

Ted Cruz says he cares about calls for his resignation as much as he cares about insults aimed at his wife.

Trump says it's "racist" the Black president got two terms and he doesn't.

Ken Starr says unless any of Trump's sperm is found on the rioters' clothes Trump couldn't possibly be impeached for inciting the coup attempt.

McDonalds just banned Donald Trump from ever eating their food again.

Trump was already going to be remembered metaphorically as a bloody s*** stain on US history, and now he's vomiting all over the pile of s*** to spite us.

Adderall just put Trump on its national do-not-prescribe list.

"You'll never abandon me like everyone else," Trump just whispered to his seven-scoop bowl of ice cream.

Trump spent all weekend stealing priceless American historical artifacts to pawn in the next few months to cover interest payments on his debts.

Trump is currently sulking around the White House with a tub of fried chicken intended for a family of six writing "I won" in grease with his finger on the walls.

BREAKING NEWS: Eric Trump currently has a nosebleed from sticking a crayon up his nostril to "color his brain yellow."

Trump signed an executive order demanding everyone send back their COVID relief checks because of how unfairly everyone is treating him.

Ivanka Trump says the senator who spends the least money on her handbags and fashion brands this year will be the senator whose state she "moves to" in order to run against in 2022.

The International Big Mac Eating Championship has announced they will no longer be hosting their 2021 annual competition at Mar-a-Lago.

Tomi Lahren has reportedly been struggling for days, but just can't make the logic math work on proving how the Capitol insurrection was really Colin Kaepernick's fault.

Ted Cruz says he couldn't live with himself unless he leaves his daughters an America he destroyed stopping at nothing to try and become president.

BREAKING NEWS: President Donald Trump is reportedly no longer using toilets in the White House...

Matt Gaetz says his 2008 DUI was because of Antifa.

Jim Jordan accidentally left his Zoom camera on while strangling several squirrels in his office during the impeachment committee hearings.

Ivanka Trump just released a pop song titled "Daddy's Ketchup."

"In the name of national unity, the investigation into what I knew about those wrestler kids getting molested should be dropped!" says Jim Jordan.

Mitch McConnell, now suddenly considering voting for convicting Trump, says three impeachment ghosts visited him last night and taught him the meaning of the Constitution.

*Fox News* is reportedly offering $10,000 for anyone who can provide information that leads to the identification of one Antifa member among the Capitol insurrectionists so *Fox* can blame the riot all on liberals.

Ivanka Trump is reportedly worried her father's cultivation of anti-Semites will hurt her presidential ambitions, and that she won't be able to win over the "Camp Auschwitz" t-shirt-wearing rioters at the Capitol insurrection.

"We should be focusing on COVID, the economy, and holding the rioters accountable, not impeachment!" say Republicans who don't want any more relief checks, economic stimulus, or to punish collaborating insurrectionist members of Congress.

"The radical, socialist Democrat communists who hate America and freedom and will stop at nothing to destroy the American way of life and culture need to be less divisive," say the majority of Congressional Republicans.

Donald Trump is reportedly pissed he got impeached twice and didn't even get one blowjob.

Donald Trump says he should be remembered and celebrated in history like George Washington for "voluntarily" giving up power.

Joe Biden says he gets to play laser tag as many days as Trump golfed.

White House staffers unanimously agree that Trump's election loss has revealed him to be the most agonizingly loud, ugly crier they've ever seen or heard. Also, he's been going through an entire bottle of ketchup every day in some kind of calming, oiled up yoga meditative ritual.

Trump claims Democrats bused in dozens of legislators from Mexico to fraudulently vote for his impeachment in the House of Representatives.

Donald Trump wants the record to show that he would have gotten COVID cases down to zero if Democrats hadn't impeached him twice.

Ted Cruz admitted he's Mothman, and terrorizes D.C. residents at night.

Ivanka Trump is reportedly eating a lot of possum to prepare for fitting in when she moves to Florida.

Donald Trump was just heard screaming at Rudy Giuliani and blaming him for his political woes, yelling out "From now on, you're working pro boner!"

Ivanka Trump just launched a new clothing brand called "Proud Girls" that has been called "paramilitary-chic," "fashionably fascist," and "extremely low-quality."

Ivanka Trump says her First Amendment rights are being violated by New York socialites who won't invite her to any parties.

Stephen Miller is reportedly freaking out because he doesn't remember where he hid all those bodies in the White House, and has found only five of the seven he hid, though the total of seven comes with a margin of error of one because he may have eaten one of the bodies and just merely forgotten about it.

Donald Jr. is currently filming a video for his Parler account with bright red, bloodshot cocaine eyes, but keeps having to start over because he can't finish the full three-minute monologue before blinking.

Trump to Don Jr.: "Stop asking me to say 'I love you!' It's weak! My father never said it to me, and I turned out totally fine and psychologically stable!"

Donald Trump: "No supporter of mine commits violence against the government... and then claims I incited them as a legal defense!"

Republicans claim a second Trump impeachment is divisive, as if ramming through a Supreme Court judge a month before an election breaking their own brand new election-year-rule with a president who didn't win the popular vote the first time and would soon lose another was a beautiful act of thoughtful, magnanimous bipartisanship.

Ivanka Trump's Guide For Women's Success In Business:
Step 1: Ask Daddy for a job in Grandpa's company
Step 2: Now you're the executive vice president, yay for your Girl Boss status!

Ivanka Trump insisted the Secret Service refer to her as "Madame Future President."

BREAKING NEWS: Matt Gaetz was found to have texted the Capitol rioters ahead of time asking them not to mess up his hair.

The only Florida country club that will accept Ivanka Trump and Jared Kushner has outhouse bathrooms and a dinner buffet with "Possum Soup Tuesdays."

BREAKING NEWS: Jared Kushner says his D.C. house's toilets were only off-limits to their Secret Service guards because he was embarrassed to let them see how often Ivanka clogs them.

The FBI's forensic investigation found that most of the feces left on the floor and smeared on the walls during the insurrection riot in the Capitol came from Jim Jordan. "Just like bullets have traceable rifling to match what gun the bullets were fired from, the colon rifling on these turds match exactly to Jim Jordan's anus," said D.C. Police Chief Thomas Harkin.

Dildos were found in three anti-gay Republican Congressmen's briefcases today after they initially refused Capitol police officers' efforts to check them in accordance with updated security protocols following the insurrection riot.

Jared and Ivanka sent out Florida mansion-warming party invitations last week to celebrate their move to Florida, but the only person who has RSVP'ed is Ted Cruz, who wasn't sent an invitation.

Donald Trump reportedly thinks Republican senators are giving him bad advice by telling him not to start a civil war because Vladimir Putin, in contrast, has been telling him it's the best idea any US president in history has ever had.

QAnon is telling believers that Donald Trump will only soon be going to jail for rape, fraud, tax evasion, and dozens of other crimes as a ruse so that he can fight the global pedophile cabal undercover from the inside of prison.

"Today we honor Martin Luther King Jr." tweets every conservative who spends every other day of the year promoting ethno-nationalism with fundamentalist zeal.

Gun-loving Lauren Boebert says it's not fair that Democrats get to bring their favorite weapon of coat-hangers into the Capitol, but she can't bring a gun to protect herself from Nancy Pelosi's baby-eating fangs.

Donald Trump just asked why "Cancel Culture" can't cancel something useful, like his business debts.

Ivanka Trump wrote a ceremonial letter to Joe Biden's incoming Daughter-Executive-Adviser, but doesn't know who to give it to.

Donald Trump thought about barricading himself in the White House by taking his son Eric as a hostage, but realized no one would believe he cares about Eric's safety.

Scientists have taxonomically added the new human species *"Homo republicanensis"* to classify Republican members of Congress who have somehow observably evolved with no backbones.

The Mar-a-Lago television screen shows Joe Biden holding Jill Biden's hand at the inauguration. A tear escapes from Donald Trump's eye and rolls down his cheek. He grabs his own hand, limp and moist, and gives it a light squeeze. "Is this love?" he wonders to himself.

QAnon believers everywhere are melting down while watching the Biden inauguration. "Why are Biden, Obama, and Pelosi not being arrested yet?" they scream aloud. "Why is Biden being allowed to give this speech? Why is Trump not being sworn in again? I ruined all my personal relationships arguing with everyone that Trump would be starting his second term today! I look like an idiot!"

Biden says the White House staff did the best they could, but the residency "still reeks of hairspray" and the bathroom carpets still have traces of orange.

Joe Biden asked the White House janitor why he keeps finding caps from Sharpie markers all over the place.

Donald Trump's second impeachment defense is that Hillary and Obama set him up at the insurrection rally. He claims he saw Obama waving a Kenyan flag, and heard Hillary screaming "Vive la Benghazi!"

Trump apologized for calling the media "the enemy of the people" for so many years, and said his impeachment trial due to the violence-inciting speech he delivered to the insurrectionist crowd has taught him how important free speech is and how it should never be punished or prosecuted for any reason.

Mitch McConnell said "F*** it," and has begun wearing his beloved turtle ties and socks. "Let them mock me!" he shouted to his bathroom mirror this morning, "I'm not ashamed of my passion for herpetoids!"

BREAKING NEWS: Joe Biden just directed all workers to arrest their employers, nationalized America's iron and steel industries, ordered all farmers to collectivize their crops, and abolished private property. America is fully communist now, just like Donald Trump said would happen!

## Donald Trump Is Suing Every Biden Voter For $5 Billion Each For "Damages To His Brand"

November 20, 2020
Washington D.C.—

President Donald Trump just launched over 80 million lawsuits, one for every American citizen counted so far who voted for Joe Biden, and addressed the lawsuits on Twitter:

"This is so unfair! All these Biden votes are rigged against me! I can't get a fair chance with any of the Biden votes! The Democrats are cheating to make 100% of Biden votes go for Biden! What are the odds that not even ONE Biden vote would go for me???"

"I'm going to have to sue all these Biden voters! PRESIDENTIAL HARASSMENT! $5 billion ought to teach them a lesson not to vote against everyone's FAVORITE President! No incumbent president has ever been treated so disrespectfully and unfairly!"

"one-way ticket moscow january 20th noon"

"is it cold in moscow?"

"does russia have extradition treaty america?"

"how many mexicans live in russia?"

"russian tax rate beauty pageants"

"did google stop working?"

"Oops! Don't mind those last tweets! Barron was borrowing my phone to do research for a school project and kept accidentally typing his Google searches into my Twitter, which I never do! #MAGA!"

# Washington D.C.

(Inspired by Langston Hughes)
by Donald J. Trump


What happens to a second term deferred?

Does it wash up
Like a deadbeat on the shore?
Or fester like a loser—
And then run again in four?
Does it stink to be noncontiguously elite?
Or disappear, passed over—
Like a banned tweet?

Maybe it just snags
Unloved by the penal code.

I'd rather explode!

## Impeached Boy Blues

(Inspired by Langston Hughes)
by Donald J. Trump


When I was in my tower
Sunshine seemed like gold.
Since I come to D.C. de
Whole damn world's turned cold.

I was a good boy,
Never done no wrong.
Just a few laws here and there
But Democrats don't play along.

I fell in love with
A Big Lie I thought was fine,
But my fans stormed the Capitol
And Nancy lost her mind.

Weary, weary,
Weary of testifying sworn.
I's so weary
I wish I'd never been born!

# More Donald Trump Headlines

- Donald Trump Spent All Morning Twitter-Feuding With A Baseball Team Of 12-Year-Olds

- Donald Trump Told John Bolton He Can Only Start One War, So He Better Choose Wisely

- A Government Audit Reveals Trump Charged Taxpayers Over $6,000 For Pay-Per-View Porn While Staying At His Own Hotels In 2017

- A Federal Audit Found Donald Trump To Be The Laziest Government Employee Since 1822

- Donald Trump Started A Charity For "Victims Of Fake News," Kept All The Donations For Himself

- Donald Trump Admits Running For President Was The Worst Decision He Has Ever Made

- Donald Trump Is Astounded To Learn Most Americans Actually Pay Their Taxes

- "Be Worried Michael Cohen Will Squeal," Say Trump Allies Who Paradoxically Swear Trump Is Innocent

- A Brand New Form Of Dementia Just Got Named After Donald Trump

- Study Confirms Trump Has Been Treated More Unfairly Than Any Human Ever

- Trump: "My Tax Returns Should Be Transparently Locked Up And Hidden Forever!"

- Jay-Z's New Album Features President Obama Freestyling On A Trump Diss Track

- President Macron: "Trump Wore Toy 'Hulk Hands' Throughout My White House Visit"

- Expert: Nostradamus Predicted Donald Trump's Pee Tape

- Donald Trump Brags That Obama Never Had An Eclipse

- Colorado Governor Ships 100 Pounds of Marijuana To White House, Begs President Trump And Jeff Sessions To Chill Out

- Trump's Doctor Claims Trump's Beach Body Is "Way Hotter" Than Obama's Was

- Trump Raved About How Skinny North Korean Girls Are, Offered To Co-Host A Miss Korean Pageant With Kim Jong Un

- Unprompted, Trump Denies That He Reinstalled President Taft's XXL Toilet And Bathtub In The White House

- A Third Species Of Marmot Just Went Extinct Supplying Fur For Donald Trump's Fake "Hair"

- Trump Claimed His Favorite President, Excluding Himself, Was Martin Luther King Jr.

- Trump Complains That The Fake News Always Posts Photos Of Him Golfing, But Never Shows Footage Of Him Weightlifting Before And After

- America Finally Found A Category Of Workers To Whom Trump Actually Pays His Debts: Porn Stars

- Local Clinic Offers Free Therapy Sessions For Any Adult Film Stars Who Have Seen Donald Trump In Tighty-Whities

- Walk-Hating Donald Trump Is Now Driving A Golf Cart Through The White House Hallways From Meeting To Meeting

- The Most Shocking Evidence Found In Michael Cohen's FBI Raid Is "Thousands" Of McDonalds Receipts

- A "239-Pound Orangutan" Was Recently Spotted Rampaging Through The Hallways At Mar-a-Lago

- New Study Finds The Ozone Layer Above Washington D.C. Totally Depleted, Trump's Hair Spray Use Suspected

- Donald Trump Says He And Osama Bin Laden Would Have Been Great Friends

- Donald Trump Admits It: "I Really Have No Idea What I'm Doing, And I'm Afraid To Ask Obama For Help"

- Donald Trump Is Concerned About His Son Barron's Moral Development Because He Hasn't Defrauded Any Charities Yet

- Donald Trump Just Interrupted His Golf Trip For A Second Impromptu Golf Trip

- Trump Has Installed Stair Chair Lifts Throughout The White House

- Trump Paid A McDonalds Cashier $150,000 To Stay Quiet About How Many Big Macs He Can Eat In One Go

- Donald Trump Left Adam Schiff A Voicemail Begging "Dude, Just Be Cool" 19 Times

- Donald Trump Wants Lindsey Graham To Be Buried In His Tomb With Him When He Dies To Continue Serving Him In The Afterlife

- Donald Trump Unironically Told John Kelly That He's Too Controversial, And Has To Go

- Obama Says Don't Worry, He Hid The REAL Nuclear Codes In A Place Trump "Would Never Think Of"

- Donald Trump Is Furious To Find Out Obama Knew Healthcare Was Complicated, But Never Told Him In Their Transition Meetings

- The Last Time Donald Trump Admitted Blame For Something Was 1957

- Trump Makes All His Grandchildren Sign Nondisclosure Agreements As Soon As They Start Talking

- Trump Claims The Trump Organization Is A Religious Institution And Therefore Not Subject To New York Taxation

- Trump Claims He's Descended From Jesus, And That's Why He Has Been So Good At Turning Debts Into Bailouts From His Dad And Creditors

- Historians Conclude That Trump Is "The Nickelback Of Presidents"

- Donald Trump Claimed Being President Is Even Worse Than Having To Spend A Day With Eric

- Trump Told His New Press Secretary He's Hoping For More Of A "North Korean Media Vibe"

- Donald Trump Dropped A Baby At A Pro-Life Rally

- Donald Trump Totally Can't Read The Room, And Is Still Ludicrously Planning To Run Again In 2020

- Trump Obstructs Justice So Much That He Accidentally Obstructed Himself Obstructing Justice

- Donald Trump Is Furious Democrats Are Using His Direct Quotes In Campaign Ads

- Trump: "Biden Will Turn Baby Jesus Gay And Socialist, And Then Abort Him!"

- A Top Evangelical Magazine Recommends That Donald Trump Be Retroactively Aborted For Humanity's Sake

- Donald Trump Claims He Looks Younger Than Pete Buttigieg

- Trump: "Mayor Pete Should Take Christian Marriage Lessons From Me!"

- Trump Says He Noticed The Other Day That Joe Biden's Birth Certificate "Looks Real Sketchy"

- Dozens Of Make-A-Wish Kids Have Requested To See Donald Trump's Tax Returns

- Trump Says Bailouts For Golf Courses, D.C. Hotels, And Florida Resorts Will Boost The Economy Tremendously

- Nancy Pelosi Filed A New Impeachment Article For Trump Being A "Whiny Little Bitch"

- Trump Reportedly Wanted To Mail Trump Hotel Coupons Along With Each Of The Stimulus Checks

- Trump Wishes He Could Fight Adam Schiff In A Duel, Laments That He's A Bigger Target Than "Pencil Neck Schiff"

- Trump Says He'd Love For John Bolton To Testify In The Impeachment Trial, But That Bolton Is Under Audit

- Trump Claims Mike Bloomberg Uses Makeup, Has Fake Hair, And Isn't A Real Billionaire

- Donald Trump Keeps Saying He Will Win "Erection 2020"

- Angela Merkel Says Donald Trump Tried To Make Out With Her At A NATO Summit In 2018

- IRS Leak: 96% Of Trump's Money Is Tied Up In A Cryptocurrency Called "Putin Bucks"

- Trump Spent 3 Hours Picking Up A Trail Of Pennies Left By Mike Bloomberg All Around The National Mall

- Trump Is Jealous That Mike Bloomberg Still Gets Loans From US Banks

- Trump: "If I'm Guilty, Why Did No Primary Witnesses Testify Against Me In The Senate Impeachment Trial?"

- Trump Is Writing His Own Tell-All Book Titled *Everything Was Perfect: A Presidential Memoir Of An Administration That Always Followed The Law*

- Trump Claims He Warned Obama About COVID-19, But That "Blacks Never Listen"

- Trump Claims His COVID Infection Is All Gone, And He Did 50 Pull-Ups This Morning

- Trump Is Jealous Obama Got "Easy Ebola" While He Got "Way Harder Coronavirus"

- Trump Is Not Sure Who To Blame For His Low Poll Numbers, But Knows It's Not His Fault

- Trump Directed The Secret Service To Reserve Rooms At His Golf Club From November 4 To January 20, But Says He's Not Worried At All About Losing Reelection Or Spending The Rest Of His Life In Jail

- Trump Says The Fake News Won't Admit He Brought "Sexy" Back To The White House

- A Leaked IRS Audit Reveals Donald Trump's Net Worth After Debts Is Just $7

- Trump Started His Own Polling Company Called "Stable Genius Polls" That Show Him Winning 85% Of The Vote

- Trump Thinks Concocting A Coma Scare Like Kim Jong Un Had Would Help His Poll Numbers

- Trump: "I'd Love To Compare School Grades With Alexandria Ocasio-Cortez, But Mine Are Under Audit!"

- Trump Wants To Cancel The Debates, Challenge Biden To A Hotdog-Eating Contest For The Presidency

- Trump Says, If Reelected, He Has A 30-Day, Fool-Proof Plan To Win The Trade War With China

- Donald Trump Is Now Questioning The Citizenship Of "Dr. Fao-Xi"

- Trump: "If I Lose Reelection, I Promise I'm Going To Be The World's Worst Sport About It!"

- Trump Called The NAACP "Rigged" For Not Including Him Among Black History Heroes

- Donald Trump's Tightly Folded Arms Betray That Even He Knows He's Going To Lose

- Donald Trump Claims He's The William Shakespeare Of Twitter, And His "Kung Flu" Tweets Were More Clever And Creative Than "*Hamlet*"

- Trump Promises He'll Win, But Says If He Loses It's Mike Pence's Fault

- Trump: "I'm Going To Win So Big, Let's Not Waste Everyone's Time Actually Counting The Votes!"

- Trump: "I Cheated Way Too Much For Democrats To Have Won Fairly!"

- Trump Says He Wants His Voters To Start Kneeling During The National Anthem To Protest His Election Loss

- Donald Trump Told Mar-A-Lago Guests That Joe Biden Is Asking For His Advice On How He Got Such A Big Inauguration Crowd Size

- Trump Suspiciously Just Mandated That Federal Prisons Start Serving "Big Mac Mondays" And "Filet-O-Fish Fridays"

- Nancy Pelosi Called Dibs On Dragging Trump Out Of The White House On January 20th If He Won't Leave

- Trump Said He Was Just About To Make COVID Disappear, But "Not Anymore!"

- Trump Called Black People "Riggers" After Claiming Their Vote Was "Rigged Against Him"

- Donald Trump, Bill Barr, and Chris Christie Are Having A Wet T-Shirt Contest To Raise Funds For Vote Recounts

- Trump Just Pardoned A Thanksgiving Turkey Named "The Trump Organization"

- Trump Hopes Inciting A Civil War To Stay In Power Won't Hurt His Nobel Peace Prize Prospects

- Trump Claims If Stormy Daniels Had Just Kept Her Mouth Shut His Presidency Would Have Been Entirely Scandal-Free

- Trump Is Relieved He Doesn't Have To Come Up With The Healthcare Plan He Impulsively Promised Anymore

- Trump Is Relieved He Doesn't Have To Come Up With The Infrastructure Plan He Impulsively Promised Anymore

- Trump Is Relieved He Doesn't Have To Come Up With A New Iran Deal He Impulsively Promised Anymore

- Trump Calls Jesus And God "Enemies Of The People" For Not Making Sure He Won Reelection

- Trump Threatened Biden If He "Ever Hurts" His Lover, North Korean Dictator Kim Jong Un

- Trump Claims After January 20th He'll Be Doing A Lot Of Reading, Praying, And Sports With Barron

- Trump Says He'll Leave The White House In Exchange For A Promise By The State Of New York Not To Investigate His Taxes, A Direct Deposit Of $421 Million, And Immunity For Incest

- Trump Is Reportedly Planning To Hide From New York Prosecutors "Saddam Hussein Style"

# **RETRACTIONS**

Following fact-checkers' assertions that this political record of the years 2017-2021 is "exhaustively fictional," the entirety of *Satire In The Trump Years: The Best Of The Halfway Post* has been retracted.

Thanks for looking at my book!

If you liked it, please leave a review of it on *Amazon, Barnes & Noble,* or anywhere else you find it. Tell your friends and family about it. Loan it to all the liberal comedy lovers you know. Request your local library get a copy. Gift it to your most conservative enemies and social media trolls!

Follow me on social media to stay current with my latest Dadaist satire:

DashMacIntyre.Medium.com
Twitter.com/HalfwayPost
Threads.net/@TheHalfwayPost
Facebook.com/TheHalfwayPost
TheHalfwayCafe.Substack.com
Spoutible.com/TheHalfwayPost
Post.News/DashMacintyre

# ABOUT THE AUTHOR

Dash MacIntyre is from St. Louis, and founded *The Halfway Post* in the summer of 2017 to craft little doses of comedic catharsis throughout the village idiot reign of Donald Trump. Follow him on Twitter @HalfwayPost to interrupt your daily doomscrolling with Dada news!

MacIntyre's latest published work is *Cabaret No Stare*, a book of prose poems, available on Amazon.